How Smart People Can Become More Successful

The Real Reasons Why Some Smart People Underachieve—And How You Can Become an Achiever

Ram V. Iyer

How Smart People Can Become More Successful
© 2025 Ram V. Iyer
All rights reserved by the author.

No part of this book may be reproduced, stored in a retrieval system, or transmitted in any form or by any means—electronic, mechanical, photocopying, recording, or otherwise—without the prior written permission of the author, except for brief quotations used in reviews or scholarly works, or as permitted under applicable copyright law.

Published by iAchiever Publishing, an imprint of Business Thinking Institute LLC

Princeton, NJ. U.S.A.

www.iAchiever.org

Requests for permission, licensing, bulk purchases, translations, or limited educational/training use (e.g., excerpts, frameworks, handouts) should be directed to the publisher.

ISBN (Print): 979-8-9987517-0-7
ISBN (eBook): 979-8-9987517-1-4

First Edition

Disclaimer
This book is for informational purposes only. The author is not a doctor, therapist, or licensed mental health professional, and this content is not a substitute for professional advice. The strategies, stories, and ideas shared are based on personal experience, research, and interviews, and should be used at the reader's own discretion.

To the smart underachievers:

Here's to your greater success.

Because when you become more successful, everyone around you benefits—your teams, organizations, families, communities, and humanity.

Table of Contents

A Message from Ram vii
Acknowledgments ix
Foreword xi
More Praise for 'How Smart People Can Become More Successful' xiii
Introduction xv

PART 1: The Foundations of Success 1
1. The Success Triad—The Essentials for Achievement 2
2. My Story & How it Informs This Book 5
3. Uncover Your Success Barriers with Inversion Thinking 10
4. Advantages & Why They Matter for Smart People 19
5. Why Disablers Must Be Addressed 27

PART 2: Understanding Smartness 34
6. Understanding Smartness 35
7. Smartness From Many Angles 43
8. Intelligence & Smartness as You Age 46
9. The Smartness Gap – Why Smart People Struggle & How to Fix It ... 54
10. The Elements of Smartness – Mindset, Behaviors, Habits & Skills ... 61
11. The Smartness Development Process—How to Build and Apply Smartness 68
12. The Earned Mindset: The Foundation for Smartness & Consistent Achievement 72
13. How Smart People Turn Intelligence & Advantages into Achievements 78
14. The Smartness Factors 84
15. The Smartness Assessment 91
16. Insights from the Smartness Assessment Data 95

PART 3: Understanding Yourself 105
17. Success: Entitlement, Destiny or Earned? 106
18. Shifting Your Paradigm from Intelligence to Smartness 112
19. Are You Excited, Fearful, Angry, or Indifferent? 117
20. Personal Judgment—The Smart Person's Ultimate Advantage 122
21. Overcoming Inner Resistance to Success 128
22. Your Why - The Driving Force Behind Success 132
23. You're Already Ahead: Leverage Your Intelligence & Other Advantages for Greater Success 137
24. Your Smartness Assessment Report—Understanding Your Enablers & Disablers 141
25. Typical Success & Failure Behaviors for Each Smartness Factor 144

PART 4: The Smartness Factors 147

THINKING SMARTNESS FACTORS 150
- 26. Detail Focus 151
- 27. Complexity Preference 155
- 28. Decision Flexibility 159
- 29. Thinking & Feeling 163
- 30. Situational Judgment 167
- 31. Thinking Range 171
- 32. Belief Reinforcement 175

ACTION SMARTNESS FACTORS 179
- 33. Action Orientation 180
- 34. Risk Tolerance 185
- 35. Self-Competence Views 189
- 36. Outward Confidence 193
- 37. Self-Reliance 198
- 38. Career Flexibility 202
- 39. Self-Advocacy 208
- 40. Need for Variety 213

RELATIONAL FACTORS 218
- 41. Emotional Intelligence 219
- 42. Interpersonal Skills 223
- 43. Teamwork 228
- 44. Personal Autonomy 233
- 45. Relational Adaptability 238
- 46. Communication & Presentation Choices 242

PART 5: Leveraging Smartness to Achieve Success 248
- 47. Bringing It All Together: The Achievement Cycle 249
- 48. Find Your Tribe & Mentors 259
- 49. What Smartness Enables You to Do 266
- 50. What Is a Successful Life? 270
- 51. Step into Your Future Now 272

About the Author 276
Introducing the Smartness Institute 277

APPENDIX 279
- Resources to Sustain & Accelerate Your Success 279

A Message from Ram

There's a silent force holding many smart people back: the illusion that being intelligent is enough to become highly successful.

For years, we've been told that intelligence guarantees success. That credentials, sharp thinking, and raw capabilities are all it takes. And maybe, deep down, you've believed that too.

But it's a seductive lie that has become an invisible enemy for many smart people. It's like a bad friend or a drug that whispers that you're already doing enough, the same one that told you to skip the workout, impulsively send the risky text, or buy crap you don't need with money you don't have.

You succeeded in school and in your early career by using your intelligence. But no one prepared you for what comes next, when intelligence alone wasn't enough. You were expected to figure it out on your own, even as everyone still expects you to become highly successful. But when it didn't happen, you were confused, frustrated, and doubting yourself. You didn't question or blame the system. You blamed yourself. You wondered, *"What's wrong with me?"* or *"What am I doing wrong?"*

Since you're smart, and everyone (including you) expects great things from you, you don't have the luxury of wondering aloud. You may not be able to talk to your colleagues, friends or family. So where do you get the answers? Who can you talk to? How do you make sense of what's holding you back? It may not be your fault—but it's your responsibility to figure it out if you want to become more successful.

I'm an MIT alum who has been in your shoes. I spent over a decade figuring this out. My discoveries and insights are in this book. It provides answers, knowledge and tools for you to achieve greater success. It could save you years of frustration—or months (years?) on a therapist's couch.

This book gives you the knowledge, insights, and tools—MIT-style: direct, no-nonsense, and practical—to develop and leverage what you truly need: Smartness. It's how you turn your intelligence and advantages into real achievement in the real world.

My mission is to expose that enemy of many smart people—and help you defeat it. You don't need to become more intelligent to become more successful—you need to get smarter at leveraging who you already are, and what you already possess.

I wrote this for people like you—smart, capable, driven—but not seeing the success you expected. Maybe you're stuck and wondering what to do. Maybe you're under-recognized. Or maybe you're just sick of watching less capable people get ahead of you.

I envision a world where smart people don't just perform—they lead. Where they're not overlooked or under-leveraged, but become the achievers who drive change—in companies, communities, and humanity.

This book starts exactly where you are right now—in the real world, with the real you.

Let's dive in.

Acknowledgments

Many people helped me climb to heights I never imagined, others saw me sink to lows I wouldn't want for anybody, and there are those who have stood by me as I made yet another 'comeback.'

They say that you gain the most clarity when you are at your lowest point. It is indeed true. Many (alleged) friends and family of convenience disappeared. I learned that understanding oneself is the best and most foundational thing one must do. And learning to rely on oneself is paramount. But… we all need help, and many people in our lives provide the help and guidance.

During the worst times, a few friends remained, without fanfare, without judgment. Kutumba Lanka, a deeply spiritual man, reminded me to look inward and trust myself. Richard Guha constantly urged me to stop underestimating my own capabilities. And Seth and Monica Rao, under the guise of dinner outings, simply made sure I didn't give up. Their quiet faith in me mattered more than they know.

A lot of the epiphanies came from speaking to several old friends from my MIT and Lucent networks. A turning point was when my friend Sean Brown at McKinsey - a fellow MIT Sloan alum - invited me to speak about my early insights at the MIT Sloan Club of Boston. That was soon after my inversion thinking epiphany and the insights about one's own 'silent killers of success.' (they're in the book). The ensuing invitation to the Harvard Alumni Association of New York City from Jyoti Singhvi, a Harvard and MIT alum, was what set me on to the challenges of smart people and also shined the light on my own challenges. The tagline of that talk's title was 'Why many smart people are not as successful as they think they should be.' Based on an unexpectedly large response that evening, I decided I would dig into the challenges of smart people and figure out how to crack the code to achieve greater success. It helped me find the answers I was seeking too. So, many thanks to the Sloan alums in Boston and the Harvard alums in New York City.

At a particularly low point in my latest comeback, I was with my friend Dr. Marshall Goldsmith, the renowned executive coach, at his condo in Manhattan. I was telling him about how tough the turnaround has been. In his inimitable way, he said, 'Ram, you'll be fine.' When pressed further, he pointed out that besides being an MIT alum, I was an immigrant in America and was raised in India—and that meant I had a success-enabling mindset. I interviewed over 100 high-achieving professionals, entrepreneurs, leaders, and more to uncover the factors behind their success. I found that they had a unique mindset (how they viewed themselves and the world around them, in their beliefs, values, and more), behaviors, and skills. I also realized that I had many similar aspects of their mindsets, behaviors, and skills. I had a solid foundation for my next comeback. Many thanks, Marshall!

My psychologist friend Strahinja always grounded me in the psychological sciences and made sure that I didn't stray into pop psychology. He remains a wonderful sounding board to this day. Our conversations, even after weeks or months, just pick up as if we just spoke a few minutes ago. The *Smartness Assessment,* which can help those who take it understand their mindset, behavioral inclinations, and skills, started as a concept I envisioned. Without Strahinja's expertise, Mahesh's smarts, and Dhana's programming prowess, the current version of the online assessments would not have been possible. That is why we have a treasure trove of assessment data that we get to analyze for insights. Insights from that data have informed many chapters in this book.

My late father, who passed away in 1998, was a guiding light who constantly raised the bar in my life. To this day, if my resolve sags, just thinking of him pulls me up quickly—I get a boost of energy right away. He is still my rock. This book is being published on April 28, 2025. Dad would have turned 92. My mother constantly reminds me that my optimism and self-confidence have helped me all my life and will continue to serve me well.

I am grateful to the hundreds of people who took the assessment that provided the data, which, when analyzed, revealed the big three challenges of highly intelligent people – excessive detail orientation (perfectionism), the constant need for variety, and poor action orientation (not acting even when one knew what to do). I found that those were the very three disablers that had held me back. I started writing six books just before the pandemic began. I didn't finish any of them. When I saw the results of the assessment data in early 2023, I knew that my constant need for variety and perfectionism were disabling my greater success, perhaps even my survival. I stopped writing all other books and put my head down to leverage the 100+ articles I've published on intelligence, *Smartness*, and success, as well as the 300+ articles I've written but never published. Once I focused on just this book, progress became much easier… and here we are. The assessment helped me, has helped over a thousand others, and can help you. I'm particularly grateful to the many leaders of alumni clubs of many of the top schools who saw the value of this work for their alumni, helping me share my findings and poking holes in my thinking along the way. Many thanks to the hundreds of assessment takers from California to the U.K. and all the way to Australia!

My daughter Anushka has seen it all—my highs, my lows, my doubts, and my drive—and has remained a steady, loyal force through every turn. She's a sharp critical thinker who listens patiently to my endless stream of ideas, rants, and raves, helping me find clarity when I can't see it myself. She's also my no-nonsense accountability coach—part living rock, part empathetic tough cookie. More than anyone, she has pushed me to grow, not just as a thinker, but as a human being. Becoming her father changed my life, anchored it and gave it more meaning.

Princeton
April 28, 2025

Foreword

Smart people are everywhere. You find them leading organizations, launching startups, earning degrees, mastering systems, solving problems, even giving advice on how others can succeed.

And yet, many of them are stuck.

Not because they're lacking intelligence—but because intelligence alone isn't enough.

I've worked with and coached Fortune 500 CEOs, Olympic athletes, Ivy League graduates, and billionaire entrepreneurs. I've worked with leaders around the world at the top of their fields and industries. And the same pattern shows up again and again: smart, capable people can fall short of their potential—not because they lack ability, but because they haven't learned how to use what they have in the right way, at the right time, for the right outcomes.

That's what this book is about.

Ram Iyer names something that's been quietly holding many smart people back for years: *The Smartness Gap*. It's that disconnect between potential and performance, between knowing and doing, between all the tools we've acquired and the outcomes we've been chasing. And he does more than name it—he helps you close it.

What I appreciate most about this book is that it doesn't ask you to become someone else. It doesn't suggest you need a new personality, another degree, or a radical reinvention of your life. Instead, it asks a far more important question:

What if you started using what you already have... better?

That requires Smartness, which Ram defines as the capability that successful smart people use more effectively than those who don't succeed.

And in this book, you'll learn how to develop it—not as a concept, but as a real, repeatable, practical capability that grows with you over time.

Ram takes something that often feels intangible—our patterns of judgment, our ability to act under pressure, our decision-making instincts—and makes it both visible and usable. He shows how disabling traits like overthinking, perfectionism, or poor action orientation aren't signs of weakness—they're simply traits that haven't yet been redirected toward better outcomes.

In that way, this book isn't just diagnostic. It's empowering. You'll come away not only with clarity about why smart people underachieve—but with a concrete process to start shifting those patterns right now.

The stories and data he shares—drawn from over 1,200 professionals who took the Smartness Assessment—are grounded, honest, and actionable. You'll see yourself in them, you'll recognize the behaviors you've justified or overlooked, and most importantly, you'll find a path forward.

And that's the powerful message at the heart of this book: Success is not the natural byproduct of intelligence. It's the result of how you apply that intelligence—consistently, wisely, and with growing self-awareness. This tendency to over-rely on one's intelligence or credentials and expect automatic success is a mindset Ram calls the Advantage Illusion. Smartness is what shatters it.

You don't have to change who you are. But you might need to change how you're showing up.

You might need to stop relying on raw ability and start building stronger habits.

You might need to stop hoping for progress—and start applying the kind of Smartness that creates it.

If you've ever felt like you *should* be further along, like your brain is working overtime but your results aren't matching your effort—this book is for you.

If you've ever looked around and wondered how someone with fewer credentials is advancing faster than you—this book is for you.

If you've ever wanted more than just ideas and insight—and instead wanted a way to turn your intelligence into consistent results—this book is for you.

Ram Iyer has done something rare here. He's offered a roadmap that honors your intelligence while challenging you to use it differently. To build momentum. To bridge the Smartness Gap. To lead yourself—and others—more effectively.

So don't just read this book. *Use* it. Engage with the assessments, reflect on the 21 Smartness Factors, and start closing the gap between what you know and what you achieve.

Because the smartest people aren't the ones with the highest IQ—they're the ones who've learned how to turn their intelligence into action.

And that's what this book will help you do.

- Dr. Marshall Goldsmith, *Thinkers50* #1 Executive Coach and New York Times bestselling author of *The Earned Life*, *Triggers*, and *What Got You Here Won't Get You There*.

More Praise for 'How Smart People Can Become More Successful'

"This is the best book I've seen for the smart but underachieving—delivered with tough love and practical wisdom. It provides more than a few million-dollar insights. I recommend this book enthusiastically!"
— **Chester Elton,** Bestselling Author, *The Carrot Principle* and *Leading With Gratitude*

"Success doesn't come from being the smartest in the room—it comes from applying it smarter. This book shows you how."
— **Desh Deshpande,** Life Member, Governing Board of MIT

"Smartness is the missing link between potential and performance, and this book is a powerful mix of data, insight, and real talk, including 21 powerful factors that can either propel or block your success. Ram nails it. Intelligence is your engine. Smartness is the steering. Ram teaches you how to drive to impact much more effectively."
— **Sean E. Brown,** MIT Sloan Alum & Career Chair, MIT Sloan Boston Alumni Association

"Ram Iyer's book delivers the tough love every smart professional needs but rarely receives. He shatters the myth that intelligence alone guarantees success and replaces it with actionable strategies anyone can use to move forward. This is the book I wish I'd had earlier in my career—it's practical, honest, and refreshingly direct. If you've ever felt stuck despite doing 'all the right things,' this book is your roadmap out."
— **Michael Vermillion,** President, Chicago Booth Alumni Club of Los Angeles

"If you've ever wondered why your intelligence and hard work haven't taken you further—this book explains why and provides a path to achieve greater success."
— **Larry Lifson,** Co-President, Northwestern Kellogg Alumni Club of Chicago West

"Often, we are so focused on creating a better world that we forget to bring those same problem-solving skills to ourselves. Ram's approach will give you a methodology to improve yourself by becoming more well-rounded. This, in turn, will make you more successful and help you to achieve what you want to achieve."
— **Mark Johnston,** 2023–24 President, MIT Club of Washington DC

"This book is a wake-up call for high-achievers. Ram shows you how to finally convert your intelligence into real-world success."
— **Marc Ingram,** President, Michigan Ross Alumni Club of Ann Arbor & Southeast Michigan

This book is a must-read for anyone wanting to live a successful and meaningful life. Ram Iyer goes beyond surface-level 'smart' to reveal a deeper, more powerful truth: smartness. It's a practical blend of habits and capabilities that turn insight into action and knowledge into real-world success.
  — **Jyoti Singhvi,** Harvard & MIT alumna, Board Member, MIT Sloan Club of NYC, CEO, The ACE Groupe

Introduction

Success isn't just about being smarter. It's about using your Smartness smartly.

In 2013, after years of building a successful business, I lost everything—money, home, confidence. My fancy degrees from MIT and two master's programs didn't save me. I had to start from scratch. That failure punched a hole through my assumptions and sent me on a ten-year hunt to figure out why smart people (people like me) can still fail hard. This book is the result: raw lessons, real data, and no-BS insights on why intelligence alone won't get you there, and what to do when it doesn't.

> *Success introduces you to the world. Failure introduces the world to you.*
> ~ Rita Hayworth

Who Are Smart People?

Smart people stand out. They demonstrate exceptional abilities: sharp judgment, quick learning, and strong problem-solving. Others rely on them in difficult situations because they deliver. Many have advanced cognitive strengths like critical thinking, creative problem-solving, and adaptive reasoning. Some are recognized through credentials, awards, or high IQ scores. Others have proven themselves through innovation, leadership, or consistent results.

Smartness is often shaped by environment: families, cultures, or communities that value education and intellectual growth. For many, being smart isn't just a trait: it's an identity. You might be known as smart by others, or you might know it about yourself. Either way, you expect more of yourself, and others do, too.

You may have wondered, "I'm smart. Why am I not more successful?" Or heard others ask, "She's so smart. Why hasn't she done more?" You're not alone.

Some smart people have elite credentials or have led major initiatives. Others have built deep expertise or amassed networks and resources. Regardless of the path, they share a common thread: they know they have more potential. Many of them want to realize it.

If you're reading this book, chances are that being "smart" has been a big part of your identity, maybe even the core of it.

But here's a simple truth that can change everything:

> *"Remember, being smart or capable isn't the goal. What matters is making it count."*

Look Around

Have you ever wondered why people with less intelligence or fewer credentials sometimes achieve more success? You're not alone. Many smart, well-qualified individuals feel stuck, unable to convert their advantages into real results. This book explains why—and what you can do about it.

The problem isn't intelligence. It's how you're using it. Many smart people unconsciously rely on the belief that intelligence alone guarantees success. But that belief distorts their decisions, behaviors, and blind spots. The breakthrough comes when they shift to a *Smartness*-centered approach, one that channels intelligence into sharper judgment, smarter actions, and real-world results.

"The greatest enemy of intelligence is not stupidity, but the illusion that intelligence alone is enough."

Smartness is what separates potential from achievement. Others succeed not because they're smarter, but because they apply what they have more effectively. That's the difference.

This book isn't about intelligence alone. It's about *Smartness*: the real driver of consistent, meaningful success.

What is Smartness?

Smartness is the ability to see things as they are, recognize what needs to be done, and take the right action. *Smartness* is a capability that anyone can learn. It's developed by cultivating mindsets, behaviors, habits, and skills that help you leverage your advantages, manage your disadvantages, and achieve greater success in the real world.

Smartness isn't the same as intelligence—it's how effectively you apply it. Intelligence is raw material; *Smartness* is the skill that shapes it into real-world results. Without *Smartness*, even the sharpest mind can get stuck in theory, complexity, or inaction. The more you develop and apply *Smartness*, the more likely you are to turn potential into meaningful achievement.

> *"Smartness is often the difference between the merely capable and the truly successful."*

Many smart people fall into what I call the *Advantage Illusion*—the belief that intelligence, credentials, or other advantages will automatically lead to success. But when intelligence isn't applied effectively, it can actually hold you back. That's what creates the *Smartness Gap*: the failure to turn potential into results through adaptability, action, and execution. Many smart people stall out because they rely on what they have, instead of developing how to use it. Smartness helps you overcome that trap by guiding you to assess situations, make better decisions, and apply your advantages intentionally—not passively relying on them all the time.

Introduction

> *"You don't need to become smarter—you need to get Smartness: the skill of turning what you have and know into achievement."*

Success isn't just a science. If it were, more people would already very successful. The real world doesn't reward formulas—it rewards judgment, timing, adaptability, execution, and achievement. That's where Smartness comes in. It's not just about knowing what to do. It's about knowing how, when, and why to do it—and then executing to achieve the desired outcome. That's an art. The good news is that you can learn it and develop it with practice.

The Smartness Factors

Many highly intelligent people remain stuck—not because they lack intelligence, but because they fail to apply it effectively alongside their other advantages. Throughout this book, we'll explore each of the *Smartness Factors* that influence success and how you can develop them.

> *"If you have high intelligence or other advantages but lack the required Smartness, you may avoid failure yet still fall short of becoming a true achiever."*

This book introduces the *Achievement Cycle*—a five-step process for turning potential into real-world success. You don't have to be a certain age, have a certain background, have a certain level of success, or be in a particular place to become more successful. You can become more capable and more successful from where you are, as you are… now! Whether you consider yourself to be already successful or consider yourself to be unsuccessful, this framework can help you become more successful.

The Five Parts of This Book

This book is structured in five parts, each building your ability to turn intelligence into achievement.

- **Part 1** lays the foundation: You'll understand the essential elements of success—aspiration, knowledge, and action—and uncover hidden barriers that smart people often overlook.
- **Part 2** introduces *Smartness*: What it is, why it matters, and how it connects intelligence with better decisions and results. It also shares key insights from 1200+ assessment-takers.
- **Part 3** helps you understand yourself: You'll assess how you're using your intelligence today and identify the habits and mindsets that help or hurt your success.
- **Part 4** breaks down the *Smartness Factors*: You'll learn how these specific mindsets, behaviors, and skills can either enable or derail your success—and how to apply them.

- **Part 5** shows you how to put it all into action: You'll use the *Achievement Cycle* to close the gap between potential and performance and build a personal roadmap for greater success.

The final chapters of this book encourage you to apply the insights and strategies from the first five parts. By reflecting on the *Smartness Factors* and leveraging your personal assessment insights, you can develop and implement your own roadmap to greater success.

If you want a structured, step-by-step guide to walk you through the process, you can purchase the *Smartness Playbook*, a separate companion to this book. The Playbook offers practical tools to systematically identify your advantages, enablers, and disablers, and helps you create and implement a personal plan for achieving greater success. Used together, this book and the Playbook provide a comprehensive, hands-on approach to enhancing your *Smartness* and leveraging your strengths.

Throughout the book, there are reflection questions that make you reflect on your life. There are also several illustrative examples. Each of those examples highlights a key truth: being smart is only as valuable as how well you apply it in real-world situations. *Smartness* is what separates those who achieve results from those who simply have potential.

Who This Book Is For

This book is for you if you're smart yet sense your achievements haven't matched your potential or expectations. Perhaps you've earned impressive credentials, built significant skills, or established a professional career, but you still feel you should achieve more. Or maybe your intelligence or talents aren't yet fully realized or broadly recognized. Recognizing your potential is a crucial first step, but true success comes from effectively applying your capabilities through strategic action. If you're particularly critical of yourself or uncomfortable with the judgment of others, this book will help you understand why—and guide you in leveraging your advantages to achieve the success you desire.

It's also for leaders, managers, or mentors who notice smart people underperforming and want to understand why and how to support them. You recognize their intelligence or talent but notice they're not fully realizing it. This book clarifies why this happens and provides practical tools—including the *Smartness Assessment*—to identify specific issues and bridge the gap between potential and results.

Even if you haven't fully recognized your own strengths or advantages yet, this book will help you discover and apply them. The only requirement is your willingness to improve how effectively you apply your capabilities and resources to achieve meaningful results.

Introduction

Whether You're in the Majority or the Minority – Smartness is Your Path to Greater Success

No matter your background, success depends on how you leverage your advantages and mitigate your disadvantages. Whether you feel the system is stacked against you or you've benefited from the system, *Smartness* is the key to navigating challenges (or opportunities) and staying ahead. The world is changing—what worked yesterday may not work tomorrow. Whether you're in the majority or minority, your success depends on how you choose to respond. *Smartness* enables you to adapt, make better decisions, follow through with actions, and succeed in real-world situations.

Simply put, Smart + *Smartness*=Greater Success

As the book title says, *Smartness* is… How Smart People Can Become More Successful

Why the Tagline, *The Real Reasons Smart People Underachieve—And How to Fix Them?*

The tagline brings up a question that many smart people ask – and offers this book as the answer to the question and a solution to address the underachievement by some smart people. *Smartness* is a set of must-have capabilities. It is often the key difference between successful and unsuccessful people. The development and application of *Smartness* can help you become more successful. If you want to achieve greater success, *Smartness* isn't optional—it is essential.

Smartness is not the domain of a privileged few. It is a capability that everyone can develop, improve, and apply—regardless of their age and current status. Whether you have significant resources or are working with limited means, you can develop and use your *Smartness*, and that will determine how well you navigate challenges, seize opportunities, and achieve greater success. And, you can develop and leverage it at any age to achieve repeatable success—again and again, for the rest of your life.

My Goals for This Book

My intent with this book is to create a resource that's:

- readable, easily understood, and practical for immediate application,
- memorable, so its principles stay with you,
- not just to make you think but also to make you act.
- a playbook for repeatable success, guiding you to greater accomplishments each time you apply its insights.

This book focuses on how to apply *Smartness* to leverage your intelligence and other advantages to achieve the outcomes you seek. No matter your ambition—

career growth, financial security, leadership, or personal fulfillment—*Smartness* is a game-changer. And it's within your reach. This book is crafted to enable the greater success you seek, guiding you on the journey to become an achiever among your peers, family, and community.

Bet on Yourself

Betting on yourself isn't a gamble—it's a smart decision. Not because you have all the answers, perfect timing, or guaranteed outcomes. You won't. You'll face hesitation, uncertainty, and maybe some failures. But you'll also build clarity, resilience, and momentum—things comfort never gives you. You'll grow wiser and sharpen your judgment. Growth doesn't come from standing still. It comes from taking calculated chances, even when things aren't certain. *Smartness* isn't about what you know—it's about the decisions you make and the actions you take, using what you know and adapting to the situation. And that's the best bet you can make.

Your Journey to Greater Success Begins Here

This book is more than just something to read—it's a guide to unleashing your potential. Here, you'll find tools to convert your intelligence into real-world achievements. Many people settle for the life they have, even when they know they're capable of more—because pursuing what they deserve feels harder than staying where they're comfortable.

Whether you seek to enhance your strengths or harness untapped potential, this book will help you think, decide, and act smarter using the advantages you have.

> *"Thinking without action is daydreaming. Acting without thinking is recklessness. Smartness is the intelligent balance of both."*

Get Set, Ready, Act!

Use this book as a guide, not as a formula. Read it cover to cover and revisit the chapters that resonate most or relate to your enablers and disablers.

The main barrier to success… is Action Orientation—the willingness to act. As you delve into this book, don't just read. Instead, take action. Use the margins and white spaces to jot down thoughts, answer the reflection questions, and take small, intentional steps daily. Remember, every step, whether a success or a learning moment, brings you closer to your goals. You can't change your past, but you can certainly choose to shape your future.

Stop waiting for the perfect moment. Stop assuming intelligence will automatically lead to success. It won't—unless you apply it smartly. Remember,

Introduction   xxi

being smart or capable isn't the goal—you already are. What matters is making it count. This book will show you how. Let's get started.

> *"Intelligence is inert unless you use Smartness to translate it into desired outcomes."*

PART 1

THE FOUNDATIONS OF SUCCESS

"The journey to success starts with understanding who you are and what you're working with. Without this foundation, every step forward may be a step off course."
~ Ram V. Iyer

Before you can leverage *Smartness* effectively, you need a strong foundation. Part 1 provides the core principles of success—what every smart person must know before applying their intelligence effectively.

In this section, we'll cover:

- **The Success Triad** – The three essential components of achievement: Aspiration, Knowledge, and Action. Without clarity about your aspirations and the requisite knowledge, you can't use your advantages or *Smartness*.
- **How real-world experiences shape success** – Through *My Story and How It Informs This Book*, I share insights from my journey that can inform your own journey.
- **Why understanding your personal barriers is critical** – How *Inversion Thinking* helps smart people uncover the hidden obstacles that prevent success. We also discuss why disablers must be identified and addressed in addition to doing the same for your advantages.

By the end of this section, you'll have the knowledge and awareness needed to build a foundation for your own long-term success.

CHAPTER 1

THE SUCCESS TRIAD—THE ESSENTIALS FOR ACHIEVEMENT

"True success is fueled by desire, built with knowledge, and realized through action."
~ Ram V. Iyer

You may want greater success, and your intelligence is an advantage, but it's not enough. To turn potential into real achievement, smart people need three forces working together: Aspiration, Knowledge, and Action. Known as the Success Triad, this concept from Hindu philosophy isn't new. It's Iccha Shakti (Aspiration), Jnana Shakti (Knowledge), and Kriya Shakti (Action). Without all three, even the smartest people fall short.

1. Aspiration (Iccha Shakti)

Aspiration is where it begins. It's your deep desire and clear intention to achieve something specific. Without it, intelligence can drift. Some smart people fall into this trap—chasing random opportunities, following trends, or getting caught up in shiny distractions. A clear aspiration gives focus. It defines *why* you do what you do and sustains your motivation through distractions and doubt. But Aspiration alone isn't enough.

2. Knowledge (Jnana Shakti)

Aspiration sets the destination, but you need knowledge to find the path. This isn't just intelligence—it's the specific skills, insights, and learning that move you forward.

Some smart people assume they already know enough. That's how they get stuck. They stop learning, fail to bridge their gaps, or think they're beyond needing help. Success demands humility and continual learning. No exceptions.

3. Action (Kriya Shakti)

Action is what drives results—or doesn't. Many intelligent people hesitate here. They overthink, wait for the perfect moment, and second-guess themselves. But the world rewards execution—not just intelligence or potential. Your actions don't have to be perfect, but they must move you forward. Success is earned again and again through deliberate action, continual learning, and adaptation.

> *"Results don't show up. Progress creates them. And that requires action."*

Are you more committed to success—or to comfort?

As kids, we dreamed big because we didn't know our limits. Then life happened. Some of us are stuck in the past, clinging to our past. Others dwell on regrets or missed opportunities. But achievers look forward: they strive to make it happen. Commitment means showing up even when it's hard, because your work has meaning, and the achievers are energized by that.

Jerry Seinfeld didn't wait for motivation or chase applause. He committed to the craft. He did the work, over and over, until excellence became a habit. That's how confidence builds. That's how *Smartness* sustains achievement.

> *"Achievement doesn't come from ease or need applause; it comes from meaning and obsession."*

Clarify Your Aspirations—and Focus on What Matters

Over the years, I've seen many people feel stuck or unfulfilled—not because they lack potential, but because they don't have clear aspirations or goals. Are you clear about what you truly want? Do you have goals that are meaningful to you?

Some people adopt aspirations that aren't their own. They follow a path someone else laid out for them—a parent's expectations, society's definition of success, or what happens to be popular in their field or friend circle. Others cling to a goal they chose years ago, even if it no longer fits who they are today. Without clarity, they drift—settling for a life that feels familiar but far less than they're capable of. It's not because they lack potential. It's because stepping toward what they truly want often feels harder than staying where they are.

There's also a common trap where people fixate on big, shiny outcomes—whether it's a certain job title, a specific salary, or recognition from others. They focus so much on the end result that they forget to think about what it will take to get there. If you want to make $10 million in the next 20 years, for example, you need more than ambition. You need to take stock of your advantages—what you have—and then figure out what inputs you can control: the skills you build, the opportunities you pursue, the network you need, etc. Only by focusing on those inputs will the goal become achievable.

This is why Aspiration is the first element of the Success Triad. It clarifies where you're headed. Without it, everything else falters.

When your aspirations are clear, and you understand what matters most to you—and why, everything else gets easier. Your choices and actions become more deliberate. You stop drifting and start moving toward something meaningful that excites you. But you have to define what you truly want and be willing to do the work that gets you there. It creates a foundation for everything else. Now, you need the knowledge to move forward and the action to make it real. That's how the Success Triad works—clarity of aspiration, purposeful learning, and deliberate action combine to drive lasting success.

John's Story: The Success Triad in Action

John always told himself he wanted to get healthier. He bounced between HIIT workouts, fitness apps, and yoga, but didn't stick with any of them because his motivation spiked but then faded.

One afternoon, chasing his kids around the park and struggling for breath, something clicked. He realized that what really mattered to him wasn't his fitness or physique, it was about being actively present in his children's lives for years to come. That became his why. He set a clear goal to run a 5K race. Not for the medal, but to prove to himself and his kids that he was still in the game, and would be around for a long time.

With that aspiration locked in, he got serious. He found a beginner's training plan, and sought guidance from a friend who ran marathons on training smarter. Then came the hard part—action. He committed to early mornings, showed up even when he didn't feel like it, and shared his runs with his kids to stay accountable and keep his motivation strong. He completed the 5K race, and even a half marathon. That's how the Success Triad works in real life—A meaningful aspiration, the right knowledge, and action that persists.

Why the Success Triad Matters to Smart People

Smart people often know about aspiration, knowledge, and action—but they don't apply them consistently. Many of them get stuck in the knowing-doing gap—knowing what to do but failing to take effective action. Our assessment data shows that 96% of smart people struggle with action orientation - hesitating, overthinking, stalling or acting hastily. By connecting aspirations with learning and execution, the *Success Triad* helps break that cycle, and turns intention into achievement. And *Smartness* is what brings them together. Without *Smartness*, even the most intelligent people often drift.

Reflection: *What's the one outcome you want—but haven't earned yet because you're missing clarity, skill, or action?*

CHAPTER 2

MY STORY & HOW IT INFORMS THIS BOOK

"One does not become enlightened solely by studying success, but by identifying and understanding one's own struggles and the relevance of lessons to our own success."
~ *Ram V. Iyer*

This book isn't just an intellectual exercise for me; it's a deeply personal journey into the intricacies of advantages like intelligence, *Smartness,* and success—mine and that of others—and the realization that *Smartness* bridges the gap between one's advantages and real-world achievements. This chapter lays the foundation for the book through my own story, illustrating the complexities that often accompany having advantages. Simply put, success blinded me. MIT, corporate leadership, and a rising career led to overconfidence. Then, failure hit, and forced me to rethink everything.

My journey may offer insights into your own—no matter your path or age. Some of my experiences may resonate with you, offering clues to who you are, why you're where you are, and what actions you must take—because your past provides clues into who you are, and your future achievements depend on what you do today. As you read on, I invite you to reflect on your life, connecting the dots to deepen your self-understanding and possibly view your future differently. Your past provides numerous clues on how you could succeed in the future—because self-understanding is the foundation of success.

My Family & Upbringing

I was born into a traditional, large (I have 57 first cousins) middle-class Brahmin family in Southern India. My father was the first one to even attend college. My father sold his share of the family's farmland to pay for his college education - a significant sacrifice and an entrepreneurial move 75 years ago. My mother, equally groundbreaking, became the first woman to finish high school—and later earned a master's degree at 76. Education wasn't just encouraged in our family; it was demanded.

As the oldest child and only son, I was the "golden boy"—expected to outshine everyone, especially my accomplished maternal cousins. That rivalry was relentless: each cousin raising the bar for the next. Between my sisters, our spouses, and me, we've earned 13 master's degrees. Now, the next generation is carrying it forward—my daughter, a biomedical engineer, is starting her MBA at

Wharton. In our family, education isn't just valued—it's how we move forward. Education has been our family's ticket to progress and greater achievements.

Driven by a culture that revered academic excellence and an educational stalwart father, my youth was directed towards scholastic achievements. I was always striving to meet my father's expectations while also seeking to outdo my maternal cousins. Each cousin sought to do better than the older ones, constantly raising the bar for the ones who followed. The dynamics of my family culture and the social pressures of growing up in a lower-middle-class family fueled my drive to excel in everything I did. Education was my ticket to greater success.

Reflection: *Consider your family background. How have your family's expectations and socio-economic status influenced your personal and professional choices? How did the pressures of academic achievement shape your self-image and career path?*

The American Dream

Coming to the U.S. for graduate school wasn't just my triumph—it was a family milestone. I was the first to leave our deeply rooted community, the first to study abroad—immigration to America where I knew nobody was a huge risk. When I got into Columbia, Chicago, Cornell, and MIT, I was ecstatic. I called my father to share the news. His response? "What took you so long?" Classic. The bar only kept moving higher. I was the first in the family to graduate from MIT—and that trailblazing started getting to my head.

Reflection: *Consider your major life milestones. What defining moments have impacted your journey to achieve greater success?*

The Career Ladder

I worked in the robotics sector in the late 1980s—long before it became popular—on underwater and mobile land robots. In the early 1990s, at Boeing, I launched cutting-edge projects to build robots for assembling the fuselages of the 777 wide-body and 757 narrow-body airplanes. At Lucent Technologies, I built a robotic assembly line for mobile phones, developed an international strategy, and headed up marketing and strategy for a $4.3 billion business. I was part of a leadership development program and one of 150 fast trackers in a company of 160,000. 12 of the 150 reported to me.

Graduating from MIT and the subsequent leadership roles at Lucent reinforced my belief that I was special, a rising star with seemingly no limits. I felt entitled to greater success. Each professional leap was a personal achievement, but it was unknowingly fueling what I now call the Advantage Illusion: the false belief that intelligence and credentials would be enough to propel me to greater successes.

When the dot-com bubble burst and the telecom sector imploded, I moved to Silicon Valley and became a venture capitalist. That fund imploded with one large bad investment, leaving me unemployed. The reality of professional instability kicked in and my trailblazing hit a wall.

I went from 'I could do no wrong' to 'I have done many wrongs.' After having tasted much success, I was now staring at the abyss because of my *Advantage Illusion*.

Reflection: *Have you ever fallen into the Advantage Illusion—believing that your intelligence or credentials would be enough to lead to greater success? What would it look like to actively challenge that belief and apply your Smartness instead?*

The Entrepreneurial Journey

After Lucent and MIT, I thought I could do no wrong. I launched multiple ventures—two failed quickly, one soared. That one took me global: Pfizer, DuPont, SONY, and others became clients; I had influential partners, did business in 16 countries and got written up in over 20 magazines. Heady times again. But as with all over-inflated balloons, the burst was around the corner. I poured six years into my fourth company, funded it myself, and ran teams across the U.S. and India. I turned down outside investment—convinced my intelligence and execution were enough. But when things started unraveling, I failed to adapt. My decision inflexibility hurt me. The entire thing collapsed, and so did the image I had of myself.

That collapse forced a reckoning. I realized I had a *Smartness Gap*—too focused on being intelligent, not enough on how I applied it. I built and took the *Smartness Assessment* during this period and uncovered the very disablers that sabotaged me: excessive detail orientation (I kept improving the product but never launched a minimum viable product); a constant need for variety (I kept adding features without market testing); and poor action orientation (I hesitated when I knew I had to act). These weren't abstract flaws—they were mine. We'll dig into them in later chapters. The turning point? Inversion Thinking—asking what I was doing to cause failure, not what I was missing or if I was the reason for the failure. That shift became the foundation for this book.

I relied too much on intelligence—assuming that it would translate to success. But intelligence without adaptability, judgment, and execution can quickly become a liability.

I believed my intelligence guaranteed success—and that belief quietly distorted how I saw the world, made decisions, and pursued success. I realized that something other than intelligence was leading to bad judgment, poor decisions and negative outcomes.

Reflection: *Think about the career risks you have taken. What drove these decisions, and how did they align with your personal values and goals?*

My Relevant Experiences

I've worn many hats—engineer, strategist, venture capitalist, founder. I've hired over 500 people, including elite university grads, engineers, leaders, and tech pros. I led marketing and strategy for a $4.3 billion business, co-founded four startups, and now I'm building my fifth. I've interviewed almost 200 high achievers for my podcasts and books, and analyzed data from 1,200 *Smartness Assessment* participants. The insight from all of that is clear: intelligence opens the door, but *Smartness* is what gets you through it. Even MONEY magazine once called me "The Comeback Kid." Everything I've learned—through wins, failures, reinvention—is in this book.

> *"Smartness is what intelligent people need to succeed outside their head—in the real world. It's what gets you results."*

Reflection: *Reflect on your own life story. What traits, experiences, or circumstances have given you an edge, and what has held you back?*

Key Takeaways

Looking back, my greatest turning point wasn't a job title, a promotion, or even an achievement—it was failure. When I lost almost everything, I finally understood: success isn't about intelligence or credentials alone. I had spent years assuming intelligence would open doors. But doors don't just open. You have to knock—sometimes repeatedly. Sometimes, you have to break them down.

What I also learned is that smart people—especially those with elite credentials or a few early wins—often struggle with self-awareness. When your identity is built around intelligence, you stop examining how you actually operate: your real strengths, your blind spots, your behaviors. Intelligence becomes a shield—and eventually, a trap.

> *"The greatest enemy of intelligence is not stupidity, but the illusion that intelligence alone is enough."*

You can be a legend in your own mind. But the world—and your competitors—don't care about your credentials. While you're basking in how smart you are, they're out executing—with sharper judgment and faster decisions.

The final, brutal realization? Entitlement kills execution. I became overconfident—believing my intelligence would always translate into success. It didn't. Intelligence only matters if it's paired with adaptability, action, and sound decision-making—the very core of *Smartness*.

That failure forced a reckoning. It introduced me to a deeper understanding of myself—and helped me see and correct my own disabling behaviors. My early successes and MIT degree bred arrogance. But failure shattered that illusion—and forced me to confront who I really was and how I actually operated.

My Story & How it Informs This Book

My failures weren't just painful. They were avoidable. Had I developed and applied *Smartness* earlier—balancing intelligence with judgment and action—I could have achieved far more.

> *"The most uncomfortable truths are often the keys to your next breakthrough. Avoiding them delays your greater success."*

Reflection: *What truth about yourself have you been dodging—because deep down, you know it's what's actually holding you back?*

You don't need to spend 10 years figuring it out like I did. Instead, just read this book, reflect, and use the companion *Smartness Playbook*. But reflection alone isn't enough. You also need the right Knowledge to make informed decisions and act. That's where we turn next.

CHAPTER 3

Uncover Your Success Barriers with Inversion Thinking

"Smart people often assume intelligence will lead them to the right answer. But the real challenge isn't the answer—it's knowing the right questions to ask."
~ Ram V. Iyer

I'm the founder and President of the iAchiever Institute and the Business Thinking Institute in Princeton, New Jersey. With over 30 years of business experience, I've seen my share of highs and lows. Despite my efforts, the spectacular business success I once envisioned has eluded me. I have the drive and credentials: two master's degrees (one from MIT), a business degree, an extensive network, and constant learning. Yet, something was holding me back from reaching the next level. Why wasn't I, an accomplished MIT graduate, more successful? I kept wondering, *"What am I missing?"* Like many smart people, I assumed intelligence, credentials, and hard work were enough. But as I later learnt, success is not just about knowing—it's about applying intelligence with adaptability, good judgment, and effective execution.

My Recent Story

About ten years ago, I was running a venture that I had spent six years building and heavily invested in. It failed spectacularly and nearly bankrupted me. I was devastated. Though I'm naturally optimistic and resilient, this setback hit me hard. I needed to understand why it happened and how I could bounce back.

I turned to mentors, friends, coaches, and experts for advice. They said I needed more capital, a better team, better technology—essentially, better everything external to me. It was the same recycled advice I'd heard many times before. While their reasons were logical, I felt something deeper was holding me back. But I had no idea what it was or how to uncover it.

Reflection: Smart people often assume intelligence alone is enough. Have you ever followed traditional 'success advice' only to realize it didn't work for you? How did thinking differently change your results?

The Aha Moment with Inversion Thinking

I chewed on their observations for weeks, and the lack of an answer gnawed at me. Then, one evening, as I was reflecting on the spectacular failure of my last venture, it hit me like a bolt of lightning: I had been asking the wrong question.

Instead of asking:
Was my failure due to what I lacked?
and
What external factors caused my failure?
I should have asked:
Did I cause my own failure?
and
Was my failure due to who I was?

I began identifying the internal disablers—weaknesses within me that had led to my failure. It was a hard question to ask and an even harder one to answer. It required brutal self-honesty. Most of us struggle with that, because facing the truth about ourselves hurts our ego. I only realized my internal barriers after repeated failures, and only when I asked the right questions.

I realized that these 'disablers' were rooted deep within my mindset—my beliefs, values, rules, principles, expectations, and self-talk. Reframing the question, using what I later learned was called 'Inversion Thinking,' changed everything. That evening, I identified three internal obstacles to my success, which are mentioned in the Acknowledgments and later in the chapter entitled 'Insights from the Smartness Assessment Data'.

Inversion Thinking helped me shift my focus from adding external solutions to uncovering internal barriers. It was a game-changer. For example, someone might suggest wearing a red jacket to boost success, but if you suffer from impostor syndrome and already feel unsuccessful, the red jacket won't make a difference.

However, identifying these internal obstacles is only the first step. Often, the biggest barriers we face are the ones we create ourselves: through patterns of self-deception, self-lies, and limiting beliefs.

Lying to Yourself

We were all raised not to lie to others—parents, teachers, and elders drilled that into us. But did anyone tell you not to lie to yourself?

The lies we tell ourselves are often far more damaging. Small missteps and justifications—those moments when we knowingly do the wrong thing and rationalize it—can snowball into bad habits that hold us back.

We all lie to ourselves. Some lies are small, others bigger. But when those lies become your truth, they shape your mindset, drive your decisions, and may lead to actions that create the very outcomes you don't want.

Recognizing and breaking these patterns is essential to removing barriers and building the foundation for true success. If you want to turn your life around or achieve greater success, start by being honest with yourself. It may be hard, but it's the foundation for true progress.

> *"Do the wrong thing once, and it's easier to do it again. That's how bad habits develop."*

Inversion Thinking helps us identify what holds us back and eliminate those obstacles. But there's a catch—it requires brutal honesty. You have to face your own weaknesses and disablers. Sometimes, that means asking others what they see, which isn't easy. Most people avoid it. But if you're a house cat looking in the mirror, what should you really be seeing?

External success often depends on internal clarity. That clarity only comes when you look inward.

Reflection: *When was the last time you looked within yourself to find the answer to a problem you were facing? Could some of your obstacles to achieving greater success be internal rather than external to you?*

I went back to my mentors, friends, and coaches, this time with a fresh perspective. The difference in our conversations was night and day. The quality of advice improved significantly, thanks to Inversion Thinking. They said, "That's an interesting way of looking at it. Let me tell you how else you screwed up!" As good friends do, they piled on, and my list of obstacles grew from three to twelve. I called them "The Silent Killers of Success." A rather simple but profound insight came from this experience:

> *"In a battle between the demons and the angels in your mind, the demons will usually win."*

These insights were so potent that I ended up sharing them in presentations at MIT and Harvard. When I spoke at the alumni club of an Ivy League university, we used the tagline, "Why are so many smart people not as successful as they think they should be?" for my talk. And guess what? Five times as many people as expected showed up. That was my cue; more people were facing this issue than I had originally thought.

I didn't stop there. I conducted more research, reading books and journals, watching videos, and speaking to classmates, colleagues, professionals, and friends. I identified over 80 reasons why some highly intelligent and smart people find it difficult to achieve greater success. I then hired two psychologists to validate my findings. With their help, we boiled over 80 reasons down to what has now become the *Smartness Factors*.

We created the *Smartness Assessment* to test whether the factors we identified applied to a broader group of smart people. I offered it to alumni from the top 15 schools globally, spanning 15 different professional groups. The analysis confirmed that the factors were highly relevant – there will be more on that in the chapter, Insights from the *Smartness Assessment* Data.

I researched each factor and found tools, worksheets, and methods to help people address them. Interestingly, many successful individuals in the same community were affected by these factors, but in enabling ways. This led to a simple realization: the *Smartness Factors* influence all smart and advantaged people—some as enablers, others as disablers. With effort, anyone can:

1. Leverage their enablers for greater success.
2. Mitigate or convert disablers into enablers.

While these factors aren't exclusive to smart people, they play a critical role in determining their success or failure.

Reflection: *Are you relying too much on intelligence without Smartness? What habits or beliefs make you assume you 'should' succeed—rather than ensuring you actually do?*

Focusing Only on Your Strengths

We are a 'good news only' society today. Everyone is expected to be positive, speak positively, and say only positive things about others. We are told about our strengths. Over time, each of us develops a 'strength bias'—believing that strengths are more common than they really are, both in ourselves and in others, and weaknesses are not. Acknowledging one's weaknesses or pointing out other people's weaknesses is almost taboo. That's when you often hear, "That's not nice!" All of us need to periodically hear the unvarnished truth if we are to truly get better. Change can only happen with awareness.

Over time, my close circle of friends and family have pointed out my strengths, but very few have pointed out my weaknesses. I guess they didn't want to offend me or jeopardize their relationship with me. On the other hand, my ego prevented me from wanting to hear or learn about my weaknesses. Over time, I trapped myself in a 'positive bubble,' primarily leveraging my strengths and ignoring my weaknesses. Many people who embrace positive psychology blindly are stuck in the same 'positive bubble.'

Your Success – Net of Strengths and Weaknesses

Let's look at how strengths and weaknesses develop—and get leveraged—over the typical lifetimes of most people. During childhood, we discover, develop, and leverage our strengths. Most of our friends and family tend to point out our strengths, not our weaknesses. Some do this to build our self-image, while others avoid highlighting our weaknesses to remain 'popular' with us. These behaviors often carry into adulthood.

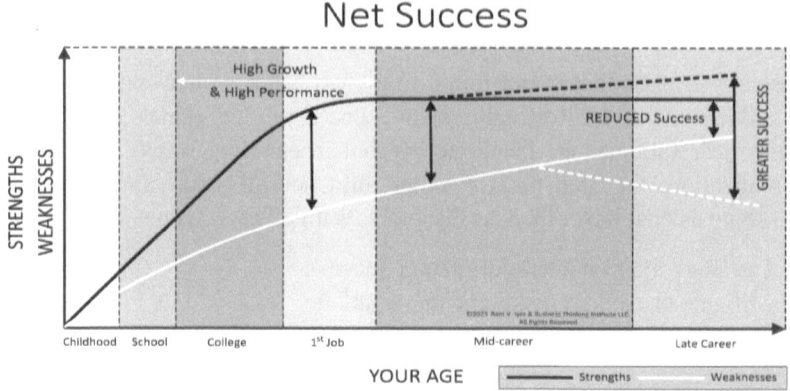

As a result, our strengths accumulate—and get leveraged more—while our weaknesses also accumulate but are largely ignored. In the graph above, the black line indicates how our strengths develop and get leveraged over age; the white line shows the growth of our weaknesses. Notice that our strengths generally plateau after we enter our first job out of college. This reflects a natural limit—each of us has only so many strengths, and leveraging them can only take us so far.

In the meantime, our weaknesses have been growing too. Most of us avoid addressing them because confronting weaknesses doesn't feel good—it doesn't align with the positive self-image we prefer to maintain. Instead, we stay in our 'strengths bubble,' deferring our weaknesses to deal with later... much later.

Over time, while our strengths plateau, our unaddressed weaknesses begin to accumulate and drag down our overall success. According to data from 1200+ people who took the *Smartness Assessment*, this shift often occurs post-college, with weaknesses starting to weigh heavier in mid-career.

You can rely on your strengths early in your career, but if you don't manage or eliminate your weaknesses, they could derail your success in mid- or late-career.

You've heard the saying, "A chain is only as strong as its weakest link." The same applies to success. Early in your career, your strengths—your enablers—often shine and carry you forward. But in mid- and late-career, it's your disablers—the weak links—that start to matter more. A single unchecked disabler can limit your progress or derail your success. That's why Smartness—the set of capabilities that helps you better leverage your enablers *and* manage or mitigate your disablers—is essential, both to be successful and to avoid failure or stagnation. It's not enough to rely on what you're good at. To achieve sustained success, you must also develop the capacity to address your success hurdles. To make smarter choices, you must first be aware of both your enablers and disablers—because informed individuals make better decisions than ignorant ones. We'll address that in the "Smartness Assessment" chapter.

In our early jobs after college, strengths are usually at their peak. Although weaknesses grow, the net gap between strengths and weaknesses still favors strengths. This period—typically the first few years after college—is often when this net positive is strongest.

By mid- and late-career, however, strengths plateau while weaknesses continue to grow, largely because we fail to address them. The gap between strengths and weaknesses narrows, making success harder to achieve. In cases where weaknesses overtake strengths, people often experience professional and personal stagnation, leading to frustration and disappointment.

At this stage of your career, improving strengths by 10%, 20%, or 50% is near impossible—you'd be fortunate to achieve even a 1% or 5% increase. On the other hand, remember our weaknesses, which we've neglected most of our lives? Reducing those weaknesses by 10%, 20%, or more is far more realistic and achievable. Focusing on minimizing weaknesses allows you to widen the gap between your strengths and weaknesses, with your strengths still dominant, ensuring your continued success.

As my friend Dr. Marshall Goldsmith aptly says in his bestselling book's title, *What Got You Here Won't Get You There,* you must, quite simply, constantly address your weaknesses to achieve sustained success.

Sometimes, progress comes down to one honest assessment: are your strengths doing more for you than your weaknesses are doing against you?

Reflection: *Do you think your current strengths and weaknesses are a net positive or a net negative?*

The Running Race Analogy

Imagine you're running a race, dressed in your best gear and fancy running shoes. How can you run faster? You might think upgrading to a sleeker pair of shoes or adding gel to your hair for aerodynamics could help. While these tweaks might offer small, incremental improvements, they are like the marginal gains we can make to our strengths later in our careers.

Now, picture yourself running with a 50-lb backpack filled with your weaknesses and disablers. Shedding even a small amount of that weight, say 5 lbs. will significantly improve your speed. Over time, as you lighten more of this baggage, you'll be able to run faster and more effortlessly, just like reducing weaknesses increases your net strengths and paves the way for greater success. In that example, practically recognizing that shedding some weight from the backpack, and having the willingness to shed it is essential for you to act – that's *Smartness*. Simply recognizing the weight isn't enough—many smart people know their weaknesses but don't act on them. *Smartness* is about identifying which burdens are limiting your progress and having the discipline to let them go. We will discuss that in detail in the chapter, Understanding Smartness, in Part 2 of the book.

Weaknesses vs. Disablers

As you explore your personal barriers to success, it's essential to distinguish between weaknesses and disablers. Weaknesses are traits or limitations—such as lacking a skill or being physically small—that might create challenges in certain situations. However, weaknesses only hold you back if they remain unmanaged.

For example, being short might be seen as a weakness in basketball because it limits certain aspects of play, like shooting the ball into the net when surrounded by tall players. If this limitation leads to constant self-doubt, excuses, or avoidance, it becomes a disabler—a mindset or behavior that actively prevents success (shooting the ball into the basket). On the other hand, a short player could focus on their strengths, such as agility, speed, or strategic thinking. They might develop a style of play that maximizes the team's effectiveness by feeding the ball to taller teammates when challenged by taller opponents. Alternatively, they could pivot to a sport like gymnastics, where height is an advantage due to a lower center of gravity and flexibility. Similarly, in professional settings, a short individual might offset perceived disadvantages by cultivating commanding interpersonal skills or presenting themselves as approachable and relatable.

Disablers are not inherent traits—they arise from how you perceive and handle your weaknesses and limitations in a given situation. These perceptions and decisions are shaped by your mindset, behaviors, and skills. By focusing on what you can control, you can turn weaknesses into neutral or even to your advantage. This ability is a fundamental step in developing *Smartness*, a concept we'll explore further in this book.

Most people, even smart people, often believe that doubling down on strengths will overcome any challenge. But real success comes from recognizing and eliminating disablers, because no amount of intelligence can compensate for blind spots that actively hold you back.

Reflection: *What is one personal weakness you've allowed to limit your success? How could you reframe it to prevent it from being a disabler?*

Acquiring More, More, and Even More

For much of my life, I believed greater success came from acquiring more—more skills, capabilities or possessions—buy one more book, attend one more program, listen to one more talk. Society constantly reinforces this mindset. We're bombarded with messages telling us that buying into the next program, getting another degree, or owning the latest thing—a bigger home or a newer car—will somehow lead to greater success.

Some of it helped. But most of the time, I would read a book, attend a seminar, or participate in a workshop and then fail to follow up. Ideas that seemed profound at the moment faded from memory within a week or two because I never put them into action. I rationalized the expense with pithy justifications like, "If I picked up even one thing, it was worth it." But let's be honest—how often can you actually recall or use even that "one thing"? Most of the time, it's money and time down the drain.

Over time, I embraced this mindset of 'more' with a relentless focus on my strengths, acquiring and building more and more. But eventually, I hit a wall. After years of focusing on my strengths, the returns diminished. There was only so much growth left to squeeze out of them.

This culture of 'more' is pervasive, fueled by FOMO (fear of missing out), and often benefits those selling it more than it benefits you. How many workshops, books, or courses have you invested in? And how many of them actually transformed your success? If you look back, you'll probably find books gathering dust, materials untouched, and dollars spent on things that didn't move the needle.

Reflection: *Make a list of personal development books and courses you've purchased or seminars you've attended (whether paid for by you or your employer). Put a checkmark next to those that truly made a difference in your life.*

Smart people often assume their intelligence alone will lead to success—but Inversion Thinking reveals the internal disablers that sabotage progress. By asking the right questions, you can bridge the gap between intelligence and real-world achievement. Inversion Thinking flips the script by focusing inward to identify the barriers that hold us back. It challenges us to ask tough questions about the internal disablers—our blind spots, habits, and mindsets—that prevent us from achieving greater success. Real breakthroughs happen not by adding more but by eliminating what's weighing us down.

True growth comes from identifying and addressing the weaknesses we've been avoiding. While the process can be uncomfortable, it's essential for unlocking our strengths and achieving sustainable success. Success isn't about doing more—it's about doing less of what holds us back. Sometimes, the breakthrough begins with brutal honesty. Start by confronting what you've been unwilling to face.

You can never become truly successful if your mindset—your beliefs, values, worldview, or self-image— is holding you back. Your mindset guides your thinking, and therefrom your actions and outcomes. If your mindset is working against you, even your greatest advantages won't help. Fix your mindset for your advantages to truly matter.

> *"Until you fix a mindset that holds you back, your advantages won't matter much."*

Reflection: *What truth about your mindset, habits, or behavior have you been avoiding—because deep down, you're uncomfortable facing it but you also know it could change everything?*

But Knowledge alone isn't enough. To succeed, you also need to recognize and leverage the advantages you already have. These advantages are often overlooked, but they play a critical role in turning insight into impact. That's what we'll explore next.

CHAPTER 4

ADVANTAGES & WHY THEY MATTER FOR SMART PEOPLE

> *"An advantage is a powerful thing, but only if you know when and how to use it."*
> ~ Ram V. Iyer

Advantage is a condition that puts one in a favorable or superior position. It gives you a leg up—a head start or an edge. It denotes a favorable or superior position and is known by many names around the world, such as **ventaja** in Spanish, **avantage** in French, ميزة (*Mīzah*) in Arabic, 优势 (*yōushì*) in Mandarin, 利点 (*Riten*) in Japanese, **Kalamangan** in Tagalog and फायदा (*Fāydā*) in Hindi, each capturing the essence of having the upper hand. In this chapter, we'll explore the different types of advantages and how understanding them is the first step toward leveraging them effectively with *Smartness*.

Just like money doesn't grow when it sits idle, advantages don't create results unless you use them well. Intelligence, credentials, and networks only move you forward when they're applied with *Smartness*. Otherwise, they can lead to overconfidence, complacency, or flat-out stagnation.

For smart people, the issue isn't just lacking advantages—it's misusing the ones they have. Many over-rely on intelligence or credentials and overlook the rest. Intelligence is the foundation, but without *Smartness*, it can become a trap. Credentials, networks, and resources can amplify success, but only when applied with timing, judgment, and intent. *Smartness* is knowing which advantage to use, when to use it, and how to use it well.

Consider this: Two people with similar advantages—such as intelligence or access to resources—may achieve vastly different outcomes. One might thrive, while the other struggles. The difference lies in how they leverage their advantages. Used effectively, advantages amplify your efforts, help you navigate obstacles, and open doors to new opportunities.

This chapter introduces three categories of advantages—Fixed, Flexible, and Situational—and explores their connection to *Smartness*, the key to transforming potential into meaningful success. By understanding your advantages and applying them wisely, you can unlock new levels of achievement.

Status reflects past achievements and may open doors, but continued success requires ongoing development. Status may open doors—but *Smartness* is what keeps them open.

> *"Raw intelligence is only half the story—what matters is how you use it."*

Reflection: *How have you been using your intelligence? Have you relied on it too much without leveraging other advantages, or have you underutilized it in key situations?*

Types of Advantages

Not all advantages are the same. Among all advantages, intelligence is the foundation—it determines how well you acquire and apply other advantages. Without intelligence and *Smartness*, even powerful advantages can be misused or wasted. Advantages vary in origin, how they're acquired, and how they can be applied to achieve greater success. To better understand and use your advantages, it helps to group them into three broad categories: Fixed, Flexible, and Situational Advantages.

1. **Fixed Advantages**
   Fixed advantages are those you're born with or acquire without significant effort. These are inherent traits or resources that provide a natural starting point for success.
   - *Examples*: High intelligence, inherited wealth, physical capabilities, or natural charisma.
   - *How They Work*: Fixed advantages give you a head start in certain areas. For instance, someone with strong analytical skills might find problem-solving easier, while someone with natural athletic ability might excel in sports.

2. **Flexible Advantages**
   Flexible advantages are those you develop and refine over time through effort and experience. These are dynamic and can grow as you build skills, relationships, and knowledge.
   - *Examples*: Negotiation skills, professional expertise, leadership capabilities, or a strong network of mentors and collaborators.
   - *How They Work*: Unlike fixed advantages, flexible advantages require deliberate effort. For example, someone who actively builds their public speaking skills can use this ability to open new career opportunities or influence others effectively.

3. **Situational Advantages**
   Situational advantages are tied to specific contexts or opportunities. They arise based on timing, environment, or unique circumstances and often require quick action to capitalize on them.
   - *Examples*: Working in a fast-growing industry, being part of a well-connected community, or running into an influential person you know.
   - *How They Work*: These advantages are often temporary and demand quick recognition and response. For instance, entrepreneurs entering the AI field during its boom can position themselves to ride the wave of growth if they act decisively. Similarly, running into an influential person

presents an immediate opportunity to build a valuable connection—if you act wisely.

Understanding these categories helps you recognize where your strengths lie and what areas might need more attention. Fixed advantages provide a strong starting point, but without flexible and situational advantages, they risk being underutilized. On the other hand, building flexible advantages and staying alert to situational opportunities ensures you remain adaptable and competitive.

Having an advantage—whether it's wealth, credentials, or a powerful network—is only the beginning. Success doesn't come from the advantage itself but from how consistently and strategically you apply it. Smart people know that real achievement requires using intelligence to adapt, act, and leverage their resources in meaningful ways. Resting on an advantage leads to stagnation; applying it wisely drives results.

Part 3 of this book will guide you in identifying your advantages, whether fixed, flexible or situational.

The Misuse of Advantages

While intelligence enables success, its misuse—overconfidence, arrogance, or inaction—can hold smart people back. Many assume that elite credentials, wealth, or networks will guarantee success, but these secondary advantages only matter if they are strategically applied with intelligence and *Smartness*. Entitlement, over-reliance, or neglect of your advantages are common pitfalls that hinder progress and prevent success – they can become disablers rather than enablers of success.

This is where The Advantage Illusion does the most damage. It convinces smart people that their intelligence or credentials are already working on their behalf—that simply having those advantages is enough. But when they stop actively applying themselves, adapting, or developing complementary strengths, they begin to stall. The illusion isn't just overconfidence. It's a quiet complacency that makes them believe they've already earned the success they haven't yet achieved.

> *"The greatest enemy of advantage is not arrogance, but the illusion that advantage alone is enough."*

1. **Entitlement:** It occurs when people assume their advantages guarantee success with little or no effort. For example, an Ivy League graduate may enter the corporate world believing their degree alone will ensure career progression. However, ignoring the need to be competitive with colleagues by building people skills or staying updated with industry developments can lead to stagnation, as others may surpass them with continuous learning and effort.
2. **Over-Reliance and Neglect**: Relying overly on a single advantage—such as wealth, intelligence, or connections—can create blind spots. It may prevent you from adapting to new challenges or developing complementary strengths.

Similarly, neglecting other advantages limits your ability to pivot or respond to changing circumstances. For instance, a professional with technical expertise but no focus on building relationships may struggle in leadership roles where collaboration is key.

> *"Any perceived advantage you don't test eventually turns into a trap."*

The key to avoiding these traps is balance. Recognize the value of each advantage, but don't let any one of them be your singular approach. *Smartness* lies in using all your advantages strategically, adapting them to different situations, and continuously developing new capabilities.

The misuse of advantages stems from a lack of awareness and intentionality. This is where *Smartness* plays a critical role. *Smartness* enables you to:

1. Recognize when an advantage can be used, or if it is being overused or neglected.
2. Use underutilized advantages when needed.
3. Avoid the pitfalls of entitlement and complacency by staying adaptable and growth-oriented.

By applying *Smartness*, you can ensure that your advantages are enablers of success rather than obstacles to it.

Reflection: *Are there advantages you've over-relied on or taken for granted? Have you neglected certain strengths that could complement your goals?*

Historical Perspectives on Advantages

History makes one thing clear: advantages open doors, but *Smartness* determines what happens next. Take Alexander the Great. He had massive advantages—royal birth, elite education, military power. But those alone didn't make him a world-shaping leader. What mattered was how he used them: with vision, adaptability, and relentless action. That's *Smartness*.

Across cultures, the lesson is the same. Confucian traditions in China, the Indian principle of *dharma*, and the Greek pursuit of *arete* all emphasize using advantages with discipline, wisdom, and integrity—not as shortcuts, but as responsibilities.

Smart people succeed not because they have advantages, but because they apply them with intention. They don't assume success, they earn it.

Cultural Perspectives on Advantages

Advantages may open doors, but *Smartness* determines whether you walk through them and what you do next.

History, philosophy, and culture all reinforce the same truth: advantages are never enough on their own. The people who succeed are the ones who use what they've got—wisely, intentionally, and repeatedly.

Across cultures, this message repeats:

- Confucian ideals emphasize humility, discipline, and lifelong learning.
- The Greek concept of arete demands full use of one's potential through excellence and integrity.
- Indian philosophy speaks to dharma—aligning action with purpose, not entitlement.

In the U.S., success is often framed as self-made, but that story usually overlooks the role of timing, privilege, and access. Meanwhile, many Eastern traditions emphasize restraint, contribution, and long-term impact—values that help smart people use their advantages with clarity and care.

Whatever the culture, *Smartness* is what turns raw advantages into real achievement. Without it, people coast or stagnate. With it, they rise.

The Research

Advantages carry both opportunity and risk. Wealth, status, education, or power can open doors—but they can also create blind spots. Smart people often overestimate their advantages, leading to complacency, overconfidence, or stagnation. Research shows how advantages shape behavior in ways that either accelerate or undermine long-term success.

1. Status Characteristics Theory (Joseph Berger)
Wealth, education, and power are status markers that shape how competence is perceived. Smart people often gain influence because of these traits, whether or not they're still earning it. This perception can lead to overconfidence. Status opens doors, but maintaining success requires continuous development.

2. The Matthew Effect (Robert K. Merton)
Initial advantages multiply. Wealth, credentials, and networks often reinforce themselves, making future success easier. Some smart people believe they succeeded **only** because of their own effort or intelligence. But they overlook the fact that external factors, like being in the right place at the right time, having access to exclusive opportunities, or benefiting from privileges (wealth, status, networks), also play a role. Sustainable success comes from leveraging a multitude of initial and newer advantages.

3. The Abundance Mindset and Complacency Trap (Stephen R. Covey)
Those with advantages often adopt an abundance mindset, seeing opportunities everywhere. But this can lead to complacency, delaying action. Smart people who feel secure can lose urgency, falling behind faster-moving competitors. Balancing confidence with continuous improvement is key.

4. Self-Fulfilling Prophecy (Robert K. Merton)
Advantages foster confidence and shape expectations, both from others and from within. But if smart people rely too much on perceived success, they risk entitlement and decline. Long-term achievement demands effort, not assumption.

5. Implicit Bias (Mahzarin Banaji & Anthony Greenwald) and **Attribution Theory** (Fritz Heider)
People often credit success to their own abilities, downplaying external factors like resources and connections. Smart people who stay grounded recognize the full picture, and keep learning. Awareness prevents entitlement and encourages adaptability.

Advantages are powerful, but they're not enough. Without self-awareness and continuous action, they can create blind spots that block growth. Smart people succeed when they leverage advantages without relying on them, combining them with humility, learning, and adaptability.

Practical Applications: Strategies to Maximize the Value of Advantages

The world thrives on favors, small and large acts of cooperation that help people achieve their goals. However, many smart people often overlook a critical factor: whether people like you, enjoy working with you, and want to help you.

For instance, imagine someone who is wealthy or graduated from a prestigious university but is disliked by colleagues. Despite their advantages, they may struggle to gain cooperation, collaboration, or support from others. This lack of goodwill can severely limit their ability to achieve their goals.

Effectively leveraging advantages requires self-awareness, humility, and the ability to adapt. These traits, each an element of *Smartness*, are what truly unlock the potential of your advantages. Here are some practical steps to ensure that your advantages are assets and not liabilities:

1. **Assess Your Advantages Regularly:** Periodically, as well as before and after significant events—with positive or negative outcomes—evaluate your current and situational advantages. Recognize both your personal and external factors that advantage you.
2. **Challenge Yourself:** Set goals that require you to grow beyond your current strengths. Avoid settling for tasks within your comfort zone, even if they yield success.
3. **Seek Feedback:** Regularly seek feedback from peers, mentors, or even critics. Constructive input helps you avoid blind spots and maintain a grounded self-view.
4. **Engage in Lifelong Learning:** Dedicate time to personal development, even in areas unrelated to your primary strengths. Expanding your knowledge base prevents overreliance on any one advantage.

5. **Give Back:** Use your advantages to support others, fostering a mindset of contribution rather than entitlement. Sharing your advantages through mentoring, volunteering, or financial support fosters humility, enhances social awareness, builds a network of supporters, and helps establish your legacy.

These strategies underscore the importance of continual growth, self-awareness, and a balanced perspective on one's achievements and advantages. By leveraging these theories, individuals can better manage their advantages to ensure lasting success.

Reflection: *Reflect on a time when you relied on an advantage rather than actively applying yourself. How did it impact your success?*

The Disabling Power of Advantages

Advantages like wealth, status, or authority are undeniably valuable, but they can also act as obstacles when taken for granted or left unchecked. Below are common pitfalls associated with advantages and strategies to mitigate their disabling effects.

1. **Entitlement**: Believing advantages guarantee success can lead to complacency, where effort diminishes, and improvement stalls. *Example:* A high-achieving graduate who coasts in their role might rely on academic credentials, only to hit career stagnation.
2. **Isolation**: Advantages can create a sense of separation, where individuals feel above others or independent of feedback, limiting collaboration. *Example:* A CEO who ignores team input, trusting solely in their position, may implement misaligned strategies that harm morale.
3. **Overconfidence in Predictable Outcomes**: Relying on advantages over skill can lead to blind spots when challenges arise. *Example:* A wealthy entrepreneur venturing into a new field may assume success is assured, only to struggle with unforeseen issues.
4. **Stagnation and Resistance to Change**: Advantages can create comfort zones, making change or innovation less appealing, which risks eroding one's edge. *Example:* A long-tenured executive resisting the adoption of new technology may fall behind as the industry advances.

Checklist to Avoid Pitfalls

1. **Adopt a Learning Mindset**: Regularly challenge yourself to grow beyond your current strengths, viewing advantages as tools that need to be regularly sharpened, not endpoints.
2. **Seek Diverse Perspectives**: Surround yourself with individuals who challenge your viewpoints, consider their perspectives, and embrace feedback to remain adaptable.
3. **Set Realistic Goals**: Define specific, achievable goals that go beyond the comfort your advantages offer. Use metrics to track progress and adapt.

4. **Practice Humility**: Recognize and acknowledge the external factors that contribute to your success, helping to prevent entitlement and isolation.
5. **Focus on Contribution**: Actively find ways to use your advantages to support others, reinforcing a mindset of service over entitlement.

Reflection: *Think of a time when one of your advantages led to complacency or overconfidence. What were the results, and how could a more balanced approach have improved the results?*

> *"Smartness bridges the gap between possessing advantages and achieving meaningful results by helping you recognize opportunities, adapt to challenges, and effectively apply your advantages in different situations."*

Having advantages doesn't guarantee anything. It's how smart people use them—what they choose to rely on, what they adapt, and how they execute—that creates real success. Intelligence may be the foundation, but it's not enough on its own. *Smartness* is what determines whether someone builds on their advantages or squanders them. And that's exactly what we'll explore in greater detail in Parts 2 and 3 of this book.

In Part 3, we'll discuss practical ways to identify and assess your own advantages in depth. You'll also learn how to overcome the disablers that may hold you back, align your actions with your goals, and consistently apply *Smartness* to navigate any situation.

Just as advantages can propel you forward, disablers—if left unrecognized—can just as easily hold you back. The next chapter dives into how smart people must identify and overcome these hidden barriers.

Even intelligence becomes a hiding place, particularly for smart people. When you stop testing yourself, you stop growing.

Reflection: *What advantage have you been hiding behind—pretending it is progress (or safe)—when deep down, you know it's become your excuse for not learning more, or stepping up or trying harder?*

This chapter lays the groundwork for identifying and leveraging your advantages effectively, setting the stage for deeper reflection in later chapters.

CHAPTER 5

WHY DISABLERS MUST BE ADDRESSED

"Enablers and enabling behaviors give us wings to soar; disablers and disabling behaviors weigh us down. To soar higher sooner, we must first shed what holds us back."
~ Ram V. Iyer

This chapter focuses on why tackling disablers is critical for success. Enablers drive momentum by enhancing your strengths, while disablers—whether internal struggles like self-doubt or external barriers like toxic environments—slow you down or derail your efforts. Ignored, they compound. But once you identify and address them, you remove roadblocks that free up your growth and accelerate progress toward your goals.

Smart people assume intelligence and skills guarantee success. But often, their biggest obstacle isn't the world. It's their own hidden resistance. These internal barriers don't just slow success; they distort decision-making, hinder adaptability, and limit execution—the core of *Smartness*.

Addressing Disablers to Unlock Potential

For smart people, disablers can be especially destructive. The more intelligent they are, the easier it becomes to rationalize poor decisions, overthink simple actions, or cling to ineffective habits. Intelligence without Smartness is like a high-performance car without a steering wheel or brakes—powerful but dangerous. Many smart people self-sabotage not because they lack ability, but because they fail to see how their behaviors are blocking their strengths. Unlike weaknesses, which are often passive, disablers are active barriers. They block momentum and drain your ability to move forward. *Smartness* is what allows them to spot and neutralize those blocks before they derail progress.

Addressing disablers involves three critical steps:

1. Recognize the Disabler: Identify the behaviors, habits, or mindsets that are holding you back.
2. Commit to Change: Develop a mindset that is open to confronting and transforming these obstacles.
3. Take Action: Replace limiting behaviors with constructive habits that align with your goals.

For example, procrastination is a common disabler that prevents progress despite good intentions. Addressing it involves identifying triggers (e.g., fear of failure), committing to taking small steps, and developing habits like creating clear priorities or seeking accountability.

How to Become More Successful

In competition, we often focus on the winner's strengths and enablers, but often fail to understand what held others back—like their mistakes, weaknesses, or disablers, which are often just as important. Life, like sports, has many competitors but only one top position. Copying the winner often backfires because their path may not align with your unique abilities or mindset. Instead, you must also focus on identifying and mitigating your own mistakes and weaknesses and observing the mistakes and weaknesses of others while leveraging your personal strengths.

Personal development must be personalized to make it more effective — to who you are, where you are, and your enablers and disablers. The *Smartness Assessment* helps pinpoint these, and this book will guide you in using your enablers effectively while mitigating (or eliminating) your disablers for greater success.

Historical Context

Throughout history, societies have recognized the role of enablers and disablers in shaping personal success. In ancient Greece, philosophers like Aristotle emphasized the concept of *arête (*excellence in character and purpose) as an enabler for a fulfilling life. Greek philosophy taught that cultivating inner strengths, such as wisdom and self-discipline, enabled individuals to overcome challenges. Still, disablers like unchecked desires and vices could derail one's path to virtue and success.

In Confucian philosophy, personal growth depended on both intrinsic virtues, like humility and diligence, and external enablers, such as supportive family and community structures. However, Confucius also warned against disablers, like pride and impulsiveness, which could undermine harmony and prevent individuals from achieving their potential. This balanced perspective highlighted the importance of recognizing and addressing one's disablers to promote individual and collective achievement.

Similarly, in Indian philosophy, the concept of *dharma*, or righteous duty, serves as a guiding enabler of personal and social success. Fulfilling one's dharma is seen as promoting harmony, while neglecting it can lead to chaos and discontent. In the *Mahabharata*, characters who embraced their duties rose above challenges, while those who ignored them faced setbacks, underscoring the importance of managing disablers.

In each of these traditions, the principle is clear: true achievement requires more than strengths or virtues alone. Success demands the proactive cultivation of enablers while addressing or avoiding disablers that can obstruct progress. These cultural insights highlight the timeless value of understanding and balancing the forces that impact one's path to success.

Reflection: Which of these cultural perspectives on strengths and weaknesses do you relate to the most?

The Research

Our understanding of enablers and disablers isn't just psychological or cultural. It's grounded in neuroscience and behavioral science. These factors operate at a fundamental level in our brains, influencing how we think, act, and make decisions. Understanding how they work gives smart people the insight to manage them more effectively.

1. The Triune Brain Model (Paul MacLean)
The triune brain model describes three parts of the brain that shape behavior:

- **The Reptilian Brain** (R-Complex): Responsible for survival instincts like fight or flight. It reacts automatically in emergencies, such as swerving when a car cuts into your lane. While useful for survival, relying on instinct alone can lead to reactive decisions that smart people need to override to avoid shortsightedness.
- **The Limbic System** (Emotional Brain): Governs emotions and social responses. It triggers anxiety before a big presentation or negotiation. Smart people who manage their emotional responses, through preparation or mindfulness, are better able to engage their reasoning brain and perform under pressure.
- **The Neocortex** (Thinking Brain): Handles reasoning, planning, and conscious decision-making. Smart people must actively engage this part to override gut reactions and emotional impulses, especially when high-stakes decisions are on the line.

2. The Role of the Basal Ganglia—The 'Lazy Brain' (Neuroscience)
The basal ganglia form habits by automating repeated behaviors. For example, driving the same route to work becomes automatic over time. This efficiency frees up mental bandwidth but also makes it harder to recognize when a change is needed. Smart people need to re-evaluate habitual behaviors to avoid repeating outdated or ineffective patterns.

3. Dopamine and Cortisol—The Chemicals Behind Habits (Neuroscience)
The brain reinforces behavior through the chemicals it releases. When someone takes positive actions—like setting a goal or making progress—it releases dopamine, creating a sense of reward that encourages them to keep going. This is how enabling behaviors, like persistence and follow-through, become habits.

But when people procrastinate or avoid difficult tasks, the brain releases cortisol, the stress hormone. High cortisol reinforces avoidance, making it harder to act the next time. Over time, this creates a cycle of inaction.

Successful people break that cycle. They focus on small wins that trigger dopamine and build momentum, rather than letting stress and avoidance take over.

4. Growth Mindset vs. Fixed Mindset (Carol Dweck)
A growth mindset fosters adaptability and persistence, encouraging people to see challenges as opportunities to improve. A fixed mindset discourages effort, causing people to avoid challenges for fear of failure. Smart people who adopt a growth mindset stay competitive by continuously learning and adapting.

5. Positive and Negative Reinforcement (B.F. Skinner)
Positive reinforcement strengthens enablers. For example, praise for contributing a new idea in a meeting encourages more contributions. Negative reinforcement, such as avoiding criticism by staying silent, can reinforce disablers like low visibility or lack of self-advocacy. Smart people stay aware of what behaviors they are reinforcing, intentionally or not.

6. Enablers and Disablers Are Dynamic (Behavioral Science)
Enablers and disablers shift depending on context, mindset, and experience. Perfectionism, for example, can drive excellence in some cases but cause procrastination when fear of failure sets in. Smart people continuously assess and adjust their behaviors to ensure enablers remain strengths and disablers don't take hold.

Understanding the science behind enablers and disablers gives smart people a distinct advantage—but only if they act on it. Success isn't just about knowing how these patterns work; it's about recognizing them in real time and making deliberate choices. The most successful individuals aren't those who avoid disablers entirely. They're the ones who identify them quickly, manage or mitigate them, and double down on the enablers to achieve greater success.

Reflection: *Which of your current habits are reinforcing enablers, and which might be making things worse? How often do you step back to re-evaluate them?*

Case Study

Take Arijit, a highly skilled software engineer in Silicon Valley, and Rosa, an entrepreneur running a popular café in Bogotá.

Arijit is a Stanford graduate who excels at creating complex algorithms that are valuable to his tech firm. However, his tendency to jump from project to project in pursuit of innovation mirrors the tendency of many people to constantly seek new challenges. Similarly, his habit of creating overly complex solutions reflects complexity bias, where individuals prefer complicated solutions over simpler ones. This makes his work difficult for others to follow and collaborate on.

On the other hand, Rosa's café became well known for its unique coffee blends, a testament to her dedication and attention to detail. But, like many who are risk-averse, she hesitated when given the chance to expand her brand internationally.

Despite clear signs of success, she feared the unknown, which held her back from potentially greater achievements.

Both Arijit and Rosa had strengths that propelled them toward success. Yet, in different contexts, those same strengths turned into obstacles, holding them back. Their experiences highlight the need to recognize when our strengths might become liabilities.

Reflection: Have you ever faced a situation where your strengths became obstacles? How did you manage it?

Practical Applications

Understanding your enablers and disablers is crucial in your journey to success. While reflecting on these aspects helps, having clear, actionable steps can make a big difference. Here are some practical ways to identify and manage them:

1. You Can Take the *Smartness Assessment*: This straightforward tool will help you identify your enablers and disablers. Visit https://www.MySmartness.com/Assessments/Smartness/ and use the discount code *SmartnessBook-2025* at checkout to access your personal assessment report for free (a $198 value).
2. Be Curious and Experiment Like a Child: Kids learn by trying, failing, and trying again. Stay curious and keep experimenting. You'll grow from every experience.
3. Set Clear Goals: Know where you're headed. Clear goals help you stay on track and recognize when an enabler might be taking you off course.
4. Seek Feedback: Ask friends, colleagues, and mentors for input. Often, others can see things in you that you might miss.
5. Keep a Journal: Regularly jot down moments when you felt empowered or hindered. Over time, you'll notice patterns that reveal your enablers and disablers.
6. Role-play Scenarios: Try out challenges in a safe, simulated environment to understand how certain strengths might turn into weaknesses depending on the context.
7. Practice Mindfulness and Meditation: Being aware of your thoughts and behaviors helps you understand when your strengths are helping or hurting.
8. Engage in Continuous Learning: Keep developing your skills and knowledge. This ensures your enablers stay relevant and you're aware of potential disablers.
9. Join Peer Groups: Surround yourself with people who can share their experiences, discuss challenges, and brainstorm solutions together.
10. Challenge Yourself: Step outside your comfort zone regularly. This can reveal hidden strengths and weaknesses that you might overlook in your day-to-day life.

11. Hire a Coach or Counselor: Sometimes, an outside perspective from a professional can help you spot blind spots and guide your growth.
12. Celebrate Successes and Analyze Failures: Acknowledge your wins, no matter how small. And when things don't go as planned, focus on what you can learn without being too hard on yourself.
13. By applying these strategies, you can gain more clarity about your enablers and disablers, and adjust your approach as needed to keep moving forward.

Reflection: Which of these twelve steps resonate the most with you? Would you use it to address your enablers and disablers?

Expert Opinion: Dr. Tomas Chamorro-Premuzic on Strengths and Disablers

Dr. Tomas Chamorro-Premuzic, a professor at both University College London and Columbia University, is an expert in business psychology and talent management. He emphasizes not just the importance of leveraging strengths but also the critical need to recognize and address weaknesses.

In his book *Why So Many Incompetent Men Become Leaders (And How to Fix It)*, Chamorro-Premuzic explores how traits like overconfidence, charisma, and narcissism, often seen as leadership strengths, can become disablers if left unchecked. Without self-awareness and conscious effort, these qualities can harm both the leader and the organization.

Chamorro-Premuzic argues that success is shaped not only by our strengths but also by how we manage our vulnerabilities. He asserts, "Ignoring our flaws can be one of the biggest barriers to greater success."

The key takeaway? Personal development requires a holistic approach that leverages our strengths and addresses our weaknesses, ensuring steady progress toward our goals. If you fear your weaknesses and vulnerabilities and avoid addressing them, they will remain significant obstacles to your success. True growth and greater achievements require the courage to confront these challenges head-on, finding ways to mitigate or eliminate their impact.

Reflection: How do Chamorro-Premuzic's insights about managing weaknesses resonate with your understanding of your own enablers and disablers?

> "Success isn't just about leveraging your enablers. It often comes from mitigating or eliminating your disablers. All else equal, the person with fewer disablers—and who makes fewer mistakes—usually outperforms those relying solely on their strengths."

In the next chapter, we'll examine specific strengths, enablers, weaknesses, and disablers to create a practical roadmap. Later in the book, we will explore the

Smartness Factors that build on this foundation, offering targeted strategies to help you close your success gap.

Reflection: *What's one disabler you've been hiding from—because deep down, you know it's not just slowing you down, it's sabotaging everything you say you want? You know it but you aren't doing anything about it.*

PART 2

UNDERSTANDING SMARTNESS

That assumption that intelligence, credentials, or other advantages should *automatically* lead to success is what I now call *The Advantage Illusion*. It's the hidden belief that having intelligence is enough. It quietly distorts how smart people assess situations, make decisions, and pursue goals. I've lived it myself. Back in Chapter 2, I described how I relied too much on intelligence, thinking it would carry me through. That mindset—unexamined and unchallenged—was a trap I didn't even know I was in.

I want to state the obvious here. Not all smart people have *The Advantage Illusion*.

Smartness bridges the gap between potential and achievement. It's how smart people use their intelligence and other advantages to make better decisions, take action, and succeed in the real world.

This part of the book explains *Smartness* in depth—what it is, how it works, and why it matters. You'll learn how *Smartness* drives success by connecting your advantages, practical intelligence, actions, and wisdom. Without *Smartness*, even the most intelligent people can stagnate. With it, they can create sustained achievement.

We'll explore how *Smartness* evolves over time, how intelligence changes with age, and why the *Smartness Factor*s matter. You'll also see the insights we gained from 1200+ participants who completed the *Smartness Assessment*.

This section gives you the foundation for repeatedly turning your advantages into achievements.

CHAPTER 6

Understanding Smartness

"Intelligence is what you have. Success comes from knowing how to use it—how to think, when to act, and when to adapt. That's Smartness."
~ Ram V. Iyer

Many people believe that intelligence and *Smartness* are the same (15% of the *Smartness Assessment* participants did), but they are different and serve different purposes. *Smartness* is how intelligent people adapt. It's dynamic, situational capability that turns potential into performance. It's what makes intelligence executable.

Intelligence is raw potential: your ability to think, reason, and learn. *Smartness* is how you apply that intelligence in real-world situations. Intelligence is about knowing; *Smartness* is about doing. Intelligence gives you possibilities, but *Smartness* turns those possibilities into achievements.

Many people confuse being smart with *Smartness*. The two are not the same. *Smartness* is not an automatic extension of intelligence. It is something different—something more.

Intelligence is raw cognitive ability: the capacity for reasoning, problem-solving, and abstract thinking. It's tempting to assume intelligence guarantees results, but real-world success depends entirely on how that intelligence is applied.

Smartness is the ability to use intelligence effectively: by making sound judgments, adapting to different situations, choosing wisely, and executing effectively. It is a learned set of capabilities, not an innate trait. Smart people do not automatically develop *Smartness*; it requires deliberate practice and experience over time. Without *Smartness*, even the most intelligent individuals can struggle to navigate complex situations, make decisions, and take action.

> **Smartness (noun) | /ˈsmɑːrtnəs/**
> *Smartness* is the ability to see things as they are, recognize what needs to be done, and take the right action. *Smartness* is a capability that anyone can learn. Smartness isn't a personality trait.It's the capability to achieve greater success. It's developed by cultivating mindsets, behaviors, habits, and skills that help you leverage your advantages, manage your disadvantages, and achieve greater success in the real world.
>
> *Smartness* is not the same as intelligence; it is about how well one applies advantages such as intelligence, wealth, credentials, and networks across various contexts. It is a learnable and improvable capability that anyone can

develop and use at any age to better assess situations, make better decisions, take action, and follow through to achieve greater success.

Key Insight: Mindset is about what you believe or how you will approach something (theory). *Smartness* is about how you achieve desired outcomes (practical) by leveraging your advantages and managing your disadvantages effectively.

Related Words: *Smart* (adjective); *Intelligence* (noun); *Wisdom* (noun); *Adaptability* (noun); *Resourcefulness* (noun); *Judgment* (noun); *Execution* (noun); *clever* (adjective)

Synonyms: *practical intelligence; savviness; astuteness; acumen; street smarts; strategic thinking*

Antonyms: *naïveté; inefficiency; shortsightedness; rigidity; poor judgment*

Usage in a Sentence:

"Success isn't guaranteed by intelligence alone—*Smartness* determines how well you apply your knowledge and resources to real-world challenges."

"Despite his intelligence, John's lack of *Smartness* in decision-making led to missed opportunities."

"Krish's street smarts helped him successfully beat a big-company competitor to land the deal. That's *Smartness* in action!"

The Foundation That Makes Smartness Work

Without *Smartness*, even the most intelligent people can struggle to navigate complex situations, make decisions, and take action. Many smart people don't see a need for *Smartness* until they hit roadblocks. *Smartness* doesn't emerge just because someone is intelligent—it requires deliberate development and consistent application.

Intelligence is what you know. *Smartness* is how you use it. Many highly intelligent people underachieve, not because they lack ability, but because they don't apply it effectively.

> *Smartness is what distinguishes intelligent people from consistently successful people.*

Smartness can only function on a foundation of Aspiration, Knowledge, and Action—what we call the Success Triad. The Success Triad creates the conditions that allow *Smartness* to work. Without all three in place, *Smartness* stalls.

- Aspiration drives effort and focus.

- Knowledge provides the raw material for better decisions.
- Action converts potential into results.

When any one of these is missing, *Smartness* cannot translate into sustained success. Think of *Smartness* as a performance enhancer. It helps you make the most of who you already are—but it can't compensate for what's missing. If Aspiration is unclear, *Smartness* has nothing to focus on. If you don't act, *Smartness* can't refine your execution. The first step toward greater success is ensuring that your Success Triad is strong. *Smartness* builds on that to maximize your results.

> *"Smartness is a performance enhancer that helps you become more successful by making the most of who you already are—but it can't compensate for what's missing."*

You're Like a Cheetah

Consider the cheetah—the fastest land animal. Your intelligence is like the cheetah's speed: raw potential. But speed alone doesn't make it a successful hunter. Hunting is a learned skill. Without it, the cheetah's speed is wasted, and it can't survive, let alone thrive.

Likewise, intelligence gives you potential—but potential alone won't make you successful. *Smartness* is a learned capability. Without it, intelligence gets wasted, and smart people stall—brilliant but stuck. Just as the cheetah must learn to hunt, smart people must develop and apply *Smartness* to get results.

Bridging the Gap Between Intelligence and Success

Intelligence is raw potential—the ability to think, reason, and learn. But potential isn't enough. *Smartness* is how well you apply that intelligence in real-world situations to create results. Intelligence is about knowing; Smartness is about doing. Intelligence gives you possibilities. *Smartness* turns those possibilities into achievements.

> *"Intelligence and Smartness are related, but are distinct capabilities. Neither one guarantees the other."*

Understanding the difference between being smart and having Smartness is the first step toward closing what I call the *Smartness* Gap—the gap between potential and achievement. Many highly intelligent people underachieve, not because they lack ability, but because they don't apply it effectively. They fail to leverage their existing advantages—whether that's intelligence, credentials, networks, or resources—into sustained success.

This book challenges you to reframe the question. Instead of asking, "Why am I not more successful?" ask, "Am I fully leveraging my existing advantages with *Smartness*?" The problem isn't that you lack potential. It's that success requires more than intelligence. It requires Smartness.

> *"Intelligence is just a tool, like a hammer. Don't confuse it with Smartness, the hand that wields it."*

Smartness is a dynamic and practical ability to recognize, leverage, and amplify all your advantages like intelligence, skills, networks, wealth, resources, and opportunities. While intelligence is undoubtedly a powerful advantage, it's only one piece of the puzzle. In everyday language, people use the word "smart" to describe quick thinking, intelligence, or adaptability. But this broad use leads many to mistakenly equate intelligence with *Smartness*, the ability to leverage advantages in real-world situations. Among the people who took the *Smartness Assessment*, about 17% believed that intelligence and Smartness are the same. They're not.

Consider this: highly successful people aren't just intelligent or highly advantaged in one area. They know how to use everything at their disposal. That's *Smartness* in action. Those who struggle to achieve their goals often fail to connect their advantages to their outcomes. They lack *Smartness*. When applied effectively, *Smartness* transforms advantages into meaningful and sustained success.

Definitions of Smartness

Traditional definitions of *Smartness*, as presented in many dictionaries, often focus narrowly on intelligence, and that's how most people interpret it. This has led to the widespread belief that *Smartness* is simply intelligence. But if intelligence alone determined success, then all highly intelligent people would automatically be successful. Yet, we know this isn't the case.

Many people with high IQs struggle to translate their intelligence into tangible achievements. Some lack the ability to adapt to changing circumstances, make sound real-world decisions, or effectively leverage opportunities. Others may be brilliant in a controlled academic or theoretical setting but fail to thrive in professional, entrepreneurial, or leadership roles that require judgment, persuasion, and resilience.

Traditional dictionary definitions (Merriam-Webster, Oxford, Collins, Macmillan) of *Smartness* often equate it with intelligence—quick thinking, cleverness, or mental sharpness. But intelligence alone doesn't guarantee success. Many highly intelligent people fail to achieve their potential because they lack the capabilities to apply what they know. This book redefines *Smartness* as a learned set of capabilities: assessing situations, deciding how to leverage one's intelligence and advantages, taking action, and adapting to outcomes.

Smartness is about turning knowledge and advantages into action. It enables individuals to assess, decide, act, and refine their approach based on outcomes. A smart person doesn't just possess intelligence: they apply it, adjust strategies based on feedback, and turn insight into results.

Some researchers refer to this capability as Adaptive Intelligence, the ability to adjust thinking and actions to meet changing situations. In this book, we call

Understanding Smartness

it *Smartness* because it reflects the practical, real-world capabilities that highly intelligent people need to develop to achieve greater success.

> *"Smartness is the ability to see things as they are, recognize what needs to be done, and take the right action by leveraging available advantages."*

It is the capability to apply one's advantages effectively in different contexts. A smart person assesses situations, determines which strengths or resources can be leveraged, identifies potential obstacles, and takes action that leads to successful outcomes. For one person, this might mean using strong communication skills to navigate corporate politics. For another, it could mean applying deep industry knowledge to solve a complex business problem.

Smartness is not a fixed trait. It's a set of practical, learnable capabilities that allow individuals to repeatedly turn their advantages into real-world achievements.

Many highly successful individuals are not necessarily those with the highest IQs or the most prestigious academic credentials. Some of the most accomplished entrepreneurs, leaders, and innovators have succeeded because they understand how to leverage their experiences, instincts, people skills, and decision-making abilities to create opportunities.

Smartness is not just about knowing what to do; it's about aligning your aspirations, knowledge, and actions to make the best use of your advantages. This interplay, known as the Success Triad, ensures that your advantages are transformed into the successful outcomes you seek. It is important to note that *Smartness* is not just about maximizing strengths; it is also about mitigating weaknesses, adapting to context, and making decisions in real-world situations.

This book builds on this broader, more actionable definition of *Smartness*. It introduces a practical framework that helps you think and act strategically, leverage your strengths, and repeatedly achieve greater success. Instead of limiting yourself to a rigid, IQ-based view of ability, you will develop a mindset and skillset that allow you to adapt, make smarter decisions, and maximize outcomes in any situation.

By embracing this expanded approach to *Smartness*, you will unlock real-world achievements far beyond what conventional notions of intelligence could ever promise.

Let's review these key definitions so we're on the same page as we move forward in this book:

- **Intelligence** is a person's cognitive ability—reasoning, problem-solving, and abstract thinking. It's about knowing: helping you learn, analyze, and solve complex problems. Often measured by IQ, intelligence reflects mental capacity but doesn't guarantee adaptability or real-world success. An intelligent person may understand business strategy yet struggle to implement it.

- **Smartness** is the practical application of intelligence, knowledge, and experience in real-world situations. It involves assessing situations, recognizing and applying your advantages effectively, taking decisive action, and refining your approach based on outcomes. Unlike intelligence, which is largely cognitive, *Smartness* is situational, learnable, and developed over time through experience, learning, and practice.

> *"Smartness is a learnable, situational set of capabilities developed through experience, learning, and practice."*

- **Smart** is a broad term people use in many different ways. It can mean intelligent, quick-witted, adaptable, or even well-presented—like being "smartly dressed." In everyday language, people often use "smart" interchangeably with intelligence or cleverness. But *Smartness*, as it's defined in this book, is something different. It's not just about being clever or having potential. *Smartness* is a learned capability, one that determines how effectively you use your intelligence and other advantages to achieve meaningful, sustained success in the real world.
- **Personality traits** are enduring characteristics that influence how individuals behave across time and situations. They include aspects like conscientiousness, openness to experience, and emotional stability. These traits matter, but unlike Smartness, they're not situational or easily learned. Smartness is not a personality trait. It's the capability to apply what you have to achieve greater success.

> *Smartness isn't a personality trait—it's the capability to achieve greater success.*

The goal of this book is not to increase your IQ but to enhance your *Smartness*, the practical ability to leverage your unique advantages for meaningful success. *Smartness* empowers you to align your aspirations, knowledge, and actions, ensuring you make the most of your strengths. By thinking strategically and making effective decisions, you can consistently turn potential into real-world achievements.

As a practical and adaptive quality, *Smartness* integrates the three pillars of the Success Triad: Aspiration, Knowledge, and Action. Developing *Smartness* enables you to leverage your advantages, navigate obstacles, and apply structured, intentional action—directing your resources and efforts toward meaningful goals with greater precision and confidence.

> *"Smartness separates the merely capable from the highly successful. The more you develop and apply your Smartness, the greater your ability to become more successful."*

While *Smartness* fuels action and drives results, wisdom deepens those efforts with insight, reflection, and a long-term perspective. Together, *Smartness* and wisdom create a powerful foundation for sustainable success: *Smartness* moves you forward, and wisdom ensures those actions are purposeful and aligned with your larger values in the long run.

Many smart people stay stuck because they're operating with a hidden assumption (sometimes even unknown to themselves): that intelligence alone guarantees success. This intelligence-centered paradigm shapes how they think, what they value, and what they overlook, often without realizing it. The real breakthrough comes when they upgrade to a *Smartness*-centered paradigm: one that turns their intelligence into execution, impact, and real-world results.

If intelligence alone guaranteed success, every smart person would be very successful. But real-world success isn't just about knowledge or IQ—it's about adaptability, execution, and judgment. Many highly intelligent people fail because they rely too much on raw intelligence while neglecting the importance and use of *Smartness*. They overanalyze, hesitate to act, or refuse to adapt, believing that intelligence alone will solve problems. Smart people succeed because they bridge the gap between intelligence and execution.

Think of intelligence as a high-performance sports car that has incredible potential. But without fuel (execution), a skilled driver (judgment), and proper navigation (adaptability), it won't reach its destination. That's where *Smartness* comes in. It's the force multiplier that ensures intelligence is applied effectively in the real world.

> *"Smartness isn't something you either have or don't. Everyone has Smartness and uses it to function. The real difference is how much they've developed it, how consistently they apply it, and whether they continue to grow it."*

Reflection: *How do you define your own ability to succeed—through innate advantages like high intelligence, wealth, and such, or your ability to adapt and apply them in various situations?*

Using Smartness

Developing and applying *Smartness* is a straightforward process. It can be used to leverage any advantage, but let's take the example of intelligence:

1. Situational Awareness – Recognize when and how to apply your intelligence effectively.
2. Decision-Making – Evaluate multiple options quickly without getting stuck in analysis paralysis.
3. Taking Action – Move forward with calculated risk, even when outcomes are uncertain.
4. Feedback & Adaptation – Learn from results and refine your approach for continuous improvement.

> *"With Smartness, intelligent people can become powerful decision-makers, trusted leaders, and consistent achievers—without changing who they are, but by better using what they already have."*

Smartness is the difference between potential and achievement. In the next chapter, we'll break down its essential components—mindsets, behaviors, habits, and skills—and how you can develop them.

Reflection: *Are you still trying to win with intelligence alone—while the world rewards those who move, adapt, and execute with Smartness?*

CHAPTER 7

Smartness From Many Angles

Now that you understand what Smartness is, let's explore how it shows up in the real world—in business, sports, personal growth, and everyday situations. Not as theory, but as something people actually use—or fail to use. These examples will help you recognize Smartness in action and begin spotting it in your own life.

In this chapter, you will see certain insights and examples repeated with a purpose—to help you see how pervasive Smartness is in our lives.

Smart people with high intelligence and other advantages often face an uncomfortable truth: Their advantages don't always translate to success. They're not where they thought they'd be, or as effective as they thought they could be.

What's missing is not more intelligence or advantages. It's Smartness—the ability to apply what you already have, deliberately and consistently, effectively.

Smartness isn't some abstract idea. It's a capability you already have and use—when you handle a tough relationship, negotiate something important, adapt under pressure, or even when you figure out how to drive your car in busy traffic. Most people develop parts of Smartness without realizing it—piecemeal, through awkward missteps, adapting over time, and picking things up by observing others. This chapter helps you put a name to it—and use it more deliberately.

> *"The world doesn't reward potential. It rewards results. That's why Smartness beats credentials—very frequently."*

The following sections give you multiple ways to see Smartness in action. Different angles. Same core insight. If you get it here, the rest of the book will make more sense—and hit deeper. Pick whichever metaphor resonates with you. Then use it.

🖉 Performance Over Intelligence
- "Smart people don't fail for lack of knowledge. They fail when they can't turn it into action. That's where Smartness comes in."
- "Expertise shows what you know. Smartness shows what you can do with it."
- "Being right doesn't change outcomes. Smartness is knowing how to get the right things done."
- "Intelligence explains the problem. Smartness delivers the solution."
- "Your experience, credentials, and other advantages matter—but without Smartness, they stall out."

⚒ Smartness Gets Results
- "Smartness is knowing when to lead the conversation, and when to reshape it."
- "A resume opens doors. Smartness keeps you in the room when things get complex."
- "Smart people are often the most overlooked—until they learn how to make their insight useful."
- "Smartness is what makes you someone people listen to when decisions matter."
- "Being the smartest person in the room only matters if people trust you to say what's relevant, timely, and useful in the moment."

🌐 Reality Doesn't Care About Theories
- "Smartness is what helps you pivot when your brilliant plan hits real-world chaos."
- "Frameworks don't fail. Execution without Smartness does."
- "The world rewards movement, not mastery. Smartness bridges that gap."
- "You don't need perfect knowledge. You need Smartness to work with the imperfect data you've got."
- "Smartness makes you valuable when the map no longer matches the terrain."

⚒ Tools & Hammers: Advantages Aren't Enough
- "A degree, title, or credential is just a tool. Smartness is the hand that swings it."
- "Being accomplished gives you the hammer. But without Smartness, you'll miss every nail."
- "Tools don't build anything by themselves. Smartness is what turns them into results."
- "Your advantage is what you were given. Smartness is what you build."
- "Smart people often mistake their tools for power. Smartness is what actually creates leverage."

♠ Poker & Chess: Strategy ≠ Success
- "In poker, the best hand doesn't always win. The smartest player does."
- "In chess, everyone starts with the same board. Smartness is how you play under pressure."
- "Smartness is what lets you act before certainty—just like in high-stakes games."
- "It's not about having better odds. It's about making better decisions with the ones you have."
- "Smart people lose games when they wait for the perfect move. Smartness gets them back in play."

Smartness From Many Angles

🏅 **Sports: Every Player Has Talent. Smartness Creates Winners.**
- "In business, as in sports, talent sets the ceiling. Smartness raises the floor."
- "The strongest player doesn't always win. The one with better timing, awareness, and adaptability does. That's Smartness."
- "Coaches pick players not for raw skill—but for Smartness under pressure."
- "Smartness is knowing when to slow down, when to strike, and when to change the play."
- "Even elite athletes train Smartness. Why should smart professionals be any different?"

💼 **Business: Knowledge Opens the Door. Smartness Closes the Deal.**
- "You can have the best ideas in the room. Smartness is what gets them adopted."
- "Smartness turns meetings into influence. It turns insight into traction."
- "A team full of experts won't deliver results without someone applying Smartness."
- "Smartness is how you lead when you don't have formal authority."
- "Business rewards action, not brilliance. Smartness is what connects the two."

Smartness isn't a personality trait. It's a learnable set of capabilities.

Reflection: Which metaphor or example resonated for you—and why?

CHAPTER 8

Intelligence & Smartness as You Age

"Intelligence is largely what you're born with; Smartness is what you build through a lifetime of learning and experience."
~ Ram V. Iyer

This chapter explores how intelligence and *Smartness* evolve over our lifetime. While intelligence is something we're born with, *Smartness* grows through experience and learning. *Smartness* determines how well you use your intelligence over time. As you age, success depends less on raw intelligence and more on your ability to adapt, execute, and apply knowledge effectively. As the old saying goes, "Books teach you a lot about the world, but the streets teach you about living." We'll examine how to use both—our natural cognitive strengths and the mindset, behaviors, and skills we develop—to navigate life's challenges, foster personal growth, and drive success. We will also examine how intelligence and *Smartness* vary with age.

Developed Intelligence

From childhood, intelligence—particularly academic skills like language, math, and problem-solving—has been the primary focus of development and recognition. Schools emphasize grades and test scores as the ultimate markers of success, and this focus continues into higher education, where test scores, degrees, and academic achievements become symbols of intellectual development.

In early adulthood, many rely on these advantages—credentials, natural talents, or access to resources—and expect them to translate into lasting success. Early wins, like good grades, a great job right out of college, or initial promotions, often reinforce this sense of entitlement as well as the illusion that success will continue with little effort.

This is when *The Advantage Illusion* begins. Some of them are convinced that what worked before will work forever—and develop a belief that they're already done enough. But as demands shift and old advantages lose their edge, the illusion cracks. Sustained success depends not on what you once had—but on how you keep evolving through *Smartness*.

However, as people move into their 30s, 40s, and 50s, the limitations of those advantages become harder to ignore. The rewards that once came easily begin to stall, leaving many feeling stuck—professionally or personally. In fact, people in their 40s and 50s made up the largest group of *Smartness Assessment*-takers. They're the ones who felt less successful—or unsuccessful—despite strong early trajectories.

Intellectual Stagnation & Poor Smartness Training

A person's intelligence doesn't decline, but their intellectual growth can stagnate. One major reason some smart people don't achieve as much as they could isn't because of their intelligence—it's because of intellectual stagnation and their poor *Smartness* training. After formal education ends, many stop actively learning, relying on outdated knowledge and skills while shifting focus to family, career, or other responsibilities. But as those responsibilities grow, the demands of work and life outpace old knowledge and skills. The world evolves, industries shift, and suddenly, what once felt like an edge starts to feel outdated.

At the same time, passive habits take over. Tasks that don't require much cognitive effort—like social media, entertainment, and routine work—replace intentional intellectual growth. And while smart people might still "learn on the job," that often just keeps them moving along—it keeps them on par with everyone else, but not ahead. Any formal training they receive is usually limited to functional skills—a programmer gets more technical training; a financial advisor learns the latest regulations—but none of it addresses what truly separates high achievers: *Smartness*. Meanwhile, those who actively develop and leverage their *Smartness* capabilities, expand their knowledge beyond their immediate function, and push beyond tasks that require little cognitive effort achieve much greater success.

Poor Smartness Training – The Missing Piece

The biggest reason smart people struggle in their mid- to late-careers isn't a lack of intelligence—it's that they received minimal training in *Smartness*.

Traditional education develops intelligence—it teaches knowledge acquisition, structured problem-solving, and credentials. But schools mostly teach theory—often about an idealized or outdated world that doesn't match reality.

- You were trained to solve problems in controlled environments—but not to navigate unpredictable, high-stakes situations.
- You were rewarded for knowledge, but not for execution.
- You were taught to work hard, but not necessarily how to think strategically and position yourself for success.
- You were taught to work in lab environments, not ones with real-world stakes.

If you landed a great job right out of college at a top company, chances are your colleagues are just as intelligent, well-educated, and capable as you are. So, what makes some people better equipped to achieve greater success than others?

Why Intelligence Alone Stops Being Enough

Early in your career, intelligence and credentials give you an advantage, but in mid- and late-career, those advantages equalize. Everyone around you is just as smart, just as qualified, just as experienced. Suddenly, raw intelligence and your credentials don't matter as much—it's how well you make situationally-appropriate decisions, act, and adapt that determines who achieves greater success.

Why Smartness Is the True Differentiator

Many smart, high-potential people—especially those who were once ahead—find themselves unprepared for senior roles, leadership, and higher levels of responsibility. Their careers have perhaps stalled, or the promotions they were expecting haven't materialized. They thought their intelligence and early advantages would be enough. But they didn't develop the execution, adaptability, and situational judgment needed for real-world success.

That's where *Smartness* becomes the ultimate separator.

Smartness is the ability to apply your intelligence, experience, and advantages in the most effective way possible across different situations. It's how you execute, adapt, and deliver results. Those who build *Smartness* thrive—rising beyond equally intelligent peers who stall out because they can't leverage what they know.

The problem? Few people know how to deliberately develop *Smartness*. Learning on the job helps, but it's slow and often lacks the insight and skilled guidance required to drive real progress. Without focused effort, on-the-job experience keeps you just in the pack, not ahead.

To outperform equally capable peers, you need more than intelligence or knowledge—you need *Smartness*. You need to apply what you know faster, more effectively, and in ways others can't match. That's why *Smartness* matters.

> *"Desire to succeed isn't the problem. Capability is—because many smart people assume they already have it, without ever developing or using their Smartness well."*

From Advantage to Success: How Smartness and Your Peers Shape the Outcome

An Earned Mindset—the belief that success must be earned through continuous effort and learning—is a core component of *Smartness*. It fosters adaptability and continuous improvement, helping people refine how they apply their intelligence and advantages over time. Dr. Anders Ericsson's well-known 10,000-Hour Rule shows that deliberate practice sharpens the ability to apply knowledge effectively—enhancing *Smartness* far beyond raw intelligence.

But practice and learning aren't enough on their own. You also need the right environment, guidance and peers to accelerate your development.

As you move through your academic and professional life, you'll find yourself surrounded by people who are just as intelligent, skilled, and advantaged as you are. You may have landed a job at Goldman Sachs, McKinsey, Bridgewater Associates, or OpenAI—beating out hundreds, maybe thousands, of others to get there. But once you're in, you'll quickly realize: your colleagues are just as smart—or even smarter—than you. So, what's your edge now? In these environments, where everyone is just as smart or advantaged as you, *Smartness* becomes the ultimate differentiator. Intelligence and credentials got you in the door. *Smartness*—your ability to adapt quickly, solve problems creatively, build strong relationships, and deliver meaningful results—is what can propel you higher.

Your peers offer a powerful mirror and a learning opportunity. Watching how they handle challenges, communicate ideas, and collaborate can give you valuable insights into how you can improve. Focus on peers who excel in areas where you need to get better—whether it's managing time, making decisions under pressure, or fostering stronger relationships.

Rather than feeling threatened by high-performing peers, use them as resources and motivation. Seek out those who are succeeding in areas you want to grow. Look for opportunities to engage with them—whether through professional networks, industry forums, or collaborative projects. High-performing peers often provide fresh approaches and unique strategies that can spark your own growth.

The truth is simple: Without continual growth, stagnation is inevitable. The modern world doesn't reward standing still. Just like a shark has to keep swimming to survive, you have to keep moving forward by continually refining your *Smartness* to stay competitive.

Success isn't just about intelligence or advantages—it's about how you apply them in different situations. *Smartness* is what separates those who keep rising from those who stall out.

Reflection: *Think of a peer whom you admire. What strengths or skills do you admire in them, and how can you develop those to enhance your own Smartness?*

Intelligence and Advantages vs. Smartness

Intelligence provides the foundation for success—but it's largely fixed. You can improve it slightly over your lifetime, but the gains are incremental. If you currently rate your intelligence at a 7 out of 10, you might raise it by 5% or 10% with sustained effort. But a leap of 25% or 50% is unlikely.

Similarly, many advantages—natural athletic ability, early-life education, first-language fluency—are hard to change, especially as we age. The circumstances we grow up in shape these advantages in ways that aren't easily reversed or expanded later in life—biology gets in the way, too.

In contrast, *Smartness* offers unlimited potential for growth. It can improve continuously—right up until your last day. If you currently rate your *Smartness* at a 5 out of 10, you could realistically raise it by 30%, 50%, or more as you sharpen your ability to respond to challenges and seize opportunities. With enough time and effort, you may even reach a 9 out of 10.

> *"The same intelligence that got you ahead in school can hold you back in the real world—unless you develop and leverage Smartness."*

As you advance in your career, your *Smartness* becomes more critical. In senior roles, the ability to apply intelligence and advantages flexibly and effectively matters far more than possessing raw intelligence or advantages. No matter where you start, you can always enhance your *Smartness*—the key is committing to continuous development.

Smartness Can Be Developed at Any Stage and Any Age

Scientific studies confirm this. Non-cognitive capabilities—like situational judgment, decision-making, and adaptability—can be developed and refined at any age.

When we say *Smartness* can be developed, we mean you can:

- Strengthen productive mindsets (e.g., Belief Reinforcement, Personal Autonomy)
- Refine behaviors (e.g., Action Orientation, Risk Tolerance, Self-Advocacy, Decision Flexibility)
- Sharpen key skills (e.g., Situational Judgment, Thinking Range, Interpersonal Skills, Emotional Intelligence)

Smartness isn't a single capability. It's a set of capabilities that you continuously build, refine, and apply to real-world situations.

Reflection: *What's one area where you can more effectively apply your intelligence and advantages? How will you build your Smartness through intentional practice?*

Smartness Curves: Growth Through Experience

Smartness is not static; it evolves as you encounter new challenges and opportunities. Intelligence and other advantages provide the foundation, but *Smartness* grows when you apply those advantages in real-world situations—a process that accelerates with more and tougher experiences and responsibilities.

> *"When the structure disappears or chaos appears, Smartness becomes your edge."*

Early in life, the focus is mostly on developing intelligence, not *Smartness*. A high school graduate may have basic *Smartness*, but higher education, internships, travel, and work experiences expose them to more complex situations that accelerate their *Smartness*. Over time, people who actively seek out real-world learning, take on harder problems, and adapt, develop *Smartness* at a much faster rate—and that gives them a lasting competitive edge. They not only improve as challenges increase, they pull ahead, because they've built the ability to apply their intelligence more effectively than others who stagnate in their comfort zone.

But not all experiences lead to smarter thinking and action. Some people repeat the same patterns and never stretch themselves. Others embrace harder challenges, learn from them, and adapt. I often tell people, *"You can't build muscles by lifting a few sheets of paper."* If you want to improve your capabilities—whether physical or mental—you need to take on heavier lifts. I saw this firsthand during my time at MIT, surrounded by people who were not just smart—but "scary smart." That environment pushed me further than I thought possible. *Smartness* grows the same way. You have to push beyond what's easy or familiar to get better faster.

This is how the gap widens between smart achievers and "the herd." Those with stronger advantages—education, resources, and networks—often accelerate faster. Those who neglect their *Smartness*—whether through lack of effort, fear of failure, or limited opportunity—stall or decline.

This is why so many careers stagnate in people's 30s, 40s, or 50s. They stop developing their *Smartness*, while others keep adapting and moving ahead. The good news? It's never too late to close the *Smartness Gap*. *Smartness* can be improved at any age.

While *Wisdom*—an advanced application of *Smartness*—is often associated with age, it is not innate. It reflects the choices and efforts made to grow and adapt over time. Two 70-year-olds, for instance, may differ significantly in their wisdom based on how they've invested in developing their *Smartness* throughout life. *Wisdom* emerges when *Smartness* is consistently refined and applied to increasingly complex challenges, combining reflection, adaptability, and long-term thinking.

Regardless of where you are today, the opportunity to enhance and leverage *Smartness* is lifelong. With intentional effort, you can expand your *Smartness* at any stage, achieving new levels of personal and professional success. Life itself is your most valuable classroom—what matters is how you choose to learn from it.

You have gotten as far as you can...

By increasing your *Smartness* now, you'll position yourself for higher levels of growth and achievement. You've likely reached the limit of success achievable with your current level of *Smartness*. To reach greater heights, you need to build on your strengths (enablers) and address your weaknesses (disablers). Without improving *Smartness*, even the most intelligent, skilled, or otherwise smart and advantaged individuals may see their progress stall. *Smartness* increasingly becomes the key differentiator among those who are otherwise highly advantaged.

> *"You've gotten as far as you can with what you've got. You must enhance your Smartness to go farther and higher."*

Career Progression & Smartness

Your first job after college is often based on your intelligence and academic credentials. However, your next promotion will probably depend on your *Smartness*. As your career progresses—especially in mid- to late-career—*Smartness* becomes the critical factor that drives promotions and career growth. Organizations consider your intelligence and capabilities as a given—you are good, like many of your peers—and value your ability to apply your skills in real-world contexts to achieve more successful outcomes, which is, essentially, your *Smartness* – factors like how you manage risks, your interpersonal and teaming skills and emotional intelligence.

This challenge is reflected in findings from the *Smartness Assessment*, which revealed that dissatisfaction with success tends to peak in mid-career:

1. Very few people notice the impact of lacking *Smartness* early in their 20s, but it becomes a bigger issue in their 30s, 40s, and later. The proxy for dissatisfaction was when they took the *Smartness Assessment* – they felt the need to find out what was holding them back.
2. The greatest dissatisfaction occurs around age 40, about 15 years after college.
3. Participants in their 40s who took the assessment outnumbered those in their 30s and 50s, while a few individuals in their 60s and 70s did take it, perhaps wondering why they hadn't achieved greater success. I even had an MIT PhD in his 80s take the assessment. I asked him, "Why?" He was wondering, "What could I have done differently to be more successful?"

These individuals are highly advantaged—often highly intelligent, educated at top schools, and initially successful—but their lack of developed *Smartness* limits further progress. This is a common challenge, but it can be overcome with the right approach, including strategies for developing *Smartness*, which are covered in Part 3 of this book.

Your Personal Development

In the past, employers often took responsibility for the personal and professional development of their employees. I remember a report from my Lucent Technologies days of a man who already had a PhD in Physics from Yale and was fully funded and supported by the corporation to attend the Columbia Business School with no requirement to reimburse the company if he left as soon as he graduated. Such arrangements, though generous, were common in the past but are now virtually non-existent, placing the responsibility for development squarely on individuals. Today, companies focus primarily on job-specific training or investing in a small group of very high-potential employees.

Many people mistakenly believe their employers should be responsible for their growth, saying, "If my employer won't pay for my training, I won't either."

This attitude is short-sighted and self-limiting. If you don't invest in your own personal development, you're simply shooting yourself in your foot! You are your biggest asset, more valuable than any credential, resource, or asset. Ironically, many readily spend thousands on vacations for short-term joy but hesitate to invest in our personal development for greater long-term success. For example, if you've paid $100,000–$300,000 for a bachelor's degree and $200,000 for an MBA, why would you hesitate to spend $5,000 or $10,000 on improving your *Smartness*? Remember, *Smartness* is a performance enhancer that helps you become more successful by making the most of who you already are. It costs far less and can deliver much higher value. Seriously. Your future success depends on what you invest in yourself today. Don't wait for others to prioritize your growth—start small—identify one area to develop and take the first step toward becoming your most capable self.

> *"Taking ownership of your personal development is the key to unlocking your full potential in an increasingly competitive and complex world."*

Unlike intelligence and many advantages, which are largely fixed, *Smartness* can be improved through deliberate effort—learning, self-reflection, and intentional practice.

Whether you're just starting out or are well-established, cultivating and leveraging *Smartness* is crucial for growth and fulfillment. The more you prioritize developing your *Smartness*, the sooner you'll see greater success. Here's something to ponder...

> *"Intelligence and knowledge without Smartness are like a load of books on the back of a horse."*

Reflection: *If you feel stuck, are you blaming the system—or is it finally time to admit you've squeezed all you can out of intelligence alone?*

CHAPTER 9

THE SMARTNESS GAP – WHY SMART PEOPLE STRUGGLE & HOW TO FIX IT

"The greatest enemy of intelligence is not stupidity, but the illusion that intelligence alone is enough."
~ Ram V. Iyer

Being smart got you here. Now, become smart enough to succeed. If intelligence alone guarantees success, why do so many smart people stall out? The answer is what I call the Smartness Gap—the failure to apply intelligence in adaptive, real-world ways. It shows up as analysis paralysis, stalled execution, poor decision-making, or missed opportunities—especially when smart people assume that intelligence, credentials, or past wins should be enough.

> *"Intelligence becomes a trap when it feels like a ticket."*

This often stems from what I call the Advantage Illusion—the false belief that intelligence or personal advantages will automatically lead to success. It's this mindset that fuels the Smartness Gap.

> *Smartness is the antidote for the Smartness Gap and the Advantage Illusion.*

It's how smart people can stop spinning in their own intelligence and start making things happen. It's how they can move from potential to progress, from hesitation to execution, from being clever to being effective. It's how they can get out of their heads—and succeed in real-world terms.

This chapter examines how the Smartness Gap shows up in real life, why it holds smart people back, and what it takes to close it and unlock greater success.

The Smartness Gap in Action – How Smart People Get Stuck

Smart people often fall into common traps that limit their success. Below are the primary ways the *Smartness Gap* manifests:

1. Overanalyzing & Perfectionism *(Smartness Factor: Detail Orientation)*
Smart people tend to analyze situations deeply, but excessive analysis can lead to inaction. They get caught in the "paralysis by analysis" cycle—constantly seeking more information or refining their plans instead of executing.

Example: A highly intelligent entrepreneur spent years perfecting his product before launch. By the time it hit the market, competitors had already taken over the space.

2. The Entitlement Trap *(Smartness Factor: Self-Competence Views)*
Smart people often assume that because they are intelligent or well-credentialed, they should automatically be successful. This sense of entitlement can create unrealistic expectations and ultimately result in frustration and stagnation.

Example: A graduate from an elite university expected promotions to happen effortlessly but struggled because he hadn't developed good interpersonal skills or a good network.

3. Decision Inflexibility *(Smartness Factor: Belief Orientation)*
Some smart people believe they know the "right" way to do things and resist adapting when circumstances change. Instead of adjusting strategies, they double down on failing approaches.

Example: A former executive refused to pivot his failing business model, convinced that his strategy would eventually work. His competitors adapted and thrived, while his company collapsed.

4. The Need for Constant Variety *(Smartness Factor: Need for Variety)*
Many smart people crave intellectual stimulation and variety. This often leads them to jump from idea to idea instead of staying focused and following through.

Example: A consultant started multiple projects but abandoned each one before it gained traction. Despite his expertise, he never built a sustainable business.

Why Smart People Stay Stuck: Playing to Not Lose Instead of Playing to Win

Smart people often swing between two extremes—pursuing achievement for the thrill of being 'the best' or working frantically to avoid looking like a failure. Their goal is not to maximize achievement but to ensure they don't look bad or fall behind their peers. Simply put, people hate losing more than they love winning. This fear-driven mindset causes even very smart people to make safe choices instead of bold ones—while less capable peers surpass them.

Breaking the Advantage Illusion: The Real Paradigm Shift

At the heart of this struggle is what the book calls *The Advantage Illusion*—the false belief that intelligence or credentials alone should lead to success. This illusion quietly distorts judgment, creates inaction or overconfidence, and causes many smart people to stall even when they have clear advantages.

Escaping *The Advantage Illusion* means shifting to a new paradigm: one where success isn't assumed—it's earned. Where intelligence isn't the objective—it's a tool for achievement. And where *Smartness*—not raw intellect—is what can drive consistent results.

> *"Smartness is the permanent antidote to the Advantage Illusion of smart people—and the key to turning them into lifelong achievers."*

Smart people don't need to become someone new. They need to stop assuming their advantages are enough and start applying them with intention. That's what the new paradigm demands. *Smartness* is how they get there.

Paradigm Shift: From Illusion to Smartness

Old Paradigm	New Paradigm
I'm smart, so I'll succeed.	I succeed when I apply my intelligence with *Smartness*.
My credentials and achievements speak for me.	My actions and adaptability create results.
If I understand it, it is all I need to succeed.	Insight without action is just potential.
I deserve success based on what I've done.	I earn success by what I do next.

How Fear of Losing Leads to Self-Sabotage

Certain behavioral tendencies reinforce this avoidance mindset, keeping smart people trapped in stagnation and underachievement. Later in this book, we will explore how the *Smartness Factors* shape how intelligence is applied—or misapplied. The most common tendencies that hold smart people back include:

- Risk Avoidance Instead of Risk Tolerance. Smart people don't always hunger for achievement. They fear visible failure, harsh judgment, and potential humiliation. Instead of betting on themselves and taking bold steps, they choose the safest paths—not because they are the best choices, but because they pose the least risk. They prefer to stay comfortably in the middle rather than risk falling, even if that means never reaching the top.
- Decision Paralysis Instead of Decision Flexibility. Smart people see too many ways things could go wrong, making them hesitate instead of acting. The result? Paralysis instead of progress, while their less hesitant peers take action and move ahead.
- Staying Comfortable Instead of Building Outward Confidence. Many smart people avoid high-stakes environments where their competence may be questioned. Instead of stepping into bigger opportunities, they stay where they feel in control, avoiding any situation where they might look bad or fail.
- Downplaying Ambition Instead of Practicing Self-Advocacy. Smart people sometimes hesitate to be openly ambitious because failure wouldn't just cost them success—it could damage their reputation. To avoid rejection

or scrutiny, they play small, keeping their ambitions private rather than boldly pursuing success.

The result? They trade the possibility of greater successes for the comfort of never failing too badly. Meanwhile, less capable or less intelligent individuals surpass them simply because they are willing to take risks and execute. Smart people may hesitate because they think they have more to lose, while those with less intelligence think they have less to lose and more willing to take bigger risks.

> *"Success is not the absence of failure."*

These common pitfalls don't mean intelligence is a disadvantage—only that it must be applied wisely. Watch yourself! The key is to develop *Smartness*: the ability to recognize when intelligence is helping you and when it's holding you back.

That's where bridging the *Smartness Gap* comes in—by shifting from overanalyzing to executing and from rigidity to adaptability.

Why Smart People Fall into This Trap

Understanding why smart people develop these self-sabotaging habits is key to overcoming them. The main reasons include:

- Intelligence Creates Blind Spots
  Smart people overestimate their own judgment, leading to resistance to feedback and alternative perspectives.

- Credentials & Achievements Build Ego
  Past successes create the illusion that future success is inevitable, which breeds stagnation.

- Success in One Area Doesn't Guarantee Success Elsewhere
  Many intelligent people assume that their expertise in one domain will translate into success in others, but real-world situations require new learning and adaptability.

Understanding why smart people fall into these traps is crucial. But awareness alone won't close the gap—only action will.

Bridging the Smartness Gap

Closing the *Smartness Gap* requires recognizing blind spots, shifting your mindset, and taking deliberate action—rather than getting trapped in overthinking or entitlement. The key is to move from analysis to execution and from assumptions to adaptability.

Every smart person has faced one or more *Smartness Gap* traps:

- Overanalyzing instead of executing.
- Assuming intelligence alone guarantees success.

- Sticking too rigidly to one way of thinking.
- Jumping from one thing to another without follow-through.

Which of these traps is holding YOU back?

Think about the biggest frustrations in your career, business, or personal growth. Are they caused by external limitations—or are they actually self-imposed barriers?

Recognizing the *Smartness Gap* is your wake-up call. The next step is figuring out how to bridge the gap.

Practical Steps to Overcome It

To overcome the *Smartness Gap*, smart people must shift their mindset and take practical steps to ensure their intelligence translates into action and results.

1. Develop Self-Awareness
Recognize if you have one (or more) of these self-sabotaging patterns. Reflect on past failures or stagnation—were they due to lack of intelligence, or misapplication of intelligence?

Action Step: Write down three situations where you got stuck. Identify whether overanalysis, entitlement, inflexibility, or distraction played a role.

2. Improve Decision Adaptability
Being smart doesn't mean always being right. Learn to adjust based on new information rather than rigidly sticking to an initial plan.

Action Step: When making a decision, ask: *"What would change my mind?"* If nothing could, you may be resisting necessary adaptation.

3. Prioritize Execution Over Analysis
Smart people often hesitate to act until everything is perfect. Shift the focus to starting and refining along the way.

Action Step: Set a "launch deadline" for your next big idea, even if it's not perfect. Take one actionable step today.

4. Shift from Entitlement to Learning
View intelligence as a tool, not a guarantee. Adopt an earned mindset—recognizing that consistent learning and persistent execution drive long-term success.

Action Step: Find someone with fewer advantages than you who has achieved more. Study how they applied *Smartness* beyond raw intelligence.

The simple yet powerful framework for doing this is the *Achievement Cycle* which we discussed in the last chapter.

> *"Success isn't about avoiding failure—it's about learning fast enough to turn failure into momentum for improvement, action, and achievement."*

The Smartness Gap and Your Next Step

Each of these *Smartness Gap* traps directly connects to key *Smartness Factors* you'll explore later in the book. For example, overcoming Overanalyzing & Perfectionism requires mastering Detail Orientation, while escaping Decision Inflexibility demands strong Belief Reinforcement.

The *Smartness Factors* are the tools that allow you to close the *Smartness Gap* and start applying your intelligence more effectively. But before you can fully leverage them, you first need to recognize which barriers are standing in your way.

The *Smartness Gap* isn't about not being smart enough. It's about not applying your intelligence effectively. Overcoming it requires recognizing blind spots, shifting your mindset, and taking deliberate action.

If you're like most smart people, your biggest obstacles aren't external. They're within you.

Reflection: *Right now, what is keeping you from the success you want?*

Is it hesitation? Overthinking? A fear of failing? Or something else you haven't yet uncovered?

The first step to closing the *Smartness Gap* is recognizing the invisible barriers standing in your way.

Recognizing the *Smartness Gap* is the first step. But knowing why smart people struggle isn't enough. You need to develop the capability to apply intelligence effectively in any situation. That capability is *Smartness*. In the next chapter, we'll break down its essential elements—mindsets, behaviors, habits, and skills.

Comparison Between Unsuccessful and Successful Smart People

A comparison of the assessment data between unsuccessful and successful smart people lays bare how *Smartness*—or the lack thereof—manifests in daily behavior, thinking patterns, and decision-making approaches. Here's a summary:

- Unsuccessful smart people often exhibit overthinking, excessive complexity, inaction, perfectionism, rigidity, and poor relational adaptability. Their intelligence becomes a liability rather than an asset. Many are trapped in cycles of over-analysis, under-action, and inflexibility. Some get stuck in self-doubt, while others are overconfident yet ineffective.
- Successful smart people balance their intelligence with action orientation, decision flexibility, emotional intelligence, risk tolerance, and practical execution. They use their intelligence strategically, act decisively, and adapt when necessary. Their relationships are leveraged intentionally, not avoided or mismanaged.

The gaps between unsuccessful and successful smart people on each *Smartness Factor* are stark and often reveal a balance problem: too much or too little of a specific trait causes underperformance.

These differences underscore why *Smartness*—not intelligence alone—makes the critical difference between potential and achievement. Now that you've explored how *Smartness* works in the real world, it's time to understand why so many smart people still struggle to succeed. The next chapter focuses on Disablers: internal and external barriers that limit *Smartness* and block success. Addressing them is critical to unlocking your full potential.

Reflection: *Are you stuck because you're not smart enough, or because you've confused being smart with knowing how to succeed?*

CHAPTER 10

The Elements of Smartness – Mindset, Behaviors, Habits & Skills

"Your intelligence sets the stage, but your mindset, behaviors, habits, skills, and actions determine the outcome."
~ Ram V. Iyer

A high-IQ individual with poor *Smartness* and weak execution will struggle, while someone with moderate intelligence but strong *Smartness* can achieve remarkable results. *Smartness* isn't just about thinking. It's about aligning your mindset, behaviors, habits, and skills with action so that intelligence translates into real-world success. *Smartness* is built—not inherited. And each of these four elements plays a critical role in turning raw intelligence into meaningful, lasting success.

Intelligence is the starting point. It's the foundational advantage that gives smart people the capacity to understand complex ideas, analyze situations, and solve problems. But intelligence alone doesn't lead to success. What separates those who achieve from those who don't is *Smartness*—how you apply intelligence through four key elements: mindset, behaviors, habits, and skills. *Smartness* turns intelligence into outcomes, and it works through a sequence that builds on itself.

Mindset shapes how smart people use their intelligence—what they notice, how they judge, and whether they act. Without the right Mindset, even exceptional intelligence gets misapplied or wasted. Some smart people fall into the trap of assuming that intelligence guarantees success. That assumption breeds entitlement, rigidity, or inaction. The Earned Mindset is the antidote: success must be earned—not assumed. We'll explore it later, alongside mindset-linked *Smartness Factors* like risk tolerance, self-competence, and the need for variety.

> *The way you see the world creates the world you see.* ~ Anonymous

Behaviors are the actions you take based on your mindset. This is where intelligence meets execution. You can have brilliant insights, but if you don't act on them—or you act on the wrong ones—intelligence doesn't matter. Smart people often get stuck here, trapped in analysis or waiting for perfect conditions. *Smartness* shows up in behavior that moves things forward.

Habits are essentially repeated behaviors. Good habits generally lead to positive outcomes, or at least help you avoid negative ones. Bad habits hold you back, even when you're smart enough to know better. They quietly undermine smart people, often without them realizing it. Good habits strengthen *Smartness*; bad habits become disablers. Habits, whether formed intentionally or not, become part of who you are. Short-term efforts—a day, a week, even a month—are like vacations. You might act differently for a while, but you'll quickly return to your old self. Real habits, built and reinforced over months and years, don't just change what you do—they shape who you become.

Good habits are how you do things the right way, over and over again. Bad habits are how you do things the wrong way, over and over again. Over time, good habits help you get better, and bad habits keep you stuck—or worse, help you get worse. Because habits run on autopilot, it's easy to miss how they're shaping your thinking, actions, and results—until the outcomes, good or bad, become too big to ignore. Bad habits come easy; good habits don't. That's why smart people have to be intentional about which habits they develop—and just as importantly, which habits they eliminate or manage.

Skills are the capabilities you develop and refine through learning and deliberate practice. Intelligence may support them, but skills are built through effort. Interpersonal skills, strategic thinking, and technical abilities aren't automatic, even for the smartest people. These skills have to be developed, sharpened, and applied in real-world situations if they're going to matter.

Connecting the Dots

Now let's connect the dots. Intelligence is the foundation—the capacity. Mindset directs where and how intelligence is applied. Behaviors put intelligence into action. Habits make those behaviors consistent. Skills sharpen your effectiveness in specific areas. Together, they define *Smartness*—and they determine whether your intelligence becomes real achievement or stays unused potential.

But there's another challenge: most people have a strength bias. They focus more on leveraging their good habits and existing strengths than on actively identifying and managing their bad habits. This bias can create blind spots. When smart people focus exclusively on what they do well, they risk allowing unproductive or harmful habits to quietly undermine their progress. This is like cancer—while invisible or not consciously apparent at first, it can silently destroy their future success. On the surface, everything may seem fine. But underneath, those bad habits are compounding, quietly eroding opportunities, damaging relationships, and draining momentum. By the time the impact becomes visible, it's often much harder to fix—or too late to avoid serious consequences. What starts as a small problem can grow into a major obstacle that blocks long-term achievement.

This is a critical difference between successful and unsuccessful people. It's not that successful people don't have bad habits—they do. The difference is that successful people are more likely to actively seek out, identify, and eliminate or manage the downsides of their bad habits, while continuing to leverage their good ones. Unsuccessful people tend to focus only on amplifying their strengths, hoping their bad habits won't matter or will somehow resolve themselves.

Over time, the cumulative effect of this difference is enormous. Smart people who actively eliminate or manage the downsides of their bad habits avoid self-sabotage, stay adaptable, and continue improving. Those who don't often find their bad habits quietly compound into major disablers that block their success.

> *"Bad habits come easy; good habits don't."*

Some factors (like certain mindsets) can be developed through books, audio, or video, while others (like hands-on behaviors and interpersonal skills) often require direct practice. Many aspects of *Smartness* benefit from a hybrid learning approach—combining self-study with in-person experiences. For instance, emotional intelligence needs both conceptual understanding (how empathy works) and real-life application to refine it.

For example, consider a large homework project. Your mindset keeps you motivated and calm. Your behaviors include breaking the project into smaller tasks, your skills (such as note-taking and time management) help you execute effectively, and repeating these approaches turns them into habits, making you more efficient each time.

Reflection: *Are your mindset, behaviors, habits, and skills helping your intelligence succeed—or quietly making sure it never does?*

Smartness & Disablers

Disablers, as discussed earlier, are obstacles that actively hinder your success. *Smartness* empowers you to confront disablers—obstacles that actively block progress—with intention and strategy. Managing, mitigating or eliminating disablers involves:

1. Recognizing the Disabler: Use self-awareness to identify behaviors, mindsets, or habits that are blocking your progress.
2. Reframing the Challenge: Shift your perspective and self-talk to view limitations as opportunities for growth.
3. Taking Intentional Action: Implement small, manageable steps to counteract the disabler and replace it with productive behaviors.

For instance, if fear of public speaking (a disabler) prevents career advancement, *Smartness* might involve reframing the fear as an opportunity to learn, practicing speeches in low-stakes environments, and gradually building confidence through experience. With *Smartness*, you can turn even the most limiting disablers into stepping stones for success.

This process is not just about individual perseverance but also about fostering adaptability in different cultural and social contexts. In the next section, we'll delve into how cultural adaptability and community connections can further elevate your journey toward sustained success.

Cultural Adaptability and the Power of Community

Certain communities around the world exemplify *Smartness* through a remarkable combination of adaptability, resourcefulness, and a long-term approach to success. The Jewish community, for instance, has consistently emphasized education, entrepreneurship, and resilience—qualities that have driven achievements across diverse fields. Their growth mindset and ability to adapt to changing circumstances illustrate how *Smartness* fosters sustained success across generations.

Similarly, Indian immigrants in the U.S. demonstrate entrepreneurial and professional excellence in a variety of sectors. Gujarati Indian business owners, particularly in the hotel and motel industry, showcase a deep commitment to growth, community support, and hard work—key drivers of their prosperity. They are said to own over half of all hotels and motels across the United States. Indian entrepreneurs have made significant contributions to the U.S. startup ecosystem. As of May 2022, immigrants founded over half (319 out of 582) of America's billion-dollar startups, with 66 of these companies having at least one founder from India—a testament to the influence of immigrant entrepreneurship. Beyond entrepreneurship, Indian leaders in the tech sector, such as Sundar Pichai (CEO of Google) and Satya Nadella (CEO of Microsoft), exemplify adaptability and innovation in navigating complex corporate landscapes.

These communities stand out as some of the most successful entrepreneurial and professional groups in the U.S. Their stories highlight how cultural adaptability, strategic use of resources, and an emphasis on education and resilience can create pathways to sustained success—an inspiring testament to real-world *Smartness*.

Personal Success Stories: The Power of Smartness

The beauty of *Smartness* lies in its ability to compensate for what you may lack in natural ability or socially valued advantages, like formal education. *Smartness* is not fixed; it grows through intentional effort, adaptability, and leveraging your advantages effectively. Not consistently applying *Smartness* can also hurt you. Here are three examples to illustrate the point.

Elon Musk illustrates the power—and pitfalls—of *Smartness* in real time. His ventures, from Tesla to SpaceX, highlight extraordinary *Smartness*: a combination of vision, calculated risk-taking, relentless innovation and execution. Musk has repeatedly leveraged his advantages—high intelligence, technical knowledge, risk-taking, media presence, and investor enthusiasm—to drive massive success. For example, without spending anything on marketing, his bold moves have often triggered surges in Tesla's stock value, increasing his net worth by billions in a matter of months. That's *Smartness* in action.

But *Smartness* isn't just about innovation—it's also about knowing when Communication Choices create risk. Public statements and social media activity

The Elements of Smartness – Mindset, Behaviors, Habits & Skills 65

that alienated key audiences, stakeholders, and partners have at times led to significant backlash. In one case, reactions to his public positioning and comments were followed by more than $100 billion in lost Tesla market capitalization. His net worth plunged by tens of billions, showing how quickly poor judgment in communication can undo years of value creation—look at the *Achievement Cycle* feedback loop.

This is the lesson: *Smartness* must be consistently applied, not just in strategy and innovation, but in communication, relationships, and reputation management. A lapse in one area can undermine success built elsewhere.

Taylor Swift exemplifies *Smartness* in action. While thousands of talented singers struggle to break through, Swift has strategically transformed herself into a billion-dollar brand (2024). With a steady stream of new songs, clever public relations, and the skillful use of social media, she has cultivated an army of raving fans who eagerly support her music and pay premium prices for her concerts. Her journey highlights how *Smartness*—more than raw talent or luck—drives exceptional and lasting success.

Queen Elizabeth II exemplifies how *Smartness* can transform inherent advantages into sustained achievement. Despite not earning a high school diploma, she became one of the longest-reigning monarchs in history. Her ancestry and title were significant advantages, but her success stemmed from a lifelong commitment to cultivating *Smartness*. Mentored by Winston Churchill, other statesmen, and palace advisors, she cultivated statecraft, diplomacy, and leadership. By embracing the traditions of the British monarchy—rich with centuries of wisdom—she continuously adapted to social and political changes, transforming her inherited role into one marked by stability, relevance, and influence. Her story underscores this book's core message: leveraging your advantages and committing to lifelong growth in *Smartness* is the key to sustained achievement.

Irrespective of your advantages, as you develop and refine your *Smartness*, you enhance your ability to navigate challenges, seize opportunities, and lay the groundwork for *Wisdom*. Over time, the reflective application of *Smartness* yields deeper insights and refined judgment—qualities often associated with *Wisdom*. In this way, *Smartness* becomes both a tool for immediate success and a pathway to achieving *Wisdom*.

In the following sections, we'll explore the depth and breadth of *Smartness*, tracing its historical roots, scientific framework, and practical implications. We'll see how cultures worldwide have valued *Smartness* and examine historical figures who have exemplified practical wisdom and adaptability. Let's start by examining the origins and evolution of *Smartness* through history.

Reflection: *Think of a time when you relied on your natural advantages, such as intelligence, resources, or credentials. How did the outcome compare to a situation where you applied Smartness to overcome a challenge or achieve greater success?*

Historical Perspectives on Smartness

Smartness is nothing new. The ability to apply intelligence, knowledge, and resources wisely has been integral to human evolution long before Charles Darwin articulated adaptability as essential for survival in his 1859 work *On the Origin of Species*. *Smartness* is not an invention of modern universities or Western thought, as some might believe. Many ancient ideas were simply relabeled in modern terms by the English language—which, as a formal system, is only about 400 years old.

Historical examples from different cultures highlight the timeless value of *Smartness*. African proverbs like "Knowledge without wisdom is like water in the sand" emphasize the need for practical application. Similarly, the ancient Chinese saying, "A wise man makes his own decisions; an ignorant man follows public opinion," underscores the importance of adaptability and informed decision-making—two hallmarks of *Smartness*.

Benjamin Franklin, one of America's Founding Fathers and a renowned inventor, exemplified *Smartness* through his practical ingenuity. Among his many contributions, Franklin invented the lightning rod to protect buildings from destruction and the odometer to measure distances, demonstrating his ability to solve real-world problems using creativity and applied knowledge.

Even literature highlights this theme. In Miguel de Cervantes' *Don Quixote*, Sancho Panza's common sense often saves Don Quixote from his misadventures, illustrating the gap between theoretical knowledge and practical wisdom. In the Middle Eastern classic *One Thousand and One Nights*, Scheherazade faces execution by a king who kills each of his wives after one day. She uses her storytelling skills to captivate him, ending each tale on a cliffhanger so he spares her life to hear more. Her clever strategy shows how *Smartness* can turn a desperate situation into an opportunity.

These historical and cultural insights underscore one enduring truth: *Smartness* is not a modern concept—it has existed across eras and geographies. It's not merely about what or who you know or have, but how effectively you apply it to achieve the outcomes you seek. By learning from these timeless lessons, you can harness your own advantages to achieve meaningful success.

The Research

Smartness goes beyond intelligence. It's about the practical application of knowledge and advantages in real life. It bridges the gap between potential and meaningful outcomes by emphasizing adaptability, resourcefulness, and the ability to assess and act effectively in dynamic situations. This chapter highlights key scientific principles that support *Smartness* as a practical, actionable skill.

1. **The Transfer of Learning** (Edward Thorndike and Robert S. Woodworth) Transfer of learning is the ability to apply knowledge and skills from one context to another. *Smartness* embodies this, enabling people to adapt

past experiences to new challenges. Taylor Swift demonstrates this by leveraging lessons from her music career to build a billion-dollar brand—pivoting from country to pop, and later into business.

2. **Problem-Solving Frameworks** (George Pólya's Four Steps)
Pólya's approach—understand the problem, devise a plan, execute, and reflect—maps directly to *Smartness*. It helps break complex challenges into manageable actions. Elon Musk applies this at Tesla: identifying inefficiencies in electric vehicles, devising plans around scalable battery tech, executing, and iterating—*Smartness* in action.

3. **Cognitive Adaptability** (Shane G. Scott and Richard Bruce)
Flexible thinking allows you to adjust to changing situations. It's a core of *Smartness*—helping you reassess, adjust plans, and make decisions under pressure.

4. **Behavioral Decision Theory** (Herbert A. Simon)
Simon's concept of bounded rationality is about making the best possible decisions with limited information and resources. *Smartness* applies this principle—pragmatic decision-making that balances speed, accuracy, and constraints. Think Scheherazade in One Thousand and One Nights: her clever use of cliffhanger stories turned limited time into survival strategy.

5. **Feedback Loops in Learning** (David A. Kolb)
Kolb's experiential learning cycle—experience, reflection, conceptualization, experimentation—captures the role of feedback in improving adaptability. *Smartness* thrives when you learn and refine as you go. Musk's iterative design process at SpaceX, where every launch informs the next, is *Smartness* fueled by feedback.

Reflection: Recall a moment when applying your knowledge, rather than merely possessing it, significantly impacted an outcome.

Smartness is dynamic. It grows through experience, reflection, and deliberate action. It isn't automatic—you have to develop and apply it intentionally. By continuously refining your mindset, behaviors, habits, and skills, you close the gap between intelligence and real-world achievement. Success isn't about what you know, who you know, or what you are capable of, but how effectively you use them.

In the next chapter, we'll shift gears to the practical side of *Smartness*. You'll discover how you could leverage your unique advantages, navigate obstacles, and align your actions with meaningful goals. The journey begins with awareness but drives outcomes only with actions. Let's dive in and bring your *Smartness* to life.

Reflection: Are your habits making your intelligence sharper—or just making your underachievement more efficient, cleverly perfecting the art of going nowhere—just in style?

CHAPTER 11

THE SMARTNESS DEVELOPMENT PROCESS—HOW TO BUILD AND APPLY SMARTNESS

"Success doesn't come from what you have—it comes from knowing how to repeatedly leverage it into achievement."
~ Ram V. Iyer

Smart people don't just need more knowledge or credentials. They can greatly benefit from applying what they already have more effectively. That's what *Smartness* is for. This chapter lays out the *Smartness Development Process*: a clear, practical system of how intelligent people can build and apply *Smartness* to achieve better, more consistent results.

This chapter shifts from what *Smartness* is to how smart people develop and apply it over time. That process has three core building blocks, like the three legs of a stool:

- The Earned Mindset sets the foundation for how effort and discipline shape outcomes.
- The *Smartness Factors* reveal the mindsets, behaviors, and skills that determine how effectively intelligence is applied.
- The *Achievement Cycle* translates *Smartness* into repeatable success.

You'll see these three ideas woven throughout the rest of the book, each with tools and examples to help you apply them in real life.

If even one leg is weak or missing, the stool becomes unstable. But when all three are strong, they support the development of your *Smartness* and help you achieve sustained success.

This is how you build *Smartness*. The more you reinforce each leg and use it, the stronger your *Smartness* becomes—and the better your results.

That's why learning by doing is the best way to develop Smartness. You don't build it by sitting on the sidelines or waiting for the perfect plan. You build it by trying things, seeing what works, and making adjustments along the way. Sometimes you'll nail it, sometimes you'll need to course-correct—and that's part of the process. The *Achievement Cycle* gives you a structure to do exactly that: act, reflect, adapt, and grow. Smartness grows when you turn action into insights and wisdom and keep moving forward.

The Three Pillars of the Smartness Development Process

The *Smartness Development Process* rests on three essential pillars, like the three legs of a stool. Each one plays a critical role in building and applying *Smartness*—and each one supports the other two pillars.

1. **Earned Mindset**
   - This is the foundation of *Smartness*.
   - An Earned Mindset is the belief that success isn't owed to you—it's earned through consistent action, good judgment, and follow-through.
   - Without an Earned Mindset, people often fall into entitlement, over-reliance on credentials, or thinking they should succeed automatically because they are intelligent. They may fail to develop their *Smartness Factors* or apply the *Achievement Cycle*.

2. **The Smartness Factors**
   - These are the mindsets, behaviors, habits, and skills that constitute *Smartness*.
   - They are practical and learnable. You develop them over time, and they build the capability you need to assess situations clearly, make better decisions, and take smarter actions.
   - The *Smartness Factors* cover three areas:
     - Thinking Factors
     - Action Factors
     - Relational Factors
   - But developing the *Smartness Factors* alone—without an Earned Mindset or applying the *Achievement Cycle*—makes them weak.

3. **The Achievement Cycle**
   - This is the process you use to apply *Smartness* consistently.
   - It guides how you act on your capabilities and translate them into real-world achievements.
   - The *Achievement Cycle* closes the gap between potential and performance by providing a five-step process you can follow repeatedly.
   - You cannot effectively apply the *Achievement Cycle* without an Earned Mindset and the development of the *Smartness Factors*.

Smart people often know what better judgment, stronger follow-through, or clearer priorities look like, but still don't apply them when it matters most. That's the gap. Developing *Smartness* is a real-world practice loop, not a conceptual model. *Smartness* is built through consistent action. Each time they challenge an unhelpful mindset, choose a smarter move, and follow through, they reinforce the system and improve their *Smartness*. It gives them a clear, structured system to develop and apply *Smartness* consistently. It connects the core elements they've already explored—mindsets, behaviors, habits, and skills—and turns them into repeatable actions that drive results.

How the Smartness Development Process Works

The *Smartness Development Process* follows a clear developmental and application cycle:

1. You develop *Smartness* by working on the *Smartness Factors*.
2. Your Earned Mindset guides how you develop and apply these factors.
3. You use the *Achievement Cycle* to take consistent, smart action—and reinforce your Earned Mindset and further develop your *Smartness Factors*.
4. You achieve results that matter.
5. These achievements reinforce and deepen your Earned Mindset, which drives you to further develop your *Smartness Factors*.

The Smartness Development Process

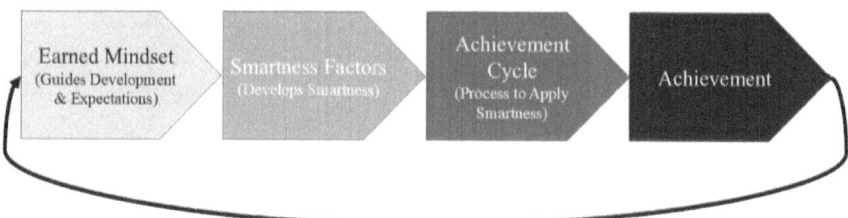

It's a self-reinforcing cycle that builds momentum and creates long-term, consistent success. The more you use this process, the more you improve in each stage of the cycle, ensuring personal development and sustained achievement.

This process works because it's grounded in real-world research and field-tested with 1200+ professionals and leaders. It's designed to be practical, adaptable, and scalable.

Smartness isn't theoretical. It's a capability you can develop, refine, and master at any age, regardless of where you're starting from. The *Smartness Development Process* gives you the tools, structure, and system to do it deliberately, rather than hoping for things to change on their own.

Remember, Success Is an Outcome. Smartness Is How You Get There.

You can't manage outcomes, but you *can* control the inputs that lead to them. *Smartness* is the most important input you have. When you develop your *Smartness*—your mindsets, behaviors, habits, and skills—you control how you act, decide, and follow through. That's what leads to success.

Don't focus on success (outcome). Focus on *Smartness (input.* The *Smartness Development Process* will help you with that. Success will follow.

The Smartness Development Process—How to Build and Apply Smartness

Next...

Overcoming disablers clears the path. But clearing the path isn't enough—you need to move forward by leveraging your advantages effectively. The next chapter shows you how to identify and maximize your personal advantages to drive greater success.

With the *Smartness Development Process* in place, it's time to go deeper. You'll start with the Earned Mindset, the foundation. Then you'll master the *Smartness Factors* and apply them through the *Achievement Cycle*.

> *"Intelligence doesn't apply itself and Smartness doesn't build itself. You need Smartness to leverage your intelligence."*

Smart people fall behind not because they lack ability, but because they delay using it. If you want results, you need momentum. And momentum starts with *Smartness*.

You've got the process. Now it's time to put it to work.

Reflection: *Are you building your Smartness like a pro—or just hoping your intelligence will figure it out for you?*

CHAPTER 12

THE EARNED MINDSET: THE FOUNDATION FOR SMARTNESS & CONSISTENT ACHIEVEMENT

"Knowledge doesn't achieve results; applying knowledge does."
~ Ram V. Iyer

For years, we've been told that success depends on mindset—especially whether we believe we can improve. Dr. Carol Dweck's work introduced the world to two belief systems: the fixed mindset (abilities are set) and the growth mindset (abilities can improve with effort). But many smart people assume that having a growth mindset is enough. It's not.

A growth mindset is just that—A belief. But beliefs don't guarantee results. It's what you do with your beliefs that matters. Smart people can have a growth mindset and still underachieve. Success comes from doing the work to earn that improvement.

> *If a growth mindset was a breakthrough in thinking, Smartness is a breakthrough in achieving.*

That's why so many intelligent, hardworking people still fall short of the success they expect. They have the belief. They have the advantages: intelligence, credentials, resources. But they struggle to turn those into real results.

Worse, some believe that belief itself is enough—that thinking "I can succeed" will make it happen. They fall into a quiet trap: mistaking positive thinking for progress. They assume that because they're capable, success will just show up. And they stop doing the work to actually earn it. Some even believe that saying "I can accomplish anything I set my mind to" could somehow make them successful—as if the declaration alone is an accomplishment.

Why? Because success demands more than belief or potential. It requires knowing when, where, and how to apply your advantages—and doing it consistently.

This is where *Smartness* comes in. *Smartness* turns mindset and advantages into real-world results. But *Smartness* can't grow in assumption or entitlement. It must be built on the foundation of the Earned Mindset.

The Earned Mindset: The Foundation of the Smartness Development Process

In the *Smartness Development Process*, Earned Mindset is the foundation that guides how *Smartness* is developed and applied. Without it, you risk falling into the traps of entitlement, passivity, and over-reliance on intelligence or credentials.

An Earned Mindset is the belief that success isn't owed to you. It's earned through consistent, intelligent action, good judgment, and follow-through.

Without an Earned Mindset, even highly intelligent people can stagnate, misjudge challenges, and underperform. They may assume past successes will automatically lead to future ones, or they may overthink and hesitate instead of acting.

With an Earned Mindset, you recognize that each success must be earned through deliberate effort and execution.

Mindset vs. Smartness: The Shift from Thinking to Action & Achievement

Fixed vs. Growth mindset Thinking	The Smartness Approach
Success is determined by whether you have a fixed or a growth mindset.	Success depends on how effectively you assess situations, make decisions, and take action.
Believing you can improve is the most important factor.	Knowing how to make decisions, take action, improve, refine your approach, and apply what you learn to achieve results.
A growth mindset focuses on persistence and effort.	*Smartness* focuses on applying effort effectively, learning from experiences, making adjustments, and repeating the cycle to achieve sustained success.
Mindset helps people overcome self-imposed limits (beliefs).	*Smartness* ensures that the mindset you choose drives productive action, helping you focus effort on what truly leads to success.

Why Many Smart People Get Stuck Without an Earned Mindset

Many highly intelligent people assume that their intelligence alone will lead to success. However, intelligence without *Smartness* often results in overthinking, hesitation, or misplaced confidence in flawed assumptions. An Earned Mindset requires actively bridging intelligence with execution—meaning that every success must be earned, not expected. Smart people who fail to develop this mindset may struggle with adapting to setbacks, misjudging real-world challenges, or believing that past successes will automatically translate into future ones. Without an Earned Mindset, even the most intelligent individuals can stagnate, failing to turn their potential into lasting achievement.

Shifting to an Earned Mindset

Shifting to an Earned Mindset requires awareness, accountability, and action. Own your results – Stop blaming circumstances or others. Take responsibility for your progress and setbacks. It means recognizing where you've been passive or reliant on external factors and making the conscious choice to take control of your growth.

Start by identifying where you might be operating with an *Entitlement* or *Destiny Mindset*. Do you assume success will come because of your past achievements, credentials, or talents? Do you wait for the right opportunity instead of creating one? These are signs that your mindset may be limiting you.

The transition to an Earned Mindset happens when you:

- Take ownership of your results, whether good or bad.
- Seek feedback and use it to improve, rather than dismissing or avoiding it, or taking it personally.
- Act deliberately, focusing on consistent effort rather than waiting for motivation or luck.
- Adapt and refine your approach instead of getting discouraged by setbacks.

Developing an Earned Mindset is a process, not a switch you flip overnight. The key is consistency—intentionally choosing, every day, to actively shape your success rather than waiting for circumstances to change.

> *"Success is not granted. It must be earned."* ~ *Unknown*

The Earned Mindset in Action

The Earned Mindset is how smart people move from potential to performance. It shows up in real-world situations—especially when things don't go as planned. Smart people with an Earned Mindset don't just believe in improvement; they act to create it. They refine their thinking, make better decisions, execute consistently, and adapt along the way.

Consider two professionals facing the same career setback—a lost promotion. One blames office politics or bad luck and remains stuck, waiting for external circumstances to shift. The other actively seeks feedback, identifies gaps, and works on self-improvement. One remains stagnant, while the other adapts, improves, and earns better opportunities.

This contrast illustrates why an Earned Mindset matters. It's not about believing you *can* grow—it's about earning it through action. Those who embrace it don't wait for success to come to them; they act to earn it.

Reflection: *Are you waiting for success, or are you actively creating it? What is one area where you can take more ownership of your growth today?*

The Earned Mindset: The Bridge Between Thinking and Execution

A growth mindset helps smart people believe in improvement, but belief alone doesn't create success—execution does. Smart people must bridge the gap between knowing and doing, and that requires an Earned Mindset.

Smartness is not a one-time event—it evolves through a continuous cycle of applying intelligence, leveraging advantages, deciding to act, learning from experience, and achieving sustained success.

Smart people often underachieve because they assume intelligence alone will carry them forward. The missing link isn't knowledge or thinking—it's execution. Success requires assessing, deciding, acting and following through consistently.

An Earned Mindset isn't just about believing you can succeed—it's about consistently earning successes through smart decision-making, adaptability, and follow-through. The world is full of people who believe they can and should succeed, but are not successful. This book provides a clear framework for turning mindset into consistent, desired real-world outcomes.

> *"Success doesn't follow a straight line—it's an iterative process. Smartness is what makes that process work in your favor."*

The Earned Mindset is the foundation of the *Smartness Development Process*. It guides how you develop the *Smartness Factors*—the mindsets, behaviors, habits, and skills that make up *Smartness*. Without an Earned Mindset, people often fail to apply those factors effectively or consistently.

Strengthening Your Earned Mindset

Building an Earned Mindset isn't a one-time shift—it's a habit that must be reinforced daily. The strongest achievers don't just apply effort when it's convenient; they commit to continuous learning, adaptability, and action.

To strengthen your Earned Mindset, focus on these key areas:

- Challenge your assumptions: Question any beliefs that suggest success is owed to you or that external factors control your outcomes.
- Build resilience: View setbacks as lessons, not failures. When things don't go as planned, adjust and move forward.

- Seek growth environments: Surround yourself with people who challenge and push you rather than those who reinforce passive thinking.
- Develop action bias: Make a habit of taking initiative instead of overanalyzing or waiting for perfect conditions.

An Earned Mindset thrives on momentum. The more you take ownership, adapt, and act, the more success you create—and the more proof you have that your growth is in your hands.

The Earned Mindset Checklist

Shifting to an Earned Mindset requires consistent effort and self-awareness. Use this checklist to assess and strengthen your approach:

- Do I take full ownership of my successes and failures, or do I blame circumstances and other people?
- When I encounter setbacks, do I analyze what I can improve, or do I dwell on what went wrong?
- Do I actively seek feedback and use it to improve, or do I avoid criticism?
- Am I willing to do the hard work required for success, or do I expect results without effort?
- Do I adapt and adjust my approach when things don't go as planned, or do I give up too soon?
- Do I take action consistently, even when conditions aren't perfect, or do I wait for the "right time"?

Success is built through repeated action. The more you commit to taking ownership, learning, and adapting, the more you reinforce the Earned Mindset—and the more success you create.

Success isn't predetermined, nor is it something you're entitled to—it's something you build through effort, adaptability, and action. The Earned Mindset is what separates those who actively create opportunities from those who wait for them.

> *"Achievement-focused people, driven by an Earned Mindset, achieve repeated success by viewing it as a continuous journey, not as a one-time achievement. "*

The key to sustaining an Earned Mindset is consistency. It's not about occasional bursts of motivation – like when on vacations - but about repeatedly making choices that reinforce ownership, learning, and growth. Every decision—how you respond to setbacks, whether you take action or hesitate, how you apply what you learn every day of your life—shapes your future success.

An Earned Mindset Requires:

- Assessing Situations Clearly – Understanding the context, recognizing opportunities and risks, and determining the right moment to act or step back.
- Making Good Decisions – Choosing actions based on logic and facts, rather than acting on impulse or wishful thinking.
- Following Through with Action (or Choosing to Wait) – Taking action when necessary—or intentionally waiting when conditions aren't favorable.

This continuous process of evaluation, decision-making, and action makes *Smartness* the next evolution in success thinking. And the *Achievement Cycle* ensures that mindset isn't just an internal belief. It's something you test, refine, and apply repeatedly to create real, repeatable success: by you, through your own actions.

How Smartness Evolves the Mindset Model

The concept of mindset was a breakthrough in understanding how belief shapes success. *Smartness* builds on this foundation by providing a clear, repeatable process that turns belief into action and action into sustained achievement.

Success isn't just about having the right mindset—it's about assessing situations, making sound decisions, and knowing when to act, how to act, and whether to act at all to achieve the outcomes you seek.

> *"If a growth mindset was a breakthrough in thinking, then an Earned Mindset, with Smartness and action, is a breakthrough in achieving."*

An Earned Mindset is the foundation of *Smartness*. When you develop an Earned Mindset, you stop waiting for success and start earning it. By developing an Earned Mindset and using *Smartness*, people can stop just believing they can succeed and start earning the success they deserve. They refine their approach, apply what they learn, and sustain their success across different challenges and opportunities in life.

Next...

In the next part of the book, we'll dive into the *Smartness Factors*—the mindsets, behaviors, habits, and skills that develop *Smartness*. These are the capabilities that allow you to consistently apply what you've learned, make better decisions, improve your action orientation and drive meaningful.

Reflection: *Are you still waiting for success to show up—or finally owning that it's your job to earn it, not someone else's?*

CHAPTER 13

How Smart People Turn Intelligence & Advantages into Achievements

"Intelligence and advantages are just enablers. Smartness is what can leverage them to turn opportunities into achievements."
~ Ram V. Iyer

Smartness isn't about knowing everything or having the highest IQ; it's about knowing how to apply what you have and your intelligence in different situations.

But before diving into how *Smartness* operates, it's important to clarify why intelligence matters—and why it's not enough.

Many smart people assume that intelligence alone is enough to guarantee success. They believe that superior reasoning, knowledge, or credentials should naturally translate into achievement. Yet, in reality, smart people often struggle because they fail to apply their intelligence in the right ways, at the right times, and with the right level of adaptability.

Intelligence Is the Core Advantage of Smart People

Relying solely on intelligence is like relying on a one-trick pony: highly limiting, insufficient and extremely noncompetitive. For many smart people, intelligence is their core advantage. It fuels their ability to learn, analyze, and solve complex problems. But intelligence is static—it doesn't increase much over one's lifetime. *Smartness*, on the other hand, is dynamic. It determines whether and how they apply their intelligence, and whether it leads to achievement or frustration. Without *Smartness*, intelligence can result in overanalysis, inaction, or poor decision-making. With *Smartness*, intelligence becomes a powerful tool for execution and adaptability.

This chapter highlights real-world examples of smart people who successfully applied *Smartness* to gain a competitive edge—and others who failed because they didn't. The key takeaway? *Smartness* isn't just what you know. It's how well you use it and execute.

Some Smart People Fail and Some Succeed

Many highly intelligent people struggle because they assume intelligence alone is enough. Leonard, a highly accomplished software engineer, assumed his technical skills alone would ensure his success. He believed his intelligence made him indispensable, but he failed to develop teamwork—an essential *Smartness Factor*. Preferring to work alone, he undervalued collaboration, relationship-building, and adaptability. Meanwhile, his less technically skilled colleagues built strong professional networks, engaged in teamwork, and navigated workplace dynamics effectively. Over time, they surpassed him in career growth. Leonard's intelligence wasn't the problem. His failure to apply *Smartness* was.

Compare Leonard's case with those who actively develop and apply Smartness. Smart people who succeed do not just rely on their credentials or technical expertise—they build strategic relationships, seize opportunities, and advocate for themselves effectively. They combine intelligence with situational judgment, decision flexibility, and action orientation to ensure their success.

For example, consider Akira, a marine biologist in La Jolla, California, who faced a rare research challenge. Instead of waiting for existing studies, she applied *Smartness Factors* like thinking range and adaptability. She pulled in experts from neurobiology, behavioral ecology, and environmental science, using an interdisciplinary approach to solve the problem. Her ability to expand her knowledge and execute decisively led to groundbreaking discoveries that reshaped marine ecology studies. Unlike Leonard, who relied only on intelligence, Akira used Smartness—strategic application, execution, and adaptability—to achieve success.

Akira succeeded not just because of her intelligence, but because she used *Smartness* to leverage her full range of advantages.

These two examples show how intelligence alone isn't enough. *Smartness* is what determines whether advantages become results—or remain unrealized.

Smart people aren't always the ones with the highest IQs. Some of the most successful people aren't the most intelligent—they're the ones who use *Smartness* to make better decisions, take action and achieve desired outcomes in the real-world.

Smartness Enables the Use of Intelligence and Advantages

Once smart people recognize the full range of advantages—including intelligence, their core advantage—they possess, the next challenge is not discovery—but activation. That's where *Smartness* plays a defining role.

Many smart people often start with clear advantages—intelligence, credentials, networks, experience, or resources. They provide a head start. But having advantages doesn't guarantee success. What separates those who consistently succeed from those who plateau or decline is whether and how they apply their advantages.

Smartness Helps You Leverage, Not Discover, Your Advantages

Smartness does not help people identify their advantages. Discovery requires awareness, reflection, and sometimes external input. Once they know what advantages they have—whether intelligence, credentials, networks, resources, or experience—*Smartness* is the critical capability that determines whether and how they leverage them. It's the difference between potential and results. Some smart people fail to apply their advantages, not because they lack intelligence, but because they lack Smartness.

Three Types of Advantages

Smartness helps smart people manage three types of advantages:

- **Fixed Advantages** are the assets they're born with or acquire early—like intelligence, family wealth, or natural charisma. These provide a head start, but they usually can't be expanded. Without Smartness, they are often underused or taken for granted.
- **Flexible Advantages** are built over time—skills, networks, expertise, reputation. These can be developed through consistent effort. Smart people with *Smartness* know how to build, adapt, and apply them to unlock greater levels of success.
- **Situational Advantages** arise unexpectedly—through timing, environment, or circumstance. Being in the right place at the right time isn't enough. *Smartness* is what helps people recognize these moments and capitalize on them before the window closes.

Smart people who succeed know which advantage to use, when to use it, and how to combine them. The rest often waste opportunities they didn't even realize they had.

The Misuse of Advantages—Why Some Smart People Get Stuck

Many smart people fail to leverage their advantages effectively. Common traps include:

- **Overreliance** on a single advantage (e.g., assuming intelligence alone guarantees success)
- **Entitlement** (believing past success or credentials should automatically translate into future results)
- **Neglect** (failing to maintain or develop other advantages, like relationships or skills)
- **Inflexibility** (refusing to adapt how they use their advantages as circumstances change)

Smartness helps prevent these traps by enabling better decisions about when and how to apply their advantages.

Smartness Can Convert Advantages into Achievements

Advantages are inert. They are just potential. They only create success only when leveraged with Smartness. For example, smart people can:

- pair intelligence with judgment and timing
- use credentials to open doors—and deliver once they're inside
- leverage networks to identify opportunities unknown to most others
- choose to apply resources with focus to achieve superior results

Smartness makes sure advantages are used deliberately, consistently, and effectively.

Managing Advantages Across Life Stages

The value of advantages shifts over time. Early in their careers, many smart people rely on intelligence (to excel academically) and credentials (to open doors). Mid-career, networks and the ability to work with and through people often matter more. Later, judgment and wisdom become the primary advantages. *Smartness* allows them to navigate these transitions, continually adjusting how they use their advantages to stay effective and relevant.

Practical Actions—How Smart People Manage Their Advantages

- Take inventory of your advantages regularly
- Identify which advantages you are underutilizing
- Challenge yourself on any overused advantages
- Build new flexible advantages over time (skills, relationships)
- Learn to move fast to capitalize on situational advantages

Smart people with *Smartness* are advantage managers. They actively orchestrate their strengths for sustained success.

So how do smart people turn intelligence into *Smartness* they can use daily? These ten approaches build practical habits that make intelligence work harder—and smarter.

Ten Suggestions for Practical Application

Smartness is the art of applying one's intelligence judiciously in various life contexts. It can be cultivated through deliberate practice. And it is crucial to apply *Smartness* in everyday life. Here are ten actionable suggestions to enhance your *Smartness* in daily life. They can not only strengthen your inherent abilities (strengths) but also leverage external factors (enablers) to enhance your overall Smartness.

1. Learn Continuously
2. Cultivate Adaptability
3. Seek Feedback
4. Act Strategically
5. Develop Emotional Intelligence
6. Take Calculated Risks
7. Practice Self-Awareness
8. Expand Thinking Range
9. Invest in Relationships
10. Close the Loop

Smart people don't fail because they lack capability—they fail because they over-rely on intelligence without applying Smartness. The most intelligent individuals often fall into the trap of analysis without action, planning without follow-through, or assuming credentials will do the heavy lifting. That's the *Smartness Gap*. Closing that gap means choosing action over perfection, adaptability over ego, and execution over entitlement. The smartest people don't just think better—they act smarter. That's how they rise. That's how they win.

Reflection: *Are you over-relying on your intelligence, credentials, or potential— and underdelivering on action? What specific change in your behavior or mindset would close that gap?*

From Intelligence to Success: The Role of Smartness

Carol Dweck's research emphasizes the importance of a growth mindset. This mindset suggests that with the right efforts, one can enhance one's intelligence and also expand and leverage one's Smartness. The late Dr. Anders Ericsson's '10,000 Hour Rule' underlines the significance of sheer practice and experience in mastering many fields. By combining the power of inherent intelligence with the honed skills of Smartness, individuals can navigate challenges with much more efficacy. Remember, you can enhance and leverage your intelligence and *Smartness* for the rest of your life.

Embracing a growth mindset, seeking mentorship, leveraging one's unique strengths (enablers), mitigating one's disablers (like biases and tendencies), and adopting a holistic view of intelligence and success with an emphasis on *Smartness* are essential to achieve greater success. Success isn't just the privilege of the intelligent. It's the fruit borne from the seed of potential, nurtured by the right practices, mindset, and smart application in various contexts.

If you leverage your intelligence but do not develop your Smartness, it could become a lifelong habit that will disable you for the rest of your life.

Understanding and Developing Smartness

For much of my life, I struggled to fully understand the distinction between intelligence and Smartness—a confusion I've found many others share. In fact, among the 1,200+ participants in the *Smartness Assessment*, 13% believe that they are the same. Yet, their differences are critical: while intelligence forms the cognitive foundation, *Smartness* is about turning potential into action—applying knowledge, skills, and resources in ways that drive meaningful success.

Initially, suggestions like 'learning through experience' felt too vague, especially since *Smartness* often depends on context. It wasn't until I reflected on my successes and failures that I realized the true power of *Smartness* lies not just in what you know, but in how you effectively apply it to achieve your goals.

Through research, assessments, and interviews with highly successful individuals, I've identified factors that influence a person's Smartness. These factors, explored in this book, are the building blocks for translating intelligence, resources, and assets into tangible success. *Smartness* isn't just valuable for personal achievement—it's essential for those in positions of influence or specialized skill to amplify their impact and create meaningful results.

As we journey through life, the ways we apply intelligence and *Smartness* naturally evolve, bringing new strengths—and sometimes challenges—that shape our success in different stages. In the next chapter, we will explore how age influences the development and impact of these qualities.

Reflection: *How much longer will you hide behind your raw intelligence—watching others with half your smarts surge ahead—before you finally leverage your Smartness to turn all that untapped potential into tangible, unstoppable results?*

CHAPTER 14

THE SMARTNESS FACTORS

"Together, our skills and mindset define our individual or collective Smartness, which influences our ability to achieve greater success."
~ Ram V. Iyer

Smartness isn't one thing. It's a system of thinking and behavioral capabilities that determine how well people apply their advantages to achieve success.

This chapter provides a brief overview of the *Smartness Factors*, which will be explored in depth in Part 4. This chapter introduces the *Smartness Factors*, core enablers that help smart people close the gap between potential and achievement. Each factor plays a different role depending on context. For example, Personal Autonomy might help a freelancer but hinder someone in a collaborative role. These factors will be explored in detail in the next 24 chapters.

The *Smartness Factors* are grouped into three categories:

- **Thinking Factors**: These affect how you analyze, interpret, and assess situations. They shape your decisions and belief formation.
- **Action Factors**: These govern what you choose to do, your follow-through, and how you execute under uncertainty.
- **Relational Factors**: These shape how you interact, collaborate, and operate within systems that require people and relationships.

The way you leverage these *Smartness Factors*—recognizing when they serve as enablers or disablers—determines how effectively you translate your advantages and potential into success. The *Smartness Factors* are pivotal to success, serving as either enablers or obstacles. By actively managing these factors, you can align your aspirations, knowledge, and actions to maximize the potential of the Success Triad for greater achievement.

Among the *Smartness Factors*, intelligence is not listed as one. Why? Because intelligence by itself is not a capability that guarantees success. It is an advantage that must be applied effectively. A person with high intelligence but low Smartness—like someone with poor Decision Flexibility and Action Orientation—may struggle far more than someone with average intelligence who is adaptive and decisive. Smart people often over-rely on intelligence as their primary advantage, making them more prone to certain disabling tendencies.

This book focuses on the *Smartness Factors*—the capabilities that determine how effectively you apply your advantages, whether intelligence, resources, skills, or something else to achieve success.

As you learn about the *Smartness Factors*, use the companion **Smartness Playbook** to assess how they apply to you and create a personalized roadmap for improvement.

The Smartness Factors

The following is a list of the *Smartness Factors* grouped by the underlying commonality – thinking, action or relational.

THINKING SMARTNESS FACTORS

1. **Detail Focus** (Realist vs. Perfectionist)
   - Enablers: Balancing precision with efficiency, applying attention to detail where it matters, and maintaining an organized, methodical approach.
   - Disablers: Perfectionism leading to inaction, over-focusing on minor details, inability to see the big picture or delegate due to a need for control, and procrastination.

2. **Complexity Preference** (Comfortable with Complexity vs. Complexity Bias)
   - Enablers: Thriving in ambiguity, recognizing patterns in complexity, and simplifying complex ideas into actionable strategies.
   - Disablers: Over-intellectualizing simple decisions, creating unnecessary complexity, struggling with ambiguity, or oversimplifying to avoid depth.

3. **Decision Flexibility** (Flexible vs. Rigid Decision-Making)
   - Enablers: Seeking counterarguments, testing assumptions, adjusting strategies based on real-world feedback, and proactively identifying when a change in direction is needed.
   - Disablers: Intellectual stubbornness, resistance to change, reliance on rigid methods, and reluctance to pivot despite new evidence.

4. **Thinking & Feeling** (Empathetic vs. Unsympathetic)
   - Enablers: Integrating logic with emotional intelligence to build trust, actively listening to different perspectives, and applying empathy to strengthen relationships and decision-making.
   - Disablers: Over-reliance on logic at the expense of empathy, difficulty relating to others, dismissing emotional concerns, or coming across as cold and insensitive.

5. **Situational Judgment** (Street-Smart vs. Lacking Street-Smarts)
   - Enablers: Quickly assessing risks and opportunities, reading people and environments accurately, adjusting strategies in real time, and applying intelligence through lived experience—not just theory.
   - Disablers: Over-reliance on book smarts, misreading social situations, undervaluing experience, and neglecting long-term thinking.

6. **Thinking Range** (Adaptive vs. Polarized Thinking)
   - Enablers: Seeing multiple angles to a problem, integrating diverse perspectives, and applying creative, flexible thinking to complex situations.
   - Disablers: Overcommitment to their viewpoint, rigid or binary (black and white) thinking, rejecting nuances, and favoring oversimplified solutions.

7. **Belief Reinforcement** (Open to Change vs. Confirmation Bias)
   - Enablers: Openness to new ideas, adjusting views based on evidence, embracing constructive feedback, and balancing confidence with humility.
   - Disablers: Assuming their intelligence makes them right, dismissing feedback from "less intelligent" people, confirmation biases instead of seeking diverse viewpoints, dogmatism, resistance to new ideas, lack of self-reflection.

ACTION SMARTNESS FACTORS

8. **Action Orientation** (Proactive vs. Reluctant to Act)
   - Enablers: Turning analysis into execution, taking initiative without over-planning, embracing forward momentum despite uncertainty, and delivering results.
   - Disablers: Hesitation due to over-analysis, reluctance to act without complete information, fear of imperfection, and over-planning as procrastination.

9. **Risk Tolerance** (Calculated Risk-Taker vs. Risk-Averse)
   - Enablers: Taking calculated risks confidently, balancing analysis with decisive action, and demonstrating resilience and adaptability.
   - Disablers: Avoidance of risks due to fear of reputational damage, excessive focus on theoretical risks over real-world opportunities, failure to take bold actions despite having the knowledge to do so, fear of failure, resistance to new experiences.

10. **Self-Competence View** (Self-Confident vs. Impostor Syndrome)
    - Enablers: Recognizing strengths and weaknesses with clarity, applying constructive feedback for continuous growth, and maintaining confidence (humbly) to act despite uncertainty.
    - Disablers: Either chronic impostor syndrome or overconfidence that leads to ignoring personal weaknesses – overestimating or underestimating one's abilities.

11. **Outward Confidence** (Self-Assured vs. Arrogant)
    - Enablers: Communicating confidence—without arrogance—through actions and presence, earning respect with presence by demonstrating competence, and inspiring others with authentic leadership.

- Disablers: Being arrogant, coming across as condescending, dismissing others' ideas, assuming respect is automatic, or intimidating others with overconfidence.

12. **Self-Reliance** (Leverages Self and Others vs. Overly Self-Reliant)
    - Enablers: Balancing leadership and delegation, leveraging collective expertise, and recognizing the strengths of others while demonstrating reliability and competence.
    - Disablers: Reluctance to delegate, resisting feedback, over-relying on personal abilities, and believing their way is always superior.

13. **Career Flexibility** (Considers Alternatives vs. Career Rigidity)
    - Enablers: Proactively identifying career opportunities, leveraging skills across industries, staying adaptable while maintaining expertise with continuous learning, and making well-timed moves before change is forced.
    - Disablers: Clinging to credentials or a fixed career identity, resisting change, and over-specializing to the point of limiting future opportunities.

14. **Self-Advocacy** (Confidently Asserting vs. Underrepresenting Self)
    - Enablers: Asserting value confidently, actively creating opportunities (not just being visible) for advancement without arrogance, and communicating achievements with clarity and self-assurance.
    - Disablers: Hesitating to self-promote, assuming merit alone will be recognized, fearing rejection, undervaluing oneself, or over-relying on others for recognition.

15. **Need for Variety** (Balanced vs. Constant Novelty Seeking)
    - Enablers: Channeling intellectual curiosity into structured exploration, maintaining focus while adapting to new experiences, and thriving in dynamic environments with creativity and flexibility.
    - Disablers: Intellectual restlessness, distraction by new ideas, difficulty committing to long-term goals, switching projects frequently and prematurely, and an excessive need for change.

RELATIONAL SMARTNESS FACTORS

16. **Emotional Intelligence** (High vs. Low Emotional Intelligence)
    - Enablers: Recognizing how emotions influence decisions, understanding and managing one's emotions, reading and responding to social cues effectively, and adjusting communication to different personalities and contexts.
    - Disablers: Overvaluing intelligence over interpersonal skills, misreading social cues, struggling with emotional regulation, and failing to adjust communication to context, inability to manage emotional reactions of others.

17. **Interpersonal Skills** (Good vs. Poor Interpersonal Skills)
    - Enablers: Building rapport, adapting communication to different personalities, balancing assertiveness with approachability, and fostering strong relationships.
    - Disablers: Struggling with small talk, poor rapport-building, difficulty navigating office politics, and ineffective communication.

18. **Teamwork** (Collaborative vs. Poor Team Player)
    - Enablers: Encouraging productive collaboration, leveraging team strengths for better outcomes, and contributing ideas while navigating group dynamics effectively and ensuring others are heard and valued.
    - Disablers: Seeing teamwork as inefficient, struggling with different working styles, resisting compromise, or avoiding collaboration altogether.

19. **Personal Autonomy** (Collaborative vs. Overly Independent)
    - Enablers: Knowing when to work independently and when to collaborate, seeking input to enhance decisions without losing autonomy, and leveraging the strengths of others to improve outcomes.
    - Disablers: Overvaluing independence, reluctance to seek help, difficulty collaborating, avoiding team involvement.

20. **Relational Adaptability** (Context-Savvy vs. Rigid Behavior)
    - Enablers: Reading social dynamics accurately, adjusting approach based on context, recognizing power structures, and shifting roles effectively between leading, collaborating, and supporting.
    - Disablers: Rigid interaction style, difficulty reading the room, discomfort with adjusting to different audiences, and failure to adapt to social dynamics.

21. **Communication Choices** (Intentional vs. Ineffective Communication)
    - Enablers: Adapting messaging to different audiences, balancing clarity with depth, simplifying complexity without losing meaning, and actively listening to enhance impact.
    - Disablers: Overloading with detail, using overly technical or abstract language, failing to adjust for context, or struggling with clarity and assertiveness.

For each factor, individuals may predominantly exhibit either enabling or disabling behaviors. However, everyone demonstrates a mix of both—depending on the situation, timing, and circumstances.

Success comes from learning to balance these factors—leveraging their enabling sides and minimizing their disablers, and depending on the situation. The *Smartness Factors* help you align your abilities with your goals and adapt as situations evolve."

Reflection: After reviewing the enabling and disabling behaviors for each Smartness Factor, which factor do you feel plays the biggest role in your current success? Which one tends to hold you back?

Smartness Factors – Some Learnable Skills, Some Behaviors, Most Mindset Elements

The majority of the *Smartness Factors* are mindset-driven, while a few are learnable skills or behaviors. Someone with an enabling mindset and the necessary skills can achieve much greater success, while someone with a disabling mindset may struggle.

Mindset is one of the most powerful determinants of *Smartness*—it shapes how you respond to challenges, make decisions, and take action. Some people naturally develop an adaptive and enabling mindset early in life, giving them a head start in *Smartness*.

But here's the key: Mindset is not permanent. If your mindset is limiting your success, you can choose to change it. It is difficult, but if you have a compelling 'why,' you can.

I've researched various methods for changing mindsets, including CBT (cognitive behavior therapy), hypnotism, Per-K, and tapping. Changing one's mindset requires time, commitment, and persistence—topics my upcoming book, **iMindset**—*Why You Do What You Do and How to Change Your Mindset for Success*, will explore in detail.

As discussed in the chapter, Understanding Smartness, some *Smartness Factors*, like Emotional Intelligence, Teamwork, and Situational Judgment, are skills that can be learned and refined through practice, training, or real-world application. Others, such as Risk Tolerance, Self-Competence Views, and Need for Variety, are mindset-driven and require shifts in elements such as beliefs, values, and personal rules.

Behavioral factors, such as Action Orientation, Interpersonal Skills, and Self-Advocacy, fall somewhere in between—they reflect both learned actions and underlying mindsets. Recognizing which factors are skills, mindsets, or behaviors helps you approach your personal development more effectively, enabling you to focus on actionable improvements that align with your goals.

Your *Smartness* is a product of the choices you make, and one of the most important choices is how you shape your own mindset.

Reflection: Reflect on a recent situation where your mindset influenced the outcome; how could a shift in mindset from disabling to enabling have changed the result?

The *Smartness Factors* are essential to everybody's success, as everybody has advantages (or strengths, if you want to see them as such) they can leverage. As you explore each factor, identify your enablers and disablers, leveraging strengths while mitigating weaknesses. Although changing skills is often straightforward, shifting a mindset takes time and persistence. Yet, with the right tools, you can cultivate a more empowering mindset, the foundation for achieving repeated success.

As you continue reading this book, place a bookmark to find this chapter easily. It will help you follow the various concepts and examples in the book more easily.

Reflection: What's the one Smartness Factor you've been ignoring because it's uncomfortable to face? Be honest—are you doubling down on strengths to avoid fixing what's actually holding you back?

CHAPTER 15

THE SMARTNESS ASSESSMENT

"You can't address a challenge you don't know about or understand."
~ Ram V. Iyer

Most smart people think they know themselves well, until their career or success plateaus. They assume intelligence is enough, only to realize too late that unseen weaknesses are limiting them. The *Smartness Assessment* makes those blind spots visible in about 15 minutes—fast.

Most people lack the self-awareness needed to fully harness their strengths or address their weaknesses. Some people think self-awareness only comes after years of meditation or countless hours on a therapist's couch. The path to unlocking your full *Smartness* is just an assessment away. Are you prepared to take the first step today? I offer a simpler solution: the *Smartness Assessment*. In just 15 minutes, it reveals your unique *Smartness* enablers and disablers, showing exactly what drives your success and what holds you back.

I've tried helping others identify their strengths and weaknesses through conversations, but despite our best intentions, it was rarely effective. Most people are uncomfortable talking about their weaknesses, making honest discussions difficult. That's why I developed the online *Smartness Assessment*. It allows you to privately and efficiently uncover your strengths and weaknesses. You'll find a link to it at the end of this chapter. You can take it at your convenience, and the results are completely confidential—shared only with you.

Developed over many years using insights from more than 1,200 smart professionals, the *Smartness Assessment* reveals which of your behaviors, mindsets, and skills are propelling you forward—and which ones are quietly holding you back. It replaces vague reflection and awkward self-analysis with a private, data-backed online tool that shows exactly what's working, what's hurting you, and what needs to shift. The *Smartness Factors* that drive real achievement have already been identified. This assessment pinpoints which ones are enabling or disabling you, without needing hours of expert coaching or endless self-assessments. In just 15 minutes on your computer, tablet, or smartphone, you'll gain personalized clarity on your *Smartness* enablers and disablers.

You could spend years trying to figure out why your progress has slowed—or you could have a clear map of what's helping you and what's getting in your way. The choice is yours.

The free *Smartness Assessment* provides a broad overview of your strengths and challenges. However, true transformation comes from understanding the specific *Smartness Factors* shaping your success. That's why I've also developed the deep-dive *Smartness Factor Assessments: twenty of them,* each focused on a key dimension of *Smartness*. These assessments provide:

- Personalized feedback on how each factor is influencing your success.
- Practical strategies to maximize enablers and minimize disablers.
- Real-world applications to help you implement changes immediately.

Consider them as your personal *Smartness* diagnostic tool—a way to uncover exactly what's working for you and where you need to adjust. These can be extremely useful because small adjustments in the right areas make the biggest impact. Readers who take these assessments report significant breakthroughs in how they approach their goals.

Reflection: *How often do you take time to reflect on what's driving your success and what might be limiting it? Are you open to learning things about yourself that you may not yet see?*

Understanding Smartness: The Unifying Framework for Achievement

In navigating personal and professional success, *Smartness* serves as the practical, adaptive capability that goes beyond intelligence or any other advantage. It's the skill of knowing how to leverage one's unique enablers and address disablers effectively in real-world scenarios. The *Smartness Assessment* doesn't measure how smart you are—it reveals how well you apply your intelligence in real-world situations. It captures the practical, adaptive side of intelligence: how you think, act, and adjust in varied, real-world conditions. With this framework in mind, let's explore how self-awareness is the first step toward boosting your *Smartness* and maximizing your potential.

Self-awareness is the first step to success.

To reach the top of the mountain, you need to know who you are (your capabilities and limitations), where you are (your current position and how far those capabilities extend), and what resources you have. For example, an out-of-shape person trying to climb a 10,000-foot mountain has very different enablers and disablers than an avid climber with ten years of experience. Each will need a different strategy to succeed.

By identifying the factors among the *Smartness Factors*, you can focus on the critical few enablers and disablers that can make the biggest difference to your greater success—a Pareto Principle (80/20) way of thinking and acting with the limited time and energy you have.

The *Smartness Assessment* doesn't just identify your strengths and weaknesses – it enumerates their advantages and disadvantages, and how you can practically leverage or mitigate them – immediately.

We live in an age of instant gratification, where many consultants promise overnight transformation. They claim your disablers will vanish, and your enablers will magically appear. By the time you realize neither happened, they've already moved on to the next gullible buyer chasing quick fixes. It's like buying a lottery ticket—hoping to be the 1 in 302 million who wins tonight.

Reflection: What would achieving greater self-awareness mean for you personally or professionally? How could it influence the choices you make moving forward?

Smart People

This book and the *Smartness Assessment* were developed for a broad set of people across the world in various professions. The assessment examines factors that affect smart people. Once you know your enablers and disablers, this book will help you understand how each factor influences your success.

1. Assessment Report: The report reflects your tendencies at the time you took the assessment, and these may shift over time depending on your mindset and the context you had in mind when taking it. If some parts of the report don't resonate, consider retaking the assessment or re-evaluating the results with different goals in mind. Keep in mind that the report is designed for a broad audience, so not every detail will apply perfectly to your situation.
2. Tailoring to Your Situation: While the assessment categorizes factors as enablers or disablers for a general audience, their relevance varies by profession. For example, an entrepreneur may need to take risks, while a doctor or tech expert will take much lower risks. View your report in the context of what you do, but be careful not to rationalize or dismiss your disablers.

Identifying your personal enablers and disablers is just the beginning. The next step is to create a plan to leverage your strengths and mitigate your weaknesses. Commitment to that plan is where real progress happens—turning ambition into achievement. We will do those towards the end of the book in Part 6.

Reflection: Which Smartness factor—enabler or disabler—do you think most urgently requires your focus, and what is the first step you'll take to address it?

You already possess advantages like elite credentials, skills, or other advantages. By identifying your enablers and disablers and working to leverage or mitigate them, you can achieve even greater success. This is not a one-time sprint but a lifelong journey of continuous improvement. Success becomes a daily habit, not tied to just one project or phase.

Remember, success and achievement are lagging indicators that follow your plan and consistent effort. It's not just about having an advantage—whether intelligence, wealth, or power—but about having a clear, personalized plan and the persistence to execute it. The *Smartness Assessment* report is a valuable starting point on this journey.

Now, you can go take the assessment to receive your personalized report on what enables and disables you, as well as where you may have a mix of both. You can access the assessment for free (a $198 value) at this link: https://*www.MySmartness.com/Assessments/Smartness*. Here's how to get your personal report:

i. Complete the assessment.
ii. When prompted to purchase your report, click on the YES button.
iii. On the checkout page, enter the discount code: *SmartnessBook-2025* to waive the fee.

Before diving into the *Smartness Factors*, we need to examine the mental operating system (the paradigm) that drives how smart people use—or fail to use—those capabilities. In the next chapter, we'll explore a powerful shift that separates potential from achievement, and the unsuccessful from the successful: moving from the intelligence paradigm to the *Smartness* paradigm.

Reflection: *Are you ready to stop relying on your intelligence to guess—and start using Smartness to know exactly what's enabling or disabling your success? How would that shift change the way you pursue your goals today?*

CHAPTER 16

INSIGHTS FROM THE SMARTNESS ASSESSMENT DATA

"The journey to realizing our full potential begins with surfacing and leveraging our strengths, confronting our internal barriers, and transforming them into stepping stones toward our greater success."
~ Ram V. Iyer

To uncover what truly drives or derails smart people, we launched the *Smartness Assessment*, taken by 1200+ professionals. The participants were self-selected people who felt they hadn't achieved the success they expected. Most were highly intelligent and credentialed, yet 85% reported feeling unsuccessful. Only 15% described themselves as successful but not satisfied with their level of success.

Through conversations with over a hundred assessment takers, I found that many had a deep desire to achieve greater success. When asked about their drive, 58% said they were highly motivated to achieve more, 34% were ambivalent (choosing the assessment option, "It would be nice if I were more successful"), and just 8% felt content.

Over the course of a year, I analyzed the assessment data and shared it with different various groups of smart people, sparking lively discussions. People questioned the factors and their definitions, leading us to validate the ones we had while also expanding the list from 15 to 21 and clarify their names.

One surprising insight: 13% of respondents equated intelligence with Smartness. They assumed intellect alone would be enough to become more successful. But the data told a different story. Those who leaned hardest on intelligence often stalled. Success came to those who applied Smartness: adapting, executing, and aligning their actions with their goals.

This chapter shares what we learned: the most common enablers, disablers, and blind spots that explain why so many smart people underachieve and what helps them break through.

Intelligence vs. Smartness

As discussed earlier, there's a clear distinction between intelligence and *Smartness*. Surprisingly, 13% of participants equated intelligence with *Smartness*—likely expecting their intellect alone to carry them. But the data proves otherwise. Many smart people assume their intelligence, credentials, or networks will naturally translate into success. But the data reveals a different story— Those who rely solely on intelligence often hit a ceiling.

Enablers / Disablers / Mixed Traits + TOS

The *Smartness Assessment* revealed that most participants exhibited a mix of enabling, disabling, and mixed traits. These were grouped into three clear categories:

- **Enablers**: Behaviors, mindsets and skills that consistently drive success
- **Disablers**: Traits that directly undermine outcomes and derail people
- **Mixed**: Behaviors that sometimes help and sometimes hinder, depending on the situation and how they're applied

Most people struggling with success exhibited mixed behaviors alongside disablers. To better understand this, I created a new metric: the *Total Obstacle Score (TOS)*. It adds together your disablers and mixed traits. For example, if you have 6 enablers, 4 disablers, and 8 mixed factors, your TOS is 12 (4+8).

Your TOS reflects how many *Smartness Factors* are standing in your way. The lower your TOS, the more effectively you're using your intelligence and other advantages. None of the 1,200+ assessment-takers had all enablers—. Everyone had at least some disablers or mixed traits.

While disablers are more severe, mixed factors affect almost everyone. Mixed traits shift with context and time, and can quietly limit success without appearing catastrophic. Many people mistakenly dismiss the mixed traits as not being detrimental. That's why addressing both disablers and mixed traits is essential if you want to move forward.

When reviewing your *Smartness Assessment* Report, focus on converting as many mixed factors into enablers, and to reduce the severity of your disablers wherever possible.

Understanding Your Total Obstacle Score (TOS)

Let's look at how mixed and severe disablers appear among the assessment takers. Below are the top disablers of the 1200+ assessment-takers:

1. **Action Orientation (95%)**: A common challenge is the inability to act in a timely manner despite knowing what needs to be done. 48% were severely disabled in this area, while 47% showed mixed behaviors.
2. **Perfectionism (92%)**: The need to be perfect or fear of judgment prevents many from moving forward. 35% were severely disabled in this area, while 56% had mixed behaviors.
3. **Novelty Seeking (88%)**: Constantly chasing new ideas without finishing old ones leads to scattered focus. 35% were severely disabled in this area, while 43% had mixed behaviors.
4. **Risk Aversion (87%)**: Fear of failure holds people back, especially those with high expectations from others. 7% were severely disabled in this area, while 80% showed mixed behaviors.

Insights from the Smartness Assessment Data

5. **Over-Dependence on Independence (82%)**: They prefer to work alone, which can be limiting in team environments. 4% were severely disabled in this area, and 78% showed mixed behaviors.
6. **Complexity Bias (81%)**: Making things more complicated than necessary to feel smart or struggling to simplify complex ideas. 12% were severely disabled in this area, while 69% had mixed behaviors.
7. **Emotional Intelligence (66%)**: Difficulty understanding or managing emotions. 4% were severely disabled in this area, and 62% exhibited mixed behaviors.
8. **Situational Judgment (65%)**: Lacking 'street smarts' or situational awareness. 1% were severely disabled in this area, while 64% had mixed behaviors.
9. **Overly Self-Reliant (60%)**: Refusing to rely on others can limit outcomes in team settings. 8% were severely disabled in this area, and 52% showed mixed behaviors.
10. **Interpersonal Skills (62%)**: Poor communication or inability to relate to others. 2% were severely disabled in this area, and 60% showed mixed behaviors.
11. **Career Flexibility (56%)**: Many are in jobs they dislike, conforming to societal norms. 3% were extremely unhappy, while 53% were moderately unhappy.
12. **Rigid Thinking (55%)**: Inflexibility in decision-making severely disabled 3% of them, and 52% showed mixed behaviors.
13. **Thinking & Feeling (50%)**: A lack of empathy impacts interpersonal situations. 2% were severely affected by this factor, while 48% exhibited mixed behaviors.
14. **Confirmation Bias (50%)**: They are unwilling to change perspectives, even when presented with new facts. 1% were severely affected, while 49% had mixed behaviors.
15. **Self-Competence Views (41%)**: Struggling with impostor syndrome and doubting personal abilities. 5% were severely affected, and 36% showed mixed behaviors.
16. **Outward Confidence (34%)**: Displaying arrogance or overconfidence. 4% were severely affected, and 30% had mixed behaviors.
17. **Polarized Thinking (26%)**: Viewing situations in black and white, with little room for nuance. 1% were severely affected, while 25% showed mixed behaviors.
18. **Teamwork (22%)**: Struggling to collaborate with others, often stemming from other factors. 1% were severely affected, while 21% showed mixed behaviors.

By understanding your TOS and addressing both severe and mixed disablers, you can take actionable steps toward greater success. Note that more than 50% of all unsuccessful and less-than-successful people have obstacles—the combination of disablers and mixed—in thirteen of the eighteen factors. Look at the text box below to understand the importance of addressing your 'mixed' factors, which can sometimes yield good results for little effort.

Now that we've identified how enablers, disablers, and mixed factors shape success, let's explore why focusing on mixed factors can deliver disproportionate results.

The Disproportionate Returns of Addressing Mixed Factors

Most people who consider themselves unsuccessful have only one or two serious disabling *Smartness Factors*, but they have numerous enabling ones. This means big obstacles are relatively few, yet most people fail to adequately leverage their numerous enablers, which could help them become much more successful. Additionally, most people ignore the large number of factors that are in the middle—the mixed factors. They are sometimes enabling and sometimes disabling; some are mildly disabling, and others are more severe. They need to be addressed as well.

On average, participants had six enablers, fewer than two major disablers, and a substantial eight mixed factors, showing that most of the potential for improvement lies in how one manages these mixed traits.

Here are three main takeaways:

- Enablers (~6 per person, on average): People already possess a core set of habits or resources that support them. Leaning on these can amplify your advantages.
- Disablers (<2 per person, on average): Most individuals don't have many truly debilitating roadblocks. Address the major ones you do have, but don't get stuck fixating on them.
- Mixed (~8 per person, on average): This is where most of the action happens. These factors can swing either way, so small shifts—like adapting a mindset or changing a habit—can convert a mixed trait from being in your way to propelling you forward. If you turn even half your mixed traits into enablers, your trajectory could change dramatically—without needing to eliminate all your disablers.

Put another way, it's not just the extremes—enablers or disablers—that explain a less-than-successful life. The real challenge often lies in how we manage the mixed factors that shift depending on the situation.

Illustrative Example (Situation–Action–Outcome):

- Situation: A student procrastinates on studying (disabler), but also seeks feedback from friends (enabler) while juggling multiple hobbies (mixed).
- Action: They tackle procrastination through accountability. They also adjust their hobby schedule to preserve creativity without losing study time.

Insights from the Smartness Assessment Data

- Outcome: Eliminating procrastination removes a major disabler. Refining hobbies converts a mixed trait into an enabler, resulting in better grades and less stress.

Factor	Average per Person	Role in Success	Key Insight
Enablers	About 6	Provide a foundation for success	Leverage them to amplify strengths
Disablers	Fewer than 2	Represent major roadblocks	Identify & mitigate to prevent setbacks
Mixed	About 8	Can either help or hinder success	Small shifts could turn them into enablers

A key takeaway is that your biggest opportunity for growth lies in managing your mixed factors effectively—these can either help or hinder your progress based on how you approach them. For example, managing mixed factors, such as channeling scattered novelty-seeking into focused creativity or turning perfectionism into high standards without paralysis, can drive rapid progress.

Ultimately, while few factors are truly disabling, many linger in the gray area of the "mixed" effect. The difference between success and stagnation often lies in two key areas: first, understanding that small adjustments to mixed factors can yield outsized results, and second, taking deliberate actions to shift mixed factors into enablers. For example, channeling scattered novelty-seeking into focused creativity or refining perfectionism into high standards—not exacting standards—without getting paralyzed can transform mixed traits into powerful enablers. Managing mixed factors effectively is a hallmark of *Smartness*—those who can recognize, adapt, and refine these factors often achieve sustained success over time.

While your advantages and enablers may keep you from outright failure, disablers can still bring you to your knees. They hold you back from achieving your full potential. And every one of the disabling or mixed factors can be mitigated or converted into enablers. In other words, you can convert each of the *Smartness Factors* into enablers of your personal success. You can also leverage every one of your enablers to achieve greater success.

When I conducted a correlation analysis of the data, I found that when certain factors disabled you, certain other factors were the main culprits. For example, the biggest causes of disabling Action Orientation (#1 disabler) were Detail Orientation (perfectionist tendencies), the excessive Need for Variety (lack of focus), risk aversion, and the tendency to make things more complex than they are or need to be. The correlation analysis showed positive and negative correlations between various factors, and they passed the common-sense test.

Reflection: *Think about a situation where your habits or behaviors have both helped and hindered you. What small shift in mindset or approach could make that factor work more consistently in your favor?*

Differences Between Unsuccessful & Successful People

Success is self-determined by the assessment-takers, not the assessment itself. About 15% of participants consider themselves successful, while 85% do not—though even those who feel successful often believe they could achieve more. Whether you see yourself as successful or not, understanding and mastering these factors can help you achieve greater success.

Here's what the data shows about the two groups:

1. Unsuccessful people have more extreme disablers than successful people—29.6% versus 22.7%.
2. The Total Obstacle Score (disablers + mixed) for the unsuccessful group is higher at 65.1%, compared to 61.7% for the successful group.
3. Successful people also have slightly more enablers—38.3%, compared to 35% for the unsuccessful.

The gap between success and the lack of success is often very small. Sometimes, it's just one more disabler or disabling behavior that makes the difference between achieving your goals and falling short.

What Holds People Back

Analyzing the *Smartness Assessment* data through two complementary lenses reveals not only how common certain disablers are but also how severely they impact individuals. When I examined the absolute prevalence of key disablers among those who consider themselves unsuccessful, I found that a whopping 96% (TOS) report issues with Action Orientation. Importantly, for about 50% of these individuals, poor Action Orientation is profoundly disabling.

Digging deeper into the underlying causes of this poor Action Orientation, we see that excessive Detail Orientation affects 93% (TOS) of unsuccessful individuals and a strong Need for Variety is reported by 90% (TOS). The data also shows that Detail Orientation is extremely disabling for about 35% of people, and the Need for Variety is extremely disabling for about 32% of the people. This suggests that overthinking, getting lost in the details and a relentless search for novelty don't merely coexist with poor Action Orientation—they actively drive it, often paralyzing progress.

Other factors such as Risk Tolerance (87%), Personal Autonomy (83%), and Complexity Preference (82%) also register as major obstacles. Although Action Orientation is the most visible symptom, these underlying issues—especially when experienced in their extreme forms—point to deeper challenges like perfectionism and an overemphasis on working independently.

Insights from the Smartness Assessment Data

Both successful and unsuccessful individuals share some common struggles; for instance, Action Orientation affects an astounding 96% of the unsuccessful people and 90% of successful people—to varying extents. However, it is the intensity of these underlying issues that differentiates the two groups – and the resulting success or failure. Unsuccessful people are far more likely to experience highly disabling levels of excessive Detail Focus and rigid Personal Autonomy. This extreme manifestation appears to be the tipping point that pushes someone from merely underperforming into a state of being truly stalled or failing.

In summary, while Action Orientation is widespread across both groups, it is the depth of its underlying drivers—excessive Detail Focus and a pronounced Need for Variety—that not only contributes to the high prevalence but also leads to significantly disabling outcomes. Recognizing and addressing these high-impact issues should be a top priority for anyone looking to convert potential into sustained success.

The Narrow Margin Between Success and Failure

The difference between success and failure is often surprisingly small. Roger Federer, one of the greatest tennis players in history, once revealed that he won just 54% of the points across his career. That's only a 4% edge over his opponents—yet it made him one of the most dominant players of all time.

While some humans pursue success as solo efforts, believing they should succeed 'on their own,' success in most endeavors is rarely achieved in isolation. The margin for success remains narrow—whether you're a solo hunter like a leopard, with just a 14%-40% success rate, or a professional like Roger Federer, whose career dominance stemmed from just a 4% edge. The data shows that addressing one more disabler or leveraging one enabler more effectively can get you closer to your goals.

The takeaway is clear: success becomes easier when you find others on a similar journey, tap into networks, and seek guidance from mentors who can help you uncover opportunities and navigate challenges. Your *Smartness Assessment Report* pinpoints specific enablers and disablers to focus on for growth.

Reflection: *Considering the narrow gap between successful and unsuccessful people, what small, actionable change can you commit to today from that report to see quick improvement in your success?*

The Big Three

For those who consider themselves unsuccessful, the three biggest disablers are

1. Poor Action Orientation,
2. Excessive Detail Focus, and
3. The constant Need for Variety (a.k.a., a lack of focus)

Together, these three factors are extremely disabling for about 32% of these individuals. Looking at the Total Obstacle Score (TOS)—which includes low, medium, and high levels of disablement—these same factors rank highest among the unsuccessful: Action Orientation (96%), Detail Focus (92%), and Need for Variety (88%).

Reflection: Do you identify with one or more of the 'Big Three' disablers? If so, what steps can you take to mitigate these factors?

Comparing Unsuccessful and Successful People

There are 10 *Smartness Factors* in which there is a 10% or greater difference between unsuccessful and successful people. The two factors with the biggest difference are Self-Reliance and Career Flexibility, followed by Practical Intelligence, Self-Competence Views, and Thinking Range.

Self-Reliance—when balanced—is a critical success factor, but when it skews too far in either direction, it becomes a major disabler. The data from 1,200 *Smartness Assessment* takers shows that 63% of unsuccessful individuals struggle with Over-Self-Reliance, compared to 44% of successful individuals. If struggling with Over-Self-Reliance is more common among those who don't reach higher success, what might that indicate? Could it be that those who resist seeking help, refuse to delegate, or struggle with collaboration end up slowing their own progress?

At the same time, what about the other extreme—Under-Self-Reliance? While the assessment data doesn't explicitly quantify its impact, we know from the research that individuals who lack Self-Reliance often struggle with confidence, decision-making, and personal ownership. Could it be that those who lean too much on others fail to develop the resilience and initiative needed for long-term success? If so, is it possible that some unsuccessful individuals don't just struggle with Over-Self-Reliance but also with Under-Self-Reliance in different situations?

Looking at the successful individuals, 44% still report struggling with Over-Self-Reliance—but clearly, they've found ways to mitigate it. What sets them apart? Does their success suggest they've learned when to ask for input, when to delegate, and when to lean on their networks? From the other side, 56% of successful individuals have figured out how to balance their Self-Reliance rather than letting it become a barrier.

That mindset—Over-Self-Reliance—is often rooted in The Advantage Illusion: the belief that intelligence should make them self-sufficient. Smart people assume that if they're truly capable, they shouldn't need help. But this illusion turns independence into isolation, weakening their ability to adapt and succeed collaboratively.

If that's the case, maybe the real issue isn't Self-Reliance itself—but the inability to recognize when outside help would accelerate progress, and when initiative must come from within. The difference between those who succeed and those who stall may lie in how well they balance independence with collaboration, and autonomy with adaptability.

The other factors with slightly smaller gaps between successful and unsuccessful individuals include Complexity Preference, Interpersonal Skills, Need for Variety, and Belief Reinforcement.

Interestingly, Action Orientation had only a 6% difference—affecting 96% of unsuccessful people and 90% of successful ones—highlighting just how widespread this challenge is. The key difference may be how successful individuals mitigate low Action Orientation. While unsuccessful individuals often allow inaction to stall them indefinitely, successful ones develop systems, accountability structures, and decision-making habits that force them to move. They may also compensate by leaning on strengths in related areas—like Career Flexibility, Self-Competence Views, or Practical Intelligence—to break through inertia and drive execution. In contrast, those who remain stuck often fall into analysis paralysis, overestimating the need for the perfect plan or perfect moment to act.

Comparing the Genders

Gender patterns from the assessment reveal that while men struggle more with confirmation bias, women face higher self-competence doubts. Understanding these tendencies can shape more effective growth strategies. Let's look at a few of the differences.

1. 83% of the men and 85% of the women who took the assessment consider themselves unsuccessful.
2. Women are more emotionally intelligent than men by a 12% margin, validating the widely held view about women and men in this regard.
3. A stereotypical advantage was apparent in women when it came to being empathetic (Thinking & Feeling factor)—56% over 46% for men.
4. Men had a greater confirmation bias (believing that they would be successful because of their high intelligence (or some other advantage) or that their thinking or action was correct) by a 7% margin.
5. When it comes to making things more complex than they need to be, women do it more than men by 5%.
6. When it comes to willingness to take risks, men are more willing than women, again by a 5% margin.
7. The biggest issue women have as compared to men is that they have greater doubts about their self-competence – impostor syndrome - by a 7% margin.
8. On the other factors, the difference between the assessment takers of the two genders is 3% or less.

Reflection: How do these comparisons align with your observations about the differences between men and women?

You now understand how smart people succeed—or get stuck. Whether you are part of the 85% seeking more success or the 15% striving for even greater heights, your struggles are shared by many, and you're not helpless—you can get better.

This chapter doesn't just list barriers; it reflects your hidden obstacles, offering insight into where you can make transformative changes. A high Total Obstacle Score isn't a permanent limitation—it's a call to action. Every disabler can be mitigated, and every enabler can be leveraged to push you further.

We've seen how common disablers like Action Orientation affect many, but knowing you're not alone can be empowering. More importantly, the small numerical differences between successful and unsuccessful people prove that mitigating even one disabler or leveraging one enabler can make a big impact.

The *Smartness Assessment* is your tool for unlocking untapped potential. It's time to act on your assessment report. As we've seen, the willingness to take timely action is often the key difference between success and stagnation.

Remember, you are not defined by your enablers and disablers but by how you use them in context to achieve the outcomes you seek.

Reflection: *You've got the data. You know your disablers. So, be honest—are you underachieving because you're actually stuck... or just unwilling to change? What's the one smartness factor you've been rationalizing—and what are you going to do about it now?*

The next part of the book delves into understanding yourself.

PART 3

UNDERSTANDING YOURSELF

The key to unlocking your greatest potential lies in understanding your greatest asset—you.
~ Ram V. Iyer

This part of the book is about understanding yourself—your greatest asset in achieving success. It emphasizes that success is a journey built upon self-awareness and the deliberate choice to leverage strengths while mitigating weaknesses. You may have ambitious goals and plans on how to accomplish them. However, the biggest asset you have is you. To truly succeed, you need to know who you are, what drives you, where you currently stand, and how you operate. You need to understand your current mindset, behaviors, and skills. The better you understand yourself, the more effectively you can apply and develop your *Smartness* to achieve the greater success you seek. Stating the obvious… **You are the biggest means to accomplishing your goals.**

As you embark on this journey of self-discovery, you'll uncover the traits and actions that have shaped your past successes (what got you here) and identify those that could propel you to even greater heights (where you want to go). Your life story so far, combined with insights from your personal *Smartness Assessment Report* (your *Smartness* enablers and disablers), will provide valuable clarity—some familiar, others perhaps new.

CHAPTER 17

SUCCESS: ENTITLEMENT, DESTINY OR EARNED?

"Your mind is a powerful tool and an excellent servant when guided by a positive mindset. Yet, it can become a dangerous master when driven by negativity, limiting beliefs, resignation or a sense of entitlement."
~ Ram V. Iyer

Have you ever wondered why some people keep achieving greater successes while others stagnate? The difference lies in how they approach success: whether they assume it will come to them or take the actions needed to achieve it. An individual's mindset—the unique lens through which they interpret challenges, opportunities, people, and the world around them—shapes whether they take action, what choices they make, and how they navigate their circumstances.

There are three fundamental ways people view success:

- The *Entitlement Mindset* assumes success is owed rather than earned. These individuals expect rewards without effort.
- The *Destiny Mindset* believes success is predetermined—by talent, luck, or external forces—rather than shaped by actions.
- People with an Earned Mindset take ownership, apply their strengths, and adapt continuously to achieve greater success.

Your mindset shapes how you handle challenges, setbacks, and opportunities. A person with an Entitlement or *Destiny Mindset* may avoid difficult situations, blame external circumstances, or wait for success to come to them. By contrast, someone with an Earned Mindset sees obstacles as learning opportunities. They take responsibility and actively work toward their goals.

This chapter explores how these mindsets influence success, why many people struggle to shift toward an Earned Mindset, and how embracing it can lead to greater achievement, resilience, and long-term success.

You may have advantages over others—whether over specific individuals or in particular situations. Does that make you feel entitled, destined, or confident (not certain) of success?

The Three Mindsets

Let's explore these three mindsets in greater detail and determine which one truly sets you on the path to meaningful success.

- **Entitlement Mindset**: "I deserve success because I'm smart."

- **Destiny Mindset**: "Success will come to me if it's meant to."
- **Earned Mindset**: "Success is built—through deliberate action."

Let's examine each one in greater detail.

The Entitlement Mindset: Expectation Without Effort

This mindset stems from what I call *The Advantage Illusion*—the belief that past wins, intelligence, or credentials automatically ensure future success. Many smart people fall into this trap early in their careers, when advantages do open doors easily.

But over time, the world changes. And if others are evolving while you're standing still, you lose your edge—and your relevance.

Sarah's Stagnation

Sarah, a tech professional with top credentials, coasted on her early reputation. She didn't adapt to new tools or trends. Others did. When she reached for bigger roles, she was overlooked. Her intelligence wasn't the problem—her assumption that it was enough was.

Reflection: *Are you relying on past achievements to carry you forward? What will you do to stay sharp and relevant?*

The Destiny Mindset: Waiting Instead of Working to Succeed

Smart people don't usually talk about "fate"—but they often behave like it matters. They assume that, because they're talented, success will eventually find them.

They wait. They imagine. They hesitate. And others, with less talent but more drive, pass them by.

Raj's Missed Potential

Raj, a brilliant entrepreneur, believed his ideas would attract investors. But while he waited, others networked, pitched, refined, and launched. His product never moved. His intelligence was real. His passivity cost him everything.

Reflection: *Are you waiting for something to happen—or making it happen?*

The Earned Mindset: Smartness in Action

The Earned Mindset bridges belief and behavior. It says: "Success doesn't come from intelligence alone. It comes from what I *do* with it."

People with this mindset don't just believe in growth—they act on it. They seek feedback, take ownership, and move forward even when it's hard. They earn it—every time.

Michael's Proactive Success
Michael knew his past wins didn't guarantee future ones. He stayed curious, built new skills, and cultivated the right relationships. His success wasn't passive. It was built—step by step.

Reflection: *Are you consistently creating your next success? What actions prove it?*

Setbacks: Catalysts for Greater Achievement

Setbacks are inevitable, no matter how much success you've had: five, ten, or even twenty years of wins don't make you immune to failure. Adapt and refine – view setbacks as signals for what needs to change, not as reasons to give up. Many who seem perpetually successful have faced numerous failures along the way—but they've learned from them, adapted, and continued to grow.

The reality is, most people hear about success but not the failures that preceded it. Repeatedly successful people with a fixed mindset can become arrogant and complacent, while those with an Earned Mindset achieve success more consistently because they see setbacks not as failures, but as learning opportunities.

While challenging, these moments aren't roadblocks but teaching moments. When you recognize and embrace them, they can improve your thinking and sharpen your *Smartness*.

A Personal Lesson in Setbacks

I've faced this firsthand. After years of professional highs, I hit a major setback when one of my ventures collapsed. Despite my prior successes, I was forced to sell my home, let go of my team, and start over completely. It was a humbling, disorienting experience. I lost my confidence and fell into a deep funk. But that setback forced me to reassess everything. I had relied too much on my past achievements and had grown overconfident, assuming my previous successes guaranteed future wins. I had stopped adapting. That realization was painful—but essential. It was a setback and a learning opportunity.

I realized something rather simple but empowering—I wasn't starting from zero, I had the benefit of experiences and some hard lessons to start with. By reflecting on these lessons honestly, I gained new insights, strengthened my *Smartness*, and improved my decision-making. I emerged stronger, more adaptable, and better equipped to rebuild my life and achieve greater success.

The Takeaway: *Smartness* Turns Setbacks into Fuel for Growth

Setbacks can derail you if you let them—but they can also serve as fuel for greater achievements. The difference lies in how you respond. With *Smartness*, you can transform both successes and failures into learning experiences, positioning yourself for even greater accomplishments.

Reflection: *Think about a recent setback—did you use it as a learning opportunity or let it hold you back? What specific lesson can you take from it to power your future?*

Comparing the Three Mindsets

To fully understand the power of the Earned Mindset, it helps to see how it contrasts with the **Entitlement and Destiny Mindsets.** Each mindset shapes how individuals approach challenges, opportunities, and their own role in success.

Mindset	How Smart People Fall into It	How Smart People Break Out of It
Entitlement	Early success made them assume intelligence alone would ensure future wins.	Recognize that intelligence is just a tool, not a guarantee, and focus on execution.
Destiny	They believe their intelligence means they are "meant" for success.	Shift to a proactive mindset—*Smartness* is about applied effort, not just raw ability.
Earned	They actively apply intelligence, refine *Smartness*, and take strategic action.	Continually learn, adapt, and execute to sustain long-term success.

The differences are clear: Those who embrace the Earned Mindset don't wait for success; they create it. And they are often the most successful.

Reflection: *Which aspects of your mindset—Entitlement, Destiny, or Earned—do you see in yourself? What is one immediate shift you can make to take more control of your success?*

Your Mindset is Foundational

Most of the *Smartness Factors* reviewed in this book (detailed in Part 4) are deeply connected to your mindset. It determines how you leverage your advantages—or allow disadvantages to hold you back. When it aligns with your goals and aspirations, it amplifies your advantages and transforms emotions into action. But when it works against you, it magnifies hesitation, self-doubt, or complacency—undermining even your greatest advantages.

> *"No advantage—intelligence, wealth, connections, credentials, skills or something else—can guarantee success until your mindset fully supports your goals."*

Your mindset is the lens through which you interpret challenges, opportunities, and setbacks. It shapes how you perceive your abilities, make decisions, and respond to adversity. A misaligned mindset holds you back, no matter how many advantages you have.

Research confirms that individuals who actively reshape their mindset develop greater resilience, improve decision-making, and create better long-term outcomes. Belief alone is not enough—success requires the consistent application of learning, adaptability, and effort.

This is where the Earned Mindset becomes critical. Unlike a fixed mindset (which assumes abilities are static) or even a growth mindset (which emphasizes the potential for improvement), an Earned Mindset bridges belief and action. It ensures that learning is not just an intellectual exercise but consistently applied in real-world situations.

By shifting to an Earned Mindset, you stop waiting for success and create it instead.

The Earned Mindset: Where Smart People Break Through

Smart people succeed not by relying on intelligence alone, but by earning success through deliberate action, ownership, and adaptability. This is the core of the Earned Mindset. It's what separates those who coast from those who grow. For a deeper look at how to develop and strengthen this mindset, see Chapter 11: The Earned Mindset – The Foundation for Smartness and Consistent Achievement.

The Role of Mindset in Achieving Success

The emotions that drive you—whether excitement, fear, anger, or even indifference—are deeply intertwined with your mindset. Mindset acts as a lens through which you interpret these emotions and decide how to respond. A growth-oriented mindset channels emotions into productive action, while a rigid or negative mindset magnifies self-doubt, procrastination, or complacency.

Your mindset determines how you perceive, react to, and manage challenges. It influences whether you see obstacles as insurmountable roadblocks (*Entitlement* or *Destiny Mindset*) or as opportunities to grow and succeed (Earned Mindset). A mindset that holds you back—filled with self-doubt or resistance to change—can undermine even your greatest advantages.

> Most of the *Smartness Factors* reviewed earlier (and detailed in Part 4) are rooted in mindset, making it foundational for success. It amplifies your advantages and transforms emotions into drivers for action. But a weak or misaligned mindset will derail even the strongest talents and resources.
>
> The *Achievement Cycle* highlights this progression: *Smartness*, practical intelligence, and wisdom precede effective action. *Smartness* is not just about your mindset—it includes behaviors, skills, and habits that determine how effectively you apply your advantages in different situations. It starts with a mindset shift—the belief that advantages are tools, not guarantees, and that real success comes from leveraging them wisely.
>
> The Earned Mindset bridges belief and execution, ensuring that learning translates into real-world application. Practical intelligence builds on this foundation by applying knowledge, experience, and situational awareness to real-world decisions. Finally, wisdom refines and enhances these decisions, ensuring they align with long-term goals and sustainable success.

You are smart. The real question is: Are you willing to earn the success you seek? Remember, smart people have the intelligence to succeed, but only those who actively develop their *Smartness*—applying knowledge, refining skills, and executing consistently—truly earn their success.

> *"Achievers are not born, they are made."*

Mindset shapes how you approach success. But even the right mindset isn't enough—you also need to harness your emotional drivers. That's where we go next.

But none of these matters if you're stuck in the wrong paradigm—clinging to the belief that intelligence guarantees success while your potential quietly rots on the vine. The next chapter exposes the hidden mental operating system that's been running the show—and shows how shifting it can change everything.

Reflection: *Are you still waiting for success to show up—or are you ready to earn it with Smartness, ownership, and persistent action—every single day?*

CHAPTER 18

SHIFTING YOUR PARADIGM FROM INTELLIGENCE TO SMARTNESS

"The way you see the world creates the world you see."
– Anonymous

Many smart people are trapped in a paradigm—a mental lens—that says intelligence alone drives success. But that belief quietly shapes what they value, how they act, and what they overlook. Shifting to a new paradigm—that success comes from how you use your intelligence—is like taking off one pair of glasses and putting on another. Suddenly, you see different paths, make smarter moves, and get better results. It's the highest-leverage change you can make—more powerful than working harder or gaining more knowledge—because it changes how you see and approach everything.

If you're a smart person, chances are your intelligence has shaped much of your identity. You've been rewarded for thinking fast, solving problems, and outperforming others intellectually. From school to early career wins, you've learned that intelligence is your superpower—and you've likely leaned on it for success.

But at a certain point, that stops being enough. You hit a ceiling. The wins don't come as easily. Other people—some even less "smart" than you—start passing you by. Yet others who are just as smart as you are able to get things done and get ahead of you. You may work harder, think more deeply, analyze longer… but results stall. What's going on?

The problem isn't that you're not smart enough. The problem is that the intelligence-first lens—the paradigm you've been operating in—is no longer serving you.

It's time to shift paradigms.

What's a Paradigm—and Why Does It Matter for Smart People?

A paradigm is the mental lens through which you interpret the world. It's your operating system—the set of assumptions, beliefs, and filters that shape what you see, what you ignore, how you solve problems, and how you define success. Paradigms aren't just ideas. They're the invisible structures behind your decisions, your reactions, and even your identity.

Smart people often operate inside a paradigm built around intelligence. Their personal identity is about being smart. Their achievements, self-worth, and confidence are rooted in their ability to think, analyze, and out-reason others.

That mindset—"I'm smart, so I'll succeed"—works early on. School rewards it. Credentials reinforce it. People admire it. But over time, some smart people get trapped in the intelligence paradigm.

But intelligence alone isn't enough.

Smart people get stuck when they fail to evolve beyond this paradigm. They double down on thinking harder instead of acting smarter. They mistake overanalysis for good judgment. They chase intellectual validation instead of real-world results.

To achieve more, smart people must shift their paradigm—from intelligence to *Smartness*.

> *"Intelligence paradigms are prisons smart people build for themselves—until they realize Smartness is the key to break out and become more successful."*

That shift is hard. It means letting go of deeply held beliefs. It means seeing yourself differently - letting go of the identity built entirely around being intelligent. It means accepting that being smart is only the starting point—not the whole game. But once that shift happens, everything changes. You stop clinging to potential and start creating results.

> *"Paradigm shifts don't just change your perspective. They change your trajectory."*

The Paradigm Shift Process: Moving from Intelligence to Smartness

You can, if you choose to, shift from the intelligence paradigm to the *Smartness* paradigm. You need to surface and change the underlying beliefs that are currently anchored in your mind.

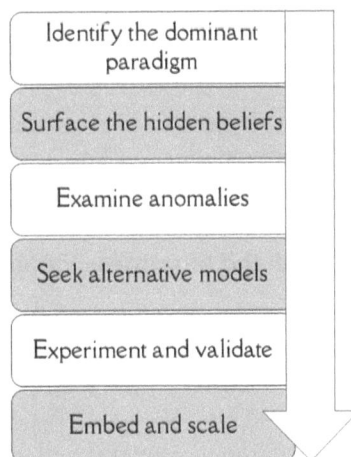

Shifting your paradigm isn't a mindset tweak—it's an identity recalibration. Here's how to replace the "intelligence will carry me" operating system with a *Smartness*-based approach that actually gets results.

1. Name Your Current Paradigm

Start by calling out the paradigm you're actually living in—not the one you claim to have. Many smart people are stuck in thoughts like:

- "If I'm the smartest person in the room, I win."
- "Thinking harder will solve this."
- "My credentials should speak for themselves."
- "If I don't have all the answers, I'll lose credibility."

These beliefs form the backbone of the intelligence paradigm—but they quietly shut down growth, collaboration, and execution.

You've named the paradigm. Good. Now let's drag the real drivers out from under the surface—because that's where they're quietly wrecking your progress.

2. Surface the Hidden Beliefs

Beneath every unproductive paradigm are protective beliefs—stories you tell yourself to stay safe but that actually hold you back. For smart people, they might sound like:

- "If I need help, maybe I'm not that smart." *(Self-Reliance and Personal Autonomy)*
- "Doing the work beneath me proves I've failed." *(Outward Confidence and Teamwork)*
- "If I try and don't win, I lose the right to be considered smart." *(Risk Tolerance and Self-Competence View)*

Those hidden beliefs? They're the puppet masters. Cut their strings—or they'll keep pulling yours.

3. Choose a New Operating Frame

Now it's time to rewrite the rules. Instead of clinging to "intelligence means success," shift to:

> *"Smartness turns intelligence into success."*

That single mental pivot changes everything. You stop hoarding knowledge and start applying it. You stop performing intelligence and start producing outcomes. You stop chasing validation—and start chasing results.

4. Install the Smartness Paradigm

If your current paradigm isn't working, you don't just drop it—you replace it. Get a new lens.

The *Smartness Paradigm* centers on the belief: *"Success comes from how I apply my intelligence—not just that I have it."* It shifts the focus from identity to behavior, from potential to action.

This new lens helps smart people:

- Stop hiding behind analysis and start choosing – combats rigidity (*Smartness Factor* - Decision Flexibility)

- Stop fearing missteps and start adapting – replaces doubt and builds resilience (Self-Competence, Risk Tolerance, Career Flexibility)
- Stop assuming outcomes and start earning them – reduces over-analysis and dependence on being the smartest (Risk Tolerance, Relational Adaptability)

You don't need a new self. You need a new lens that gives you an empowering way of seeing the world and yourself.

5. Rewire Through Action

This is the step most smart people skip—and the one that could change everything. They often say, "I get it" and even believe it—but then do nothing. I've done that. You probably have too.

New beliefs are useless unless your behavior proves them.

The data from the *Smartness Assessment* indicates that Action Orientation negatively affects an astounding 96% of unsuccessful people. Smartness only strengthens when it's practiced.

Every time you:

- Choose movement over overthinking,
- Accept feedback instead of defending your image,
- Ask for help instead of protecting your ego,
- Do something bold before you're fully ready…

…you reinforce the *Smartness Paradigm*.

Over time, Smartness becomes your default—because you've earned it through repetition, discomfort, and guts.

From Potential to Success

Smart people don't need more intelligence. They need to reframe how they see themselves—and success. This isn't about abandoning your intelligence. It's about upgrading how you use it. *Smartness* is the new lens. The new metric. The new path.

> *"You can become more successful by becoming the kind of smart that actually wins—Smartness."*

It's time to stop proving how smart you are—and start becoming the kind of smart that actually wins.

Reflection: *What outdated paradigm has been steering your life while you weren't looking? Which beliefs once made you feel safe—but now keep you small, stuck, and underachieving? What doors do you think will open the moment you stop clinging to intelligence—and start living through Smartness?*

"Sometimes the hardest part of getting better is letting go of who you used to be."

Once you've broken out of the intelligence paradigm and adopted a *Smartness*-based lens, everything hinges on how you apply it. That's where Personal Judgment comes in. It's not a *Smartness Factor* but it's the force that determines how smart people assess situations, weigh options, and choose what to do next. Without it, even the smartest paradigm stalls. With it, *Smartness* becomes a multiplier.

CHAPTER 19

Are You Excited, Fearful, Angry, or Indifferent?

"The drive to succeed starts with emotion – excitement, fear, anger or indifference. "
~ Ram V. Iyer

Remember, emotion creates motion. And while emotions have many origins, that variation matters more than most smart people realize. Some feel inspired by big dreams. Others feel pressure to meet expectations. Some are tired of underperforming. Others are just numb—in a detached, almost Zen state. What drives them shapes how they show up, how much energy they bring, and how they tackle their success journey.

The *Smartness Assessment* data confirms this. When asked what best describes their current motivation for success, responses clustered into four dominant categories:

- Excitement (Pleasure)
- Fear or Pressure (Pain)
- Frustration or Resentment (Anger)
- Numbness or Apathy (Indifference)

Each emotion points to something deeper. Each one shapes how people behave under pressure—and whether they follow through or stall.

Reflection: *Reflect on your achievements. How do you define success for yourself? What drives your desire to succeed?*

What Motivates People?

Decades ago, at a Tony Robbins seminar, I learned people are motivated by two things: to gain pleasure or avoid pain. If motivated by pleasure, it's like chasing a carrot—driven by desire. If avoiding pain, it's like running from a stick—driven by fear.

Reflection: *Are you primarily motivated by chasing rewards (pleasure) or avoiding setbacks (pain)? How has this shaped your decisions and results so far?*

I've found that pain and pleasure are genuine catalysts for change. One could excite you, and the other could make you fearful. Smart people often swing between two extremes—pursuing achievement for the thrill of being 'the best' or working frantically to avoid looking like a failure. But there's more to the story. Two other emotional states—Anger and Indifference—play crucial roles in the desire to achieve greater success.

1. Pleasure: The Pull Toward Greater Success
For many, success is fueled by excitement—the thrill of achievement, recognition, or fulfillment. This is "carrot" motivation—a desire to gain something meaningful. Pleasure-driven people set ambitious goals, visualize success, and stay energized by anticipation. But if rewards seem too distant, their motivation fades. That's why a strong 'why' and achievable milestones matter.

2. Pain: The Push Away from Failure or Discomfort
Others are driven by pain—pushing to escape failure or discomfort. This "stick" motivation fuels effort to avoid setbacks, struggles, or inadequacy. It drives action but can also lead to burnout or short-term thinking if not balanced with a long-term focus.

3. Anger: A Powerful but Risky Motivator
Many smart people get angry—at others or themselves. They feel they should be further ahead, should be doing better. Anger can drive sharp focus and resolve— or, mismanaged, it becomes corrosive: blame, self-sabotage, perfectionism.

After setbacks, smart people face a choice: grow or grow bitter. Some get stuck in self-pity. Others evolve and ask, "What needs to change in me?" Pain is inevitable. But whether it becomes an anchor or a catalyst—that's their decision.

Anger can be your catalyst or it can drag you down.
Used well, anger can be fuel. It can drive intense focus, determination, and the resolve to push forward. Mismanaged, it becomes corrosive. It leads to blame, self-sabotage, second-guessing, avoidance, or perfectionism.

And then comes the choice.

When smart people face failure, they can sink into self-pity—or use the pain to grow.

Some replay setbacks, blaming the world. Others ask, "What has to change in me so I become better, not bitter?"

Pain is inevitable. But whether it's an anchor or a catalyst—that's up to them.

Smart achievers turn setbacks into pivot points, not stopping points.

> *"Achieving greater success boils down to whether you use your past to become better—or stay bitter."*

Reflection: *How can you reframe a past failure to unlock a smarter, more focused path forward?*

4. Indifference: The Quiet Barrier to Achievement
Indifference is worse than fear—at least fear sparks action. Indifferent people hover near success but never commit. They settle, rationalize mediocrity, and shield themselves from discomfort.

True contentment is fine. But many confuse it with lazy complacency. They claim satisfaction while quietly avoiding effort. If you want more and do nothing, that's not peace. That's hiding.

Not everyone needs to chase success. Some people are truly content with what they've built and see no reason to push further. If you truly prioritize other things, that's fine. But many mistake complacency for contentment—convincing themselves they're satisfied when, deep down, they're just avoiding effort. If deep down you want more but do nothing, that's not contentment, that's lazy complacence disguised as acceptance.

> *"I hate being a nobody more than I hate trying and failing."*

Reflection: *Are there areas in your life where you might be settling for less than you're capable of? What steps can you take to move beyond complacency?*

Upgrade Your Mindset for Success

Your mindset is the foundation for how you process emotions—whether excitement, fear, anger, or indifference. It shapes how you channel these emotions into action. *Smartness* isn't just about intelligence; it's about directing that intelligence effectively. As discussed earlier, emotions fuel motivation, but it's your mindset that determines whether you translate them into meaningful action.

The wrong mindset can leave even the brightest minds stuck, while the right one can turn smart people into achievers.

Developing an Earned Mindset, an applied form of the growth mindset, — helps you channel these emotions into productive actions: transforming fear into preparation, excitement into momentum, and anger into constructive change. On the other hand, a *Destiny Mindset* leads to stagnation, reinforcing self-doubt and inaction.

Most of the *Smartness Factors* involve one's mindset, making it critical for sustained success. Even the greatest advantages—whether intelligence, resources, connections, or something else—can be wasted if one's mindset doesn't support action.

If your current mindset is limiting you, focus on upgrading to an Earned Mindset—seeing your advantages as tools, not guarantees. This shift ensures that emotions fuel growth rather than paralysis.

> *"A mindset that undermines you must be rebuilt to support your goals— until it does, no advantage will lead you to greater achievements."*

Steps to Upgrade Your Mindset:

- Identify Limiting Beliefs – What internal narratives are preventing you from acting on your full potential?
- Challenge Negative Self-Talk – Replace self-doubt with constructive affirmations and evidence-based confidence.
- Adopt a Learning Perspective – View failures as stepping stones rather than final verdicts.
- Surround Yourself with Growth-Oriented People – Your mindset is influenced by those you interact with regularly.

Reshaping your mindset isn't just possible—it's essential for achieving your full potential.

Reflection: Is your mindset helping or hindering you? If it's holding you back, what steps can you take today to reshape it so your emotions work for you rather than against you?

Emotions and Personal Judgment

Emotions drive action, but how you interpret and respond to them determines your outcomes. Excitement can fuel bold moves, fear can lead to hesitation, anger can drive action, and indifference can cause inaction. But without sound judgment, emotions alone won't guarantee success. Many people make decisions clouded by unchecked emotions—reacting impulsively or avoiding action altogether.

This is where Personal Judgment becomes critical. Understanding your emotions is only the first step. The real challenge is applying smart, balanced decision-making in the face of those emotions. In the next chapter, we explore how good judgment enables you to make the right choices, even in uncertain or emotionally charged situations.

It's time to decide whether you ready to chase the carrot, avoid the stick, redirect your anger, or shake off indifference. If you choose to commit, this book can guide you to go from where you are to where you could be, from who you are to who you could become. The path to success depends on your mindset. Quite simply, if you don't like your life as it stands, …

> *"Change your mindset, change your life!"* ~ *Unknown*

Reflection: *Have you ever felt anger or frustration push you to take action? Or has indifference ever held you back? How can you channel these emotions more effectively toward your goals?*

Smartness isn't just about knowing what to do—it requires action and follow-through. But taking action isn't just driven by what you know or feel; it depends on the quality of your judgment. Recognizing your emotions is only part of the equation. What you do next—and whether it leads to success—depends on your ability to make sound decisions. In the next chapter, we'll explore why Personal Judgment is the ultimate advantage smart people can develop, and how it shapes every decision you make.

Reflection: *Which emotion is running your life right now—excitement, fear, anger, or indifference—and is it fueling your next move or helping you rationalize doing nothing and stay stuck?*

CHAPTER 20

PERSONAL JUDGMENT—THE SMART PERSON'S ULTIMATE ADVANTAGE

"Effective decision-making hinges on contextual judgment. Individuals skilled at it achieve greater success, while those who aren't achieve lesser success."
~ Ram V. Iyer

Smartness depends on good judgment. No matter how intelligent someone is, success comes down to how they evaluate various situations, weigh trade-offs, and make choices.

Personal judgment determines whether smart people move forward or stall—because it shapes whether to act (or not), what to do (or not), and where to act (or not).

Judgment is not the same as smartness—and it doesn't come first. *Smartness* is the broader capability: the ability to assess situations, apply intelligence and advantages, and adapt over time. Judgment is complementary to Smartness—it works alongside it, shaping how well smart people interpret situations and make choices. *Smartness* doesn't depend on judgment. But when judgment falters, *Smartness* often stalls with it.

Good judgment turns *Smartness* into real-world results. Poor judgment turns it into frustration.

If intelligence is the engine, *Smartness* is the full performance system—and judgment is the driver who makes driving decisions.

This chapter will help smart people sharpen their judgment, avoid self-sabotage, and turn intelligence into lasting success.

What is Judgment?

Judgment is the ability to evaluate a situation, synthesize information, and make a decision based on what matters most – to you. It's the personal process of weighing options, considering trade-offs, and determining the best course of action. Your judgment is shaped by how you view the situation, the people involved, the stakes, and your own values, capabilities, and priorities. Unlike rules or formulas, judgment is uniquely yours—and it improves with practice, reflection, and experience. You may seek somebody else's opinion, but your judgment of a situation and what to do is uniquely yours. That's why it's often referred to as personal judgment.

Judgment sits at the heart of the *Achievement Cycle* because it integrates mindset, behavior, and skill into effective decisions. Each *Smartness Factor*

Personal Judgment—The Smart Person's Ultimate Advantage

contributes to your ability to exercise sound judgment. Decision Flexibility helps you adapt, Emotional Intelligence supports interpersonal dynamics, Situational Judgment sharpens context awareness, and Self-Competence shapes your confidence in making tough calls.

Judgment is both a skill you can build and a process you refine over time. It's the connective tissue that links every aspect of Smartness.

Why does judgment matter? Because every decision, big or small, shapes the trajectory of your life. From career moves to personal choices, judgment allows you to adapt to changing situations, balance competing priorities, and align your actions with your values and goals. It's the invisible hand steering you through uncertainty and complexity. Poor judgment can derail progress and squander opportunities, while good judgment turns knowledge, resources, and advantages into meaningful outcomes.

> *"Judgment is not just about making the 'right' choice—it's about making the right choice for you."*

Based on the outcome, your personal judgment could be poor or good. Say you're offered a higher-paying job in another city. It could be a great career move, but relocating would disrupt your family's life. Do you take it? Judgment is about weighing the trade-offs—career growth vs. personal stability—and making the best choice for your situation. You consider the facts, but ultimately, the decision comes down to your personal judgment.

Effective personal judgment is closely tied to Smartness. It depends on knowing what enables or disables good decisions—not just through knowledge, but through context, mindset, and available resources.

Judgment draws from your mindset, behavior, and skills—channeled through the *Smartness Factors* that influence success. These factors aren't good or bad on their own; their value depends on the situation and how they're applied.

Judgment demands flexibility, adaptability, and the willingness to learn from experience. It's shaped by your beliefs, biases, values, behavior, skills, and advantages—and must be continuously refined. Those with sound judgment consistently outperform those who rely on rigid rules or reactive decisions.

This chapter explores how judgment shapes decisions, connects to Smartness, and helps you navigate complex situations more effectively.

Reflection: *What patterns do you notice about how you make decisions under pressure? Are there specific triggers (words, behaviors, or certain people) that affect the clarity of your judgment?*

Historical Perspectives on Judgment

Good judgment has shaped personal and societal success for centuries. Ancient civilizations valued wisdom, foresight, and the balance between logic and intuition.

For the Greeks, it was a moral and intellectual virtue. Egyptians applied strategic foresight; Chinese traditions emphasized ethical, practical wisdom. Indian philosophy emphasized discernment (*viveka*), context-driven action (*dharma*), and inner clarity (*pragya*) as foundations for sound judgment.

Over time, thinkers merged knowledge and ethics, viewing judgment as a mindset, not just a skill. The Renaissance blended creativity with intellect; the Enlightenment advanced rationality. Today, psychology and neuroscience offer insights—like cognitive bias and dual-process thinking—that past philosophers couldn't access. From Aristotle to Kahneman, the lesson holds: sound judgment bridges the gap between knowledge and action.

Understanding Judgment in Today's World

Today, psychology and cognitive science offer deeper insights into judgment. A mix of thought processes, emotions, and experiences shapes how we decide. Our brains rely on two modes: fast, intuitive thinking (System 1) and slower, deliberate reasoning (System 2). Both are essential, but they must be balanced to handle complexity.

Emotions and subconscious biases also play a bigger role than we think. Gut instincts can guide us—but unchecked bias can mislead us. Strong judgment integrates instinct with reflection, blending insight with analysis.

Seen through both historical and modern lenses, judgment is a timeless virtue and a practical skill. It's not just knowing what to do—it's knowing how to approach decisions with clarity and adaptability.

Sharpening Your Judgment: Practical Strategies for Better Decision-Making

Judgment isn't theoretical—it's practical. These strategies, grounded in the *Achievement Cycle*, help you make thoughtful, adaptable decisions aligned with your goals. By balancing instinct and analysis, managing biases, and seeking diverse input, you can strengthen judgment across all areas of life.

Here are ten strategies drawn from leading psychological and cognitive theories to help you build better decision-making habits:

1. **Understand Cognitive Biases**
   Cognitive biases—like confirmation bias, overconfidence, and anchoring—can distort judgment.

   Suggested action: Learn to spot common biases and pause to ask if they're shaping your thinking.

2. **Embrace Kahneman's Dual-Process Thinking**
   Kahneman's theory distinguishes between fast (System 1) and slow (System 2) thinking.

Suggested action: For big decisions, slow down—gather more information and engage System 2.

3. **Apply the Hierarchy of Value**
   Hartman and Byrum identify three value levels: systemic, extrinsic, and intrinsic.
   Suggested action: Evaluate decisions from all three angles—big picture, tangible results, and personal meaning.

4. **Develop Emotional Intelligence**
   Emotions deeply influence decisions—especially under stress.
   Suggested action: Build emotional awareness and manage your state before major decisions.

5. **Use Fast and Frugal Heuristics**
   Gigerenzer shows that simple decision rules work well under pressure or limited info.
   Suggested action: Identify reliable shortcuts for repeated decisions—then use them with confidence.

6. **Engage in Scenario Analysis**
   Premortem thinking helps anticipate what could go wrong.
   Suggested action: Before big decisions, visualize possible failures—and plan for them.

7. **Seek Diverse Perspectives**
   Tetlock's research shows diverse input improves accuracy and reduces bias.
   Suggested action: Talk to people with different viewpoints before making complex decisions.

8. **Reflect on Past Decisions**
   Reviewing choices reveals behavioral patterns and blind spots.
   Suggested action: Keep a decision log and regularly revisit what worked—and what didn't.

9. **Commit to Continuous Learning**
   Expanding knowledge improves decision range and depth.
   Suggested action: Make learning routine—through reading, conversations, or workshops.

10. **Practice Mindfulness**
    Mindfulness improves focus, clarity, and regulation in decision-making.
    Suggested action: Add short daily mindfulness practices to reduce reactivity and improve focus.

By integrating these strategies into your daily life, you can strengthen your judgment skills, leading to more thoughtful and effective decisions.

The Power of Good Judgment

Good judgment shapes every part of success—from strategy to relationships. When decisions are made with clarity, they lead to:

1. Strategic Thinking: Anticipate and plan for better outcomes.
2. Risk Management: Spot and address problems early.
3. Better Problem-Solving: Find smarter solutions by exploring angles.
4. Stronger Relationships: Build trust and credibility.
5. Resilience: Stay clear-headed and responsive under pressure.

Action Steps:
1. Review past decisions to see what worked—and why.
2. Balance instinct with analysis in key decisions.
3. Get diverse input to broaden your perspective.
4. Stay informed to make smarter choices.
5. Build emotional intelligence to weigh broader impacts.

The Consequences of Poor Judgment

Poor judgment can stall progress and trigger avoidable setbacks:

1. Bad Decisions: Lead to missed chances or damaging outcomes.
2. Overlooked Risks: Cause mistakes that could've been prevented.
3. Strained Relationships: Undermine trust and credibility.
4. Weaker Problem-Solving: Limits solutions and leads to repeat errors.
5. More Stress: Erodes confidence and mental clarity.

Action Steps:
1. Reflect on past mistakes and adapt your approach.
2. Get input or mentorship on high-stakes decisions.
3. Analyze options and seek varied viewpoints.
4. Stay open to feedback and learning.
5. Manage stress to stay clear-headed under pressure.

Reflection: Think of a major decision you're currently facing. How can you apply the lessons in this chapter to make a better decision informed by good judgment?

Judgment is a skill that can be developed and honed over a lifetime. Its foundation lies in understanding yourself—your mindset, behaviors, skills, and advantages—while being mindful of the context in which decisions are made. Balancing fast, intuitive thinking with slower, analytical reasoning is key to better judgment.

For over twenty years, I have believed that judgment is one of the most critical attributes for success. Only recently have I fully understood how it affects our choices and outcomes. Nobody is born with good judgment. It is cultivated

Personal Judgment—The Smart Person's Ultimate Advantage

through experience, reflection, and learning from both successes and failures over one's lifetime.

By improving your judgment, you can approach challenges with greater clarity, reduce risks, and make better choices that align with your goals. In the end, good judgment smoothens your path to lasting success and enables you to turn your aspirations into achievements.

But sound judgment depends on knowing yourself—what empowers you and what holds you back. That's why understanding your *Smartness* Profile—your Enablers and Disablers—is essential. That's where we go next.

Reflection: *Think of a situation when your judgment really counted—did it make you successful or blow up in your face? And more importantly, what have you done since then to develop better judgment?*

CHAPTER 21

OVERCOMING INNER RESISTANCE TO SUCCESS

"I embrace who I am today and choose who I will be in the future."
~ Ram V. Iyer

Before we move forward, let's confront one of the biggest success barriers—internal resistance to change.

> *"Many people get stuck because they wish they were someone else instead of leveraging who they are today and intentionally shaping their future."*

Success isn't just about external action—it's also about overcoming internal blockers like fear, self-doubt, and procrastination. These often operate beneath the surface. Sometimes we hide them. Other times we don't even recognize them. Either way, they hold us back. When you have internal resistance, you cannot lift a single finger!

You might set ambitious goals and create a solid plan—then stall, not from lack of skill, but because something inside resists change. All of us have faced moments where we want to act, but... something seems to be preventing us from taking any action. That's inner resistance.

Many of these blocks come from habits—mental and behavioral patterns that were once helpful but eventually become constraints. The problem is they form slowly, and by the time they limit us, they feel normal. The most dangerous habits feel fine—until you realize they're holding you back, and by then, they're hard to break.

> *"Some of the most dangerous habits feel fine—until you realize they're holding you back, but by then, you can't break them."*

They could also stem from your mindset – what you believe or value, rules you live by, or assumptions you make.

That's why self-awareness and intentional effort are essential to breaking free.

Reflection: *Think about a time when you felt 'stuck' in pursuing a goal. Was it due to external obstacles, or do you think some internal resistance was at play?*

Understanding Inner Resistance

Inner resistance is the invisible force that blocks change, even when we know it's necessary. It shows up as procrastination, self-sabotage, or avoidance, often disguised as excuses.

It can stem from several deeply ingrained factors:

- **Fear of Vulnerability**: Avoiding situations where flaws might be exposed. The ego works to 'protect' us—even if it limits growth.
- **Identity Preservation**: Resisting change to protect an identity we've grown attached to—whether self-imposed or shaped by others. We often cling to a false version of ourselves rather than accept change.
- **Comfort Zone**: Choosing the familiar, even when it's unfulfilling, over the discomfort of growth. Often tied to personal risk tolerance.
- **Biological Laziness** (physical or mental): The instinct to conserve energy and avoid effort—especially when rewards feel distant or uncertain.

After you recognize these triggers, you can begin dismantling their hold on your actions and decisions.

Reflection: *What's one way you've noticed inner resistance show up in your life, and how has it held you back?*

The Psychological Barriers to Success

1. **Fear of Vulnerability.** We avoid situations that expose our flaws, mistaking vulnerability for weakness. But dodging feedback and growth opportunities keeps us stuck.
2. **Social Comparison.** Comparison is the thief of joy—but it's human nature. Instead of focusing on progress, we fixate on others' success. This creates pressure, envy, or the urge to chase someone else's version of success. There will always be someone ahead—trying to match them could be an endless chase.
3. **Sunk Cost Fallacy.** The sunk cost fallacy traps us in unproductive situations because of past investments. Whether we stick with a failing project or remain in a dead-end job, the thought of the time, money, or effort already spent often prevents us from cutting our losses. Success, however, is about making decisions based on what's best for your future, not what you did or spent in the past.
4. **Cognitive Dissonance.** When our self-image doesn't align with our actions, it creates mental conflict—dissonance. For instance, we might see ourselves as achievers, yet our actions—like procrastinating or avoiding challenges—often tell a different story. This internal conflict can lead to avoidance and stagnation. Resolving cognitive dissonance requires honesty, recognizing where we fall short, and taking deliberate steps to close the gap.

Reflection: *Which of these psychological barriers resonates most with you, and what's one small step you could take to overcome it?*

Breaking Free from Resistance: Reframing It as Growth

Resistance is often misinterpreted as a sign of failure or inadequacy, but it's actually a natural part of personal growth. When you encounter resistance, it's a signal that you're stepping out of your comfort zone and about to learn something. Instead of giving up or avoiding it, ask yourself: *"What can I learn from this situation?"* Reframing resistance as an opportunity to learn shifts the narrative from avoidance to learning.

Steps to Overcome Resistance
There are some proven approaches to break free from resistance:

1. Identify Triggers: Pay attention to the thoughts, situations, or behaviors that spark resistance. Is it fear of failure, uncertainty, or perfectionism? Look for patterns and break them by changing your behavior.
2. Start Small: Set manageable, bite-sized goals that build momentum and confidence. For example, instead of tackling an entire project, commit to working on it for just 10 minutes a day.
3. Shift Your Mindset: Replace self-defeating thoughts with empowering ones. When resistance says, "I can't do this," respond with, "I can figure it out."
4. Seek Support: Share your challenges with mentors, coaches, or trusted friends who can offer guidance and accountability.

Practical Tools

1. Journaling: Write down your moments of resistance and what you did to overcome them. This helps you identify patterns and celebrate progress.
2. Visualization: Picture yourself successfully navigating through resistance and achieving your goals.
3. Reflection: Take time to pause and evaluate what's working and what needs adjustment. Past patterns leave clues you can use.

Reflection: *What's one specific area in your life where resistance keeps holding you back, and what immediate step can you take to reframe it as an opportunity for growth?*

Leveraging Smartness to Overcome Resistance

Inner resistance isn't just an obstacle—it's an opportunity to apply your *Smartness* enablers to move forward. The key lies in recognizing how these enablers can help you break through barriers and transform resistance into momentum. Here are three *Smartness Factors* that can help overcome resistance. You can read more about these and other factors in Part 2 of this book.

1. Emotional Intelligence: Resistance often stirs up feelings of fear, frustration, or doubt. Emotional intelligence enables you to recognize and regulate these emotions, transforming them into motivators rather

than obstacles. For example, instead of being paralyzed by fear, you can reframe it as excitement for the challenge ahead.
2. Decision Flexibility: Overcoming resistance often requires adapting to new circumstances or letting go of unproductive habits. Decision flexibility allows you to pivot when necessary, focusing on what's effective rather than what's familiar.
3. Self-Competence Views: Believing in your ability to succeed is a powerful antidote to resistance. By cultivating confidence in your skills and judgment, you can approach challenges with a mindset of possibility rather than defeat.

By leveraging these enablers, you can take a proactive approach to tackling resistance. Instead of letting inner barriers dictate your actions, you can use them as stepping stones toward greater success.

Reflection: *Which Smartness enabler(s)—Emotional Intelligence, Decision Flexibility, or Self-Competence Views—can you use to overcome a current challenge?*

Every day, you have a choice—to embrace who you are today and intentionally shape who you want to be in the future. The smartest people understand that success isn't about wishing for a different starting point; it's about making the most of who you are and where you are now, and then taking action to work towards your desired goal.

Resistance isn't the enemy—it's a signal that growth is within reach. By reframing resistance as an opportunity and applying the tools from this chapter, you can transform it from a barrier into a catalyst for progress. Success isn't defined by the absence of resistance but by how effectively you move through it. Each small, intentional step builds momentum, helping you overcome challenges and create a foundation for lasting achievement.

But even with momentum, you need a deeper reason to keep going, especially when the path gets tough. That reason is your Why. And that's where we're headed next.

Reflection: *Are you resisting success because change is hard—or because staying stuck feels safer than pushing to achieve more?*

CHAPTER 22

YOUR WHY - THE DRIVING FORCE BEHIND SUCCESS

"Your 'Why' gives your goals meaning, transforming your advantages into momentum and your challenges into lessons that guide you toward success."
~ Ram V. Iyer

Desires are free, but achieving meaningful goals requires effort and trade-offs. While we can dream without limits, turning those dreams into reality demands dedication, sacrifice, and hard work. It often means giving up leisure time, investing resources, and making difficult choices. Along the way, you—and those around you—may ask, "Why is this goal so important to me?"

Without a compelling answer, it's easy to lose motivation when obstacles arise or when setbacks test your resolve. Are you clear about why you're pursuing your goals, or are you still searching for that deeper purpose? Take a moment to reflect. Your Why is the force that will keep you moving forward, even when the path gets tough. Write down what truly excites and drives you—what's at the core of your ambitions.

After interviewing over a hundred people who took the *Smartness Assessment*, I found two drivers of success beyond the original *Smartness Factors*. These aren't just for the so-called smart crowd—they apply to everybody.

1. A strong desire for success, and
2. Having a powerful emotional reason, or 'why,' driving that desire.

Without these two drivers, even the most capable person may struggle to reach their potential. This clarity of purpose enables the practical application of one's advantages. Without a strong 'why,' even the greatest goals can feel hollow.

Think about this: Our assessment data shows that 54% of people responded with, "I absolutely want to become much more successful." Others said, "It would be nice if I became more successful." Which group do you think is more likely to achieve their goals?

What truly drives you? Are you clear on the reasons you're chasing success, or are you still searching for that powerful 'why'?
Success isn't a one-size-fits-all measure; it's deeply personal. Some people may start with advantages—whether it's wealth, family connections, or the right environment—but true success is about having a desire and an emotionally charged reason to persevere until you achieve your goals. This desire, fueled by a personal 'why,' is what sets people apart.

Your 'why' needs to be more than a passing thought. It's easy to say, 'I want to be successful,' but will you say it with the same conviction tomorrow, next week, and next month? What drives you? Why do you want it? Your 'why' could be intrinsic, deeply personal, or even extrinsic, influenced by the expectations of others. Many people lack a 'why,' others have a weak one, most (I have noticed) have a borrowed one (they repeat what they've read or heard), but only a few have a strong, intrinsic motivation that pushes them forward. When you know your 'why,' challenges become tests of strength, and setbacks transform into valuable lessons.

This chapter is about understanding and embracing your 'why.' Take a moment to consider what truly motivates you—your own reasons can be the ultimate catalyst for success. Don't wait for tomorrow—clarifying your 'why' today could be the first step to transforming every goal you set. Success is personal, and so is the 'why' behind it. Define yours with conviction.

Reflection: *Think about your own life or career and pick one significant accomplishment. Can you identify what motivated you to persevere until you accomplished that goal?*

The Power of the 'Why'

Your 'why' is your emotional fuel. It can be a 'carrot' pulling you toward a goal or a 'stick' pushing you away from something undesirable. As Simon Sinek highlights in *Start with Why: How Great Leaders Inspire Everyone to Take Action*, knowing your 'why' is essential for lasting success.

A marathon runner honoring a loved one, a parent going back to school for their kids, an artist creating for the love of it—each succeeds because their 'Why' is stronger than their struggles.

While discipline can get you far, it often fades over time. A core intrinsic motivation is different—it's resilient, keeping you focused and motivated when willpower alone might fail.

Reflection: *Think of a time when you were highly motivated to achieve something. What was the emotional 'why' behind this drive, and how did it shape your efforts?*

The Role of Intrinsic Motivation

Research shows that people who pursue goals for personal fulfillment—not external rewards—are more likely to succeed. A teacher driven by a love of teaching, for example, stays committed even when things get tough.

Reflection: Identify a goal or activity you pursue because it brings you intrinsic joy – you do it because you enjoy doing it. How does this differ from tasks you do for external rewards (to please others or to get a reward from others)?

Emotional Resonance of the 'Why'

Emotions are integral to our 'why.' Research from the University of Rochester shows that goals pursued for personal, intrinsic reasons yield greater satisfaction. Imagine an entrepreneur who starts a business to create something meaningful rather than just for financial gain. Their passion and commitment often translate into greater satisfaction and success.

Grab a notebook or open up your favorite app on your computer or tablet, and write down one goal that excites you. Then ask yourself: Why do I want this? Keep drilling down with 'Why?'—repeatedly if you have to—until you uncover the deepest reason behind your desire. You're not just looking for surface answers; dig until you find the core purpose that fuels this goal.

Vision, Values, and Success

A clear vision aligned with personal values can significantly impact success. A study published in The Leadership Quarterly highlights how leaders with a clear, value-driven vision tend to be more effective. Consider a company leader whose vision for environmental sustainability drives their business strategy, leading to innovative practices and success in their field.

Reflection: Reflect on your most important goals. How do they align with your personal values (what you value more or less, like money or relationships) and emotional aspirations? Are they truly meaningful to you?

Overcoming Challenges with a Strong 'Why'

A solid 'why' can be an anchor during tough times. For example, an athlete recovering from injury, driven by the goal to compete again, can face rehabilitation with unwavering determination, turning setbacks into comebacks.

Your 'why' is the heart of your pursuit of greater success. It's about the journey and the fulfillment that comes with chasing something that truly matters to you. Identifying and embracing this driving force can transform the path to success from a chore or duty into a purposeful and passionate journey.

Reflection: *Think of a significant challenge you faced. Did your underlying 'why' help you navigate and overcome this obstacle?*

Are you Setting Goals for the Right Reasons?

Have you noticed that most annual plans and New Year's resolutions don't succeed? Many goals are set with good intentions but never achieved. Why? In my experience, it's because people often use these goals to distract themselves from the real changes they need to make.

Think about it: resolutions are often influenced by feelings of disappointment, societal pressure, or fleeting bursts of motivation. Instead of addressing deeper issues, they can become a way to avoid confronting what truly needs attention. For example, if your goal is to stop overeating or avoid junk food, have you ever asked yourself why you overeat or choose junk food in the first place? Is it due to stress? Or because you compare yourself to others and feel self-conscious?

Setting such goals might make you feel like you're working toward self-improvement, giving a temporary sense of progress. But don't confuse activity with intentionally addressing the root cause of your challenges. Without tackling the deeper issues, these efforts often fall short.

Psychological research, such as the concept of *Immunity to Change* by Lisa Lahey and Robert Kegan, shows that we often resist making deeper changes—even when we know they're necessary—because we subconsciously cling to our comfort zones.

Real, lasting change requires more than just setting goals. It demands identifying and addressing the root causes of your challenges and finding a compelling reason—a strong "why"—to sustain your effort over time.

> *"We sometimes make resolutions in order to avoid confronting what really bothers us or holds us back."*

This pattern of avoidance is linked to a hidden resistance to change, often underpinned by beliefs and habits that keep us stagnant. Without addressing this resistance, achieving the desired change will remain elusive.

This resistance, embedded in deep-seated beliefs and habits, acts as a defense mechanism. Attempting change without confronting these underlying factors is like trying to bypass our psychological immune system, which often fails to enact lasting change. This concept underscores the importance of identifying and working through these subconscious barriers for genuine transformation.

> *"What we say we want is driven by our conscious mind. However, what we're willing to do is shaped by our subconscious mindset—our beliefs, values, rules, habits, and motivations (or lack thereof)—some of which we may not even be aware of."*

Many books discuss the importance of one's 'why.' I strongly recommend that you read some of them.

> *"Your 'why' is the wind beneath your wings. Discover it, and let it fuel your journey to greater success. "*

Reflection: *Reflecting on your current goals, are they driven more by external expectations or your own deeply felt reasons? How might this influence their outcome?*

When you're clear on your Why, you unlock your drive to act. But drive alone isn't enough. You also need to use your existing advantages—your intelligence, skills, networks, and resources—to move forward with purpose and power. In the next chapter, we'll explore how smart people leverage their existing advantages to achieve even greater success.

Reflection: *Are you doing what fires you up—or just chasing goals that look good but aren't yours and feel empty as hell?*

CHAPTER 23

YOU'RE ALREADY AHEAD: LEVERAGE YOUR INTELLIGENCE & OTHER ADVANTAGES FOR GREATER SUCCESS

"Why would you want to be like everybody else when you can be an achiever with your advantages?"
~ Ram V. Iyer

I know you want to become more successful, even if it sometimes feels like the odds are stacked against you. You're not starting from scratch. You've already climbed higher than most. Now it's about pushing higher. To reach the top, you need to recognize where you stand and use the intelligence, skills, and resources you already have.

Every success story begins with a foundation—your unique advantages. These are the traits, skills, and resources that give you an edge, whether you recognize them or not. Yet, simply possessing advantages isn't enough; the difference lies in how you choose to use them.

Many people fail to fully leverage what they have, either because they underestimate their potential or feel weighed down by challenges. But recognizing that you're already ahead, in some way, can shift your mindset. This chapter will explore why actively embracing and using your advantages is critical for achieving greater success—and how you can begin to see them as tools to propel you forward.

Reflection: *List three advantages you have right now. How can you maximize them today?*

Think for a moment...

If you're reading this book, you're literate—a privilege many in the world do not have. Chances are, you've had access to education, perhaps even higher education, and you're driven by ambition. Your intelligence, skills, and experiences give you an edge—but only if you use them. What will you do today to move forward?

Pause for a moment and let this sink in: compared to the majority of the global population, you've achieved more, possess more, and have more opportunities at your fingertips. Reflect on your journey so far. What milestones have you achieved that once felt out of reach? What strengths or resources did you rely on to overcome challenges? Are you maximizing those same tools to climb even higher today?

The Research

Dr. Raj Chetty, a Stanford researcher for the National Bureau of Economic Research, studies how socioeconomic factors—like education, family background, and neighborhood environments—impact economic mobility in the U.S. His work highlights that quality education and supportive neighborhoods strongly shape life trajectories. For those with advantages like intelligence, education, or leadership, the path to success tends to be smoother, with easier access to opportunities and a higher likelihood of achievement. Many people with great advantages still struggle, while others with fewer advantages excel because they use their *Smartness* to navigate challenges and seize opportunities.

> *"Smartness is the differentiator between those who maximize their advantages and those who waste them."*

Chetty's research also reveals a harsh truth: most people are bound by their parents' socioeconomic status, and moving from lower to upper income is extremely difficult. For those already in higher income and education brackets, success often comes more easily. Simply put, place and opportunity are closely linked, so capitalizing on advantages—such as the town you grew up in, networks, or educational legacies—can lead to faster, easier, and more significant growth. In the next section, let's examine some of these advantages.

Foundations of Success: Intelligence, Leadership, Education, Wealth, and Networks

Several key foundations often distinguish those on a fast track to success: intelligence, leadership qualities, elite credentials, wealth, and strategic networks. Let's explore how each of these advantages can be leveraged for even greater achievement.

- **Intelligence and Leadership**
  High intelligence and strong leadership skills provide a significant edge. Those with these qualities often excel in fast-changing fields where quick adaptation and innovation are crucial. For example, a scientist with exceptional analytical skills and the ability to synthesize complex data can drive groundbreaking research and lead teams to transformative discoveries. Similarly, a tech entrepreneur with strong leadership and problem-solving abilities is well-positioned to thrive in competitive markets. These qualities, combined with the support of peers or mentors, can drive meaningful success.

- **Education, Titles and Credentials**
  Education acts as a powerful foundation. It is a turbocharger that expands your knowledge and increases your ability to learn. Graduates of elite schools or holders of advanced degrees (doctors, engineers, lawyers) often enter highly paid careers. Similarly, if you have prestigious titles or credentials,

leveraging them—through lifelong learning and application—can enhance your trajectory.

Reflection: How does your education give you an edge in reaching your goals?

- **Wealth**
  Wealth not only provides stability but also opens doors to exclusive opportunities that can accelerate success. Those from affluent backgrounds or family businesses often find that opportunities come to them, giving them access to resources and ventures that may be out of reach for others. However, wealth alone is not enough; knowing how to invest and manage this advantage effectively is critical.

  Reflection: If you have wealth, how has it contributed to or hindered your success?

- **Strategic Networks**
  Social networks amplify each of these foundations, providing access to resources, mentorship, and industry connections. Whether through alumni groups or professional organizations, strategic networks reveal new opportunities and connect you to influential individuals. Membership in groups like YPO, EO, or Tiger 21 grants access to high-value circles where opportunities seek the members, not the other way around.

  Reflection: What networks are you a part of that could accelerate your success?

Overcoming Entitlement with Smartness and Strategy

However, possessing these advantages does not guarantee success. First and foremost, as this book points out, you need to know how to leverage your *Smartness* enablers (while also mitigating your disablers) to become more successful. You also need a strategic approach to overcome the typical challenges of entitlement and complacency. Successful individuals must recognize the significance of their starting point and actively seek ways to amplify their impact for greater personal, professional, and community success. **This book will help you address the issues raised in this paragraph.**

> *"When your Smartness matches your advantages, you can become an achiever."*

For those who already stand on higher ground, the call to action is two-fold. First, there's a personal imperative: use your advantages to fuel your greater achievement. Simply feeling good about your education, skills, or wealth isn't enough—you need to make strategic investments in personal growth, education, and your network. A better and more successful you benefits not only yourself but also those around you.

Second, you have a broader societal responsibility. Your unique advantages can be a ladder for others, helping them reach new heights. By sharing insights, connections, and support—whether through mentorship, opening doors, or offering advice as a consultant—you create a ripple effect. Helping others succeed builds a legacy that extends far beyond personal achievements. Remember, the more people you uplift, the greater the impact you make.

Understanding that you're already ahead is the first step. But knowing where you stand isn't enough—you need to know which aspects of your mindset, which of your behaviors and traits are helping you, and which are holding you back. That's where your personal *Smartness Assessment* comes in. In the next chapter, we'll walk through how to use your *Smartness Assessment Report* to understand your enablers and disablers—and how to take targeted action for greater success.

Reflection: *You've got what billions don't—brains, education, and opportunities. Are you making it count, or just coasting while the world waits for you to achieve something spectacular with them?*

CHAPTER 24

YOUR SMARTNESS ASSESSMENT REPORT—UNDERSTANDING YOUR ENABLERS & DISABLERS

"Knowing yourself is the beginning of all wisdom on the path to achievement."
~ Ram V. Iyer

If you want to reach your full potential, you need to know what's helping or hurting you—you need self-awareness. The *Smartness Assessment* pinpoints the enablers that currently drive your success and the disablers that hold you back. That is your starting point.

Besides identifying your enablers and disablers, it identifies a third set of factors labeled as 'Mixed'—which are factors in which you have some enabling and some disabling behaviors. By identifying and understanding these, you can take targeted action to maximize your strengths while addressing obstacles, and make smarter decisions. It's like having a roadmap revealing the highways and the hurdles on your way to achievement.

You can access the assessment for free (a $198 value) at this link: https://www.MySmartness.com/Assessments/Smartness and get your personal *Smartness Assessment Report*. Here's how to get your personal report:

i. Complete the assessment.
ii. When prompted to purchase your report, click on the YES button.
iii. On the checkout page, enter the discount code: *SmartnessBook-2025* to waive the fee.

Making Sense of Your Smartness Assessment Report

If you have your report, let's continue. At the beginning of the report, you will be given a numeric count of the number of enablers, disablers, and mixed factors. Write them down below:

Enablers: _____ ; Disablers: _____ ; Mixed: _____

Add the number of Disablers and Mixed, which we call the Total Obstacle Score (TOS): _____ .

I have found that while Disablers are extremely disabling, almost everybody is affected by the 'Mixed' factors which are sometimes disabling or somewhat disabling. You need to mitigate both your disablers and mixed factors.

Next, let's clearly identify the classification of each of the *Smartness Factors* from your report. For each factor, circle either Enabling, Disabling or Mixed by referring to your report:

Factor 1 - Action Orientation   Enabling/Disabling/Mixed
Factor 2 - Detail Focus   Enabling/Disabling/Mixed
Factor 3 - Need for Variety   Enabling/Disabling/Mixed
Factor 4 - Risk Tolerance   Enabling/Disabling/Mixed
Factor 5 - Complexity Preference   Enabling/Disabling/Mixed
Factor 6 - Belief Reinforcement   Enabling/Disabling/Mixed
Factor 7 - Personal Autonomy   Enabling/Disabling/Mixed
Factor 8 - Thinking & Feeling   Enabling/Disabling/Mixed
Factor 9 - Emotional Intelligence   Enabling/Disabling/Mixed
Factor 10 - Decision Flexibility   Enabling/Disabling/Mixed
Factor 11 - Situational Judgment   Enabling/Disabling/Mixed
Factor 12 - Self-competence Views   Enabling/Disabling/Mixed
Factor 13 - Interpersonal Skills   Enabling/Disabling/Mixed
Factor 14 – Outward Confidence   Enabling/Disabling/Mixed
Factor 15 – Self-Reliance   Enabling/Disabling/Mixed
Factor 16 - Career Flexibility   Enabling/Disabling/Mixed
Factor 17 - Thinking Range   Enabling/Disabling/Mixed
Factor 18 – Teamwork   Enabling/Disabling/Mixed
Factor 19 – Self-Advocacy   Enabling/Disabling/Mixed
Factor 20 – Relational Adaptability   Enabling/Disabling/Mixed

Place a * against the factors that are your known BIG ENABLERS and BIG DISABLERS—you may already have a strong sense. We will return to this list in the companion *Smartness Playbook*.

Reflection: What's one enabler from your Smartness Profile you can intentionally leverage to achieve a real goal you're working on? Similarly, what is one disabling factor that you could mitigate over the next 30 days that could make a big difference?

I strongly encourage you to take the *Smartness Assessment* so that the chapters in Part 4 of this book are more personal and practical by helping you understand what enables or disables your success. We will delve deeply into each of the *Smartness Factors*. You'll gain a clear understanding of how these factors can either enable or disable your success, depending on how they are applied. This exploration will build on what you've discovered about yourself in Part 3, including insights from your personal *Smartness Assessment Report*, equipping you with the knowledge to navigate challenges and maximize your advantages.

Then, in Part 5, we'll bring everything together by aligning what you've learned about your advantages and the *Smartness Factors* with practical tools and strategies to craft a plan for purposeful action and meaningful achievements.

Reflection: Now that you know what's helping and hurting you, are you ready to do something about it, or just going to file it away and stay exactly where you are?

But first, we'll start with a clear picture of what typical success and failure behaviors look like across all the *Smartness Factors*. Recognizing these patterns will help you focus on what matters most. That's where we're headed next.

CHAPTER 25

TYPICAL SUCCESS & FAILURE BEHAVIORS FOR EACH SMARTNESS FACTOR

"Success or failure is largely within your control, depending on how you frame situations and choose to act."
~ Ram V. Iyer

By now, you've likely reviewed your *Smartness Assessment* and have a sense of where you excel and where you struggle. The table below breaks down the *Smartness Factors* into two key areas:
1. Typical enabling behaviors that accelerate success
2. Typical disabling behaviors that slow you down or hold you back

These are generalizations across the entire population. The impact of each *Smartness Factor* varies based on your profession, personal strengths, and circumstances. For instance, extreme detail orientation is a critical enabler if you're a NASA engineer designing spacecraft, where precision down to the millimeter can mean the difference between mission success and catastrophic failure. But if you're running a high-volume grocery store, obsessing over the exact alignment of canned goods on the shelves could hurt your business. Use this table to interpret your assessment results within the context of these generalizations:

Table: The Smartness Factors: Enabling & Disabling Behaviors

#	Smartness Factor	Typical Enabling Behaviors	Typical Disabling Behaviors
1	Action Orientation	Takes timely action, moves forward despite uncertainty, executes plans	Procrastinates, overthinks, delays decisions, hesitates to act, or is paralyzed.
2	Detail Focus	Pays attention to important details, ensures accuracy and precision	Gets lost in details, suffers from perfectionism, misses the big picture
3	Need for Variety	Adapts well to new experiences, enjoys learning new skills, stays engaged	Struggles with consistency, gets distracted, lacks sustained focus
4	Risk Tolerance	Takes calculated risks, embraces new opportunities, innovates	Avoids risks by overanalyzing and struggling with uncertainty.

5	Complexity Preference	Handles complex problems, thrives in intellectually demanding situations	Overcomplicates simple issues, struggles with execution, gets stuck in analysis
6	Belief Reinforcement	Stays confident in decisions, applies past learning effectively	Clings to outdated beliefs, resistant to new ideas, ignores feedback
7	Personal Autonomy	Self-driven, takes initiative, independently solves problems	Resists collaboration, struggles with authority, avoids guidance
8	Thinking & Feeling	Balances logic with empathy, makes well-rounded decisions	Overly emotional or overly rational, lacks balance in judgment
9	Emotional Intelligence	Understands and manages emotions well, reads social cues effectively	Lacks self-awareness, struggles with interpersonal interactions
10	Decision Flexibility	Adjusts decisions based on new information, adapts as needed	Stubborn in decisions, slow to change course, inflexible mindset
11	Situational Judgment	Understands context before acting, adapts approach accordingly	Applies one-size-fits-all thinking, misreads situations
12	Self-Competence Views	Has a realistic view of own abilities, continuously improves	Overestimates or underestimates own competence, lacks self-awareness
13	Interpersonal Skills	Builds strong relationships, communicates effectively	Struggles with collaboration, lacks networking abilities
14	Outward Confidence	Projects confidence, earns trust, asserts self effectively	Appears insecure or arrogant, struggles with credibility
15	Self-Reliance	Takes responsibility, solves problems independently	Avoids asking for help, resists teamwork, struggles in crisis
16	Career Flexibility	Adapts to career changes, explores new opportunities	Stuck in outdated career path, fears change, resists upskilling
17	Thinking Range	Can think strategically and tactically, adjusts thinking style as needed	Too narrowly focused or too broad, struggles with adaptability

18	Teamwork	Works well in teams, collaborates effectively	Prefers working alone, struggles with group dynamics
19	Self-Advocacy	Speaks up for self, negotiates well, asserts value	Hesitates to self-promote, always avoids conflict, struggles with visibility
20	Relational Adaptability	Adapts behavior to different people and situations without losing effectiveness.	Uses the same rigid approach in all interactions, struggling to read social cues and adjust.
21	Communication Choices	Chooses the right communication method and tone for the audience and context, leading to clear understanding, stronger relationships, and better outcomes.	s inappropriate communication channels or tone, causing confusion, misunderstandings, damaged relationships, or missed opportunities.

Making Sense of Your Smartness Profile

Now that you've seen the typical enabling and disabling behaviors, the question is: How do your own behaviors compare? We'll address your personal assessment report and how to use it to develop a plan to achieve greater success in Part 5 and in the Playbook at the end of the book.

Being smart and having advantages isn't enough. Success comes from how you use them. Your strengths will take you far, but only if you also address your weaknesses. If you are unhappy with your current level of success, you need to do both.

Reflection*: After seeing the success and failure patterns laid bare, which of your disabling Smartness Factors are you ready to stop rationalizing—and start dismantling—before they drag you down any further?*

PART 4
THE SMARTNESS FACTORS

"Neither strengths nor weaknesses are inherently advantageous or disadvantageous all the time; it depends on the situation and how you, as an individual, use them. That depends on your individual Smartness."
~ Ram V. Iyer

Throughout this book, we've emphasized that success relies on how effectively you choose to apply (or not) your *Smartness* in various situations.

Success depends not just on the advantages you possess, but on how you use your *Smartness*—your mindset, behaviors, and habits—determines their use. Neither advantages nor disadvantages, strengths nor weaknesses, are inherently good or bad all the time; their impact on your greater success depends entirely on how you choose to apply them. Since *Smartness* is a set of capabilities within your control, you can develop and modify them. You can choose to use your *Smartness* in enabling ways to turn your advantages to achieve greater success, or in disabling ways that will hold you back or even cause you to fail.

Through research and analysis of thousands of assessments, we've identified a set of *Smartness Factors* that determine whether your advantages work for or against you. In the *Smartness Development Process*, these factors sit between your Earned Mindset and the *Achievement Cycle*. They are the capabilities you draw on to consistently make good decisions, take action, and sustain success. You apply these *Smartness Factors* through the *Achievement Cycle*—a process that ensures consistent action and real achievement.

You already have some of these factors at different levels of strength. The goal is to develop them deliberately, so they become reliable drivers of achievement.

Three Domains of Smartness Factors

The *Smartness Factors* are grouped into three categories that reflect the key areas where *Smartness* is applied:

1. **Thinking Factors**
   These factors shape how you process information, assess situations, and make decisions.
   They improve your ability to think flexibly, exercise good judgment, and broaden your thinking range.

2. **Action Factors**
   These factors drive how you take action, follow through, and build momentum.
   They include action orientation, risk tolerance, self-competence, and more.

3. **Relational Factors**
   These factors define how you relate to others, build trust, and navigate relationships.
   They enable you to collaborate effectively, manage interpersonal dynamics, and maintain personal autonomy when needed.

Each domain complements the others, and together, they form a comprehensive set of capabilities that make *Smartness* a practical tool for achieving success.

You can use your *Smartness Factors* to:

- Either apply intelligence to drive innovation or let it trap you in overthinking.
- Either leverage wealth to create opportunities or let it dull your ambition.
- Either wield power to influence effectively or become weak and irrelevant.
- Either use credentials to fuel continuous growth or rely on them so much that you stagnate.
- Either make a strong first impression with good looks or fail to back it up with substance and impact.

These factors are the foundation of *Smartness* and are applied through the *Achievement Cycle*.

Each of the next 21 chapters will explore one *Smartness* factor in depth, helping you understand:

- How this factor influences success.
- What enablers and disablers look like in action.
- How to modify your mindset, behaviors, and habits to maximize your success.

Each of the following 21 chapters covers the *Smartness Factors* I've identified so far. They're written to stand alone—so you can read them individually or as a continuum. Many chapters are interconnected, and links are made between them where useful.

As you read—especially the *Smartness Assessment* data sections—pay attention to how these factors differ between successful and unsuccessful people. Don't be fooled by the small differences between these two groups. Remember, success often stems from small differences between the 'winners' and the 'runners-up'. As an analogy, the difference between the winner of a 100-meter running race and the first runner-up is often just thousandths of a second. So, if you're ahead, use that lead—but don't become complacent. If you're slightly behind, remember:

even small improvements can dramatically boost your chances of becoming more successful.

Other Smartness Factors

As we analyze *Smartness Assessment* data and I speak to people, new factors continue to emerge. We will refine and expand these in future assessments. Use these 21 identified factors as your foundation, while staying open to new insights that enhance real-world success. For the latest updates on *Smartness Factors,* please check www.MySmartness.com periodically or join the email list to stay informed.

A Deeper Understanding of Each Smartness Factor

To apply these insights effectively, you must understand how exactly each of the *Smartness Factors* enables or disables your success. It's not enough to know that Action Orientation is a disabler—you must determine whether it stems from haste, procrastination, or overthinking – the details of what aspect of Action Orientation disables you. Likewise, if it's an enabler, pinpointing how exactly it benefits you can help you achieve greater success.

The *Smartness Factor Assessments*—like the Action Orientation Assessment—analyze your mindset, behaviors, and patterns to reveal what's driving or hindering your success. If overthinking is your biggest obstacle, recognizing it allows for targeted improvement.

You can do that for each of the *Smartness Factors*. With these insights, you can make informed choices about what to maintain, modify, or improve and what to leverage or mitigate.

You can take the *Smartness Factor Assessments* at *www.MySmartness.com/ Assessments* to gain clarity on your *Smartness Factors* and achieve greater success.

In the chapters ahead, we'll delve into each of these *Smartness Factors*, exploring how you can harness them to maximize your success and avoid their potential pitfalls. The 21 *Smartness Factors* are classified into three groups – thinking, action and relational, based on what behaviors are predominant. Each of them develops *Smartness* and are applied through the *Achievement Cycle*.

Are you ready to unlock your potential? Let's begin.

THINKING SMARTNESS FACTORS

CHAPTER 26

DETAIL FOCUS

"Don't fear perfection—you'll never reach it. Stop chasing endless details—they'll never be enough. Instead, develop judgment to recognize when something is 'good enough,' and you'll thrive."
~ Ram V. Iyer

Smart people often believe their intelligence shields them from mistakes. But it's often the smallest details that trip them up. Detail Focus—how well they manage the critical elements others overlook—can make or break their success. It's not just about avoiding errors; it's how big ideas actually work.

But there's a catch: many smart people get lost in the weeds. Perfectionism kicks in. They obsess over every minor detail, endlessly refining and reworking, convinced that the tiniest flaw will derail everything. Instead of driving progress, their intelligence traps them in a loop of over-polishing.

Amit, a brilliant engineer, dazzled on paper but failed in execution because he dismissed the small things as "beneath him." Others grind to a halt from over-tweaking, thinking they're protecting quality, when they're really just avoiding the next step.

When smart people neglect Detail Focus, they create avoidable failures. When they master it—knowing when details matter and when they don't—their intelligence becomes unstoppable.

Reflection: *Given what you do professionally, is Detail Focus an asset or a liability? Are you a good judge of when something is good enough?*

Smartness Assessment Data Analysis

In a survey of 1,200+ smart people, Detail Focus was the second most disabling factor. 92% of unsuccessful respondents cited it as a disabler. Even among successful individuals, 71% reported difficulty. Gender differences showed 86% of women struggle with Detail Focus, compared to 81% of men. Women lean toward perfectionism; men tend to overlook details.

The performance gap is stark. Smart people who master Detail Focus deliver higher-quality work, avoid errors, and consistently finish what they start. Those who obsess over details or ignore them stall projects, damage credibility, and miss advancement opportunities. Perfectionism, procrastination, and the inability to "let go" are common traps.

Detail Focus strongly correlates with Thinking Range, Complexity Preference, and Practical Intelligence. Those who balance these use Detail Focus to sharpen execution without losing the big picture. Without that balance, they bury themselves in minutiae or leave gaps that derail execution. Success hinges on knowing which details matter—and when to move forward.

Reflection: How does your Detail Focus affect your willingness to take risk or explore other options? Does it help you succeed, or does it hold you back?

Enabling Aspects of Detail Focus

When used effectively, Detail Focus can significantly enhance success across various fields:

1. Raises quality—essential in medicine, engineering, and law.
2. Improves creativity—by identifying new angles in writing, programming, or design.
3. Strengthens problem-solving—by finding root causes in research, business, and engineering.
4. Prevents costly errors—boosting productivity in medicine, business, and research.

Reflection: How can Detail Focus benefit you in your line of work?

Checklist to Harness Enabling Aspects of Detail Focus

1. Prioritize accuracy where precision drives impact.
2. Use detail skills to improve systems, processes, or products.
3. Uncover hidden problems and develop creative solutions.
4. Create error-checking routines to minimize mistakes.
5. Block distractions to focus deeply on critical tasks.

Disabling Aspects of the Factor

Detail Focus also has significant disabling aspects when taken to extremes (imbalanced):

Too much Detail Focus:

1. Perfectionism delays action under the excuse of "getting it perfect."
2. Smart people obsess over low-impact details.
3. They micromanage and can't delegate, slowing progress.
4. Obsession with precision increases stress and burnout.
5. They lose perspective, impairing decisions and shutting down creativity.

Too little Detail Focus:

1. Critical errors slip through, undermining quality.
2. Rushing leads to sloppy results and lost credibility.
3. Skipping steps causes rework, delays, and mistakes.
4. Speed sacrifices accuracy and erodes trust.

Detail Focus 153

5. Big ideas collapse due to poor execution.

Checklist to Mitigate Disabling Aspects of Detail Focus

To prevent too much Detail Focus:
- Set strict deadlines to avoid endless revisions.
- Prioritize impact and let go of low-leverage details.

To prevent too little Detail Focus:
- Build review points to catch critical errors.
- Break complex work into manageable steps.

To maintain balance:
- Regularly assess whether detail level matches task importance.
- Align Detail Focus with goals—precision should drive progress.

By implementing these approaches, individuals can mitigate the disabling aspects of Detail Focus, balancing their pursuit of excellence with practical efficiency and mental well-being.

Reflection: *How can you adjust your focus on details to ensure that it does not hinder your growth, productivity, and well-being?*

Smartness in Action

Amit was a strategic thinker whose big-picture ideas often lost impact because his work overlooked important details. After a costly mistake on a client project due to a simple error, he realized he needed to balance his focus. By slowing down and double-checking his work, he rebuilt trust and gained a reputation for delivering both insight and accuracy.

In contrast, Lena was meticulous to a fault. She spent so much time perfecting minor details that she regularly missed deadlines, frustrating her team and stalling her projects. When she learned to distinguish between what mattered and what didn't, her efficiency improved—and her ability to execute on time made her a more effective leader.

Mastering Detail Focus enables smart people to balance precision with efficiency, ensuring critical specifics are addressed without getting trapped in minutiae. Over time, this sharpens their ability to deliver consistently high-quality work, reinforcing trust and credibility. In the *Achievement Cycle*, Detail Focus builds the foundation for reliable performance—essential for sustaining long-term success.

> *"Smartness is knowing when precision drives progress—and when perfection just gets in the way."*

Smart people tend to often overinvest in precision, obsessing over details that delay progress or exhaust others. Their sharp eye for accuracy becomes a trap when they lose sight of the bigger picture. To become more successful, smart people should ask "Is this detail mission-critical?", pause before perfecting, and seek external feedback to know when to stop refining. They need to prioritize what moves the needle, not what merely satisfies their high standards.

Engaging with detail is essential, but it's only part of the equation. The next *Smartness Factor*—Complexity Preference—shows how smart people expand their thinking to manage complexity, without losing focus or getting overwhelmed.

For Deeper Insights

How does this factor show up in your life? Do your mindset, behaviors, and habits reflect a strength or a hurdle? Take the **Detail Focus Assessment** (*www.MySmartness.com/Assessments*) to identify your behavioral tendencies—whether you are a *Detail Perfectionist, Balanced Detail-Oriented Achiever, Big Picture Thinker,* or an *Overly Generalist.*

Reflection: *When it comes to details, are you burying yourself in perfection—or skipping the basics and blowing the execution? What's one shift you can make to keep Detail Focus from getting in your way?*

CHAPTER 27

COMPLEXITY PREFERENCE

"The ability to simplify means to eliminate the unnecessary so that the necessary may speak."
~ Hans Hofmann

Complexity Preference reflects how well smart people navigate complicated ideas, situations, or environments—and how effectively they manage multiple variables without oversimplifying or shutting down.

Some prefer simplicity: clarity, structure, and linear paths. Others thrive in ambiguity, loving puzzles and shifting dynamics. Neither is inherently better. But today's success often requires engaging with complexity—not avoiding it.

Many smart people love complexity. It's often their way of proving they're the smartest in the room. But too often, Complexity Preference becomes a trap—where they overcomplicate problems, pile on nuance, and make simple solutions harder than they need to be. Instead of driving results, they stall in elaborate models, endless analysis, and intellectual posturing.

Consider Mateo, a strategist who built intricate frameworks for every project. His ideas dazzled—until nothing got finished. The work collapsed under its own weight, and his team burned out. Complexity Preference is a double-edged sword: it fuels insight when used well, but crushes progress when unchecked. Mastering it means knowing when depth adds value—and when simplicity is the smarter move.

Reflection: *Where in your work or life are you adding unnecessary complexity to prove your intelligence—when a simpler path would deliver better results?*

Smartness Assessment Data Analysis

Complexity Preference marks a major dividing line between successful and unsuccessful smart people. In the *Smartness Assessment*, 81% of less successful participants identified it as a disabler, compared to 71% of successful ones. This 10% gap is one of the widest across all *Smartness Factors*.

Many smart people misuse Complexity Preference by adding unnecessary layers to prove their intelligence rather than drive results. The outcome? Confusion, delays, and team frustration.

Those who apply this factor well excel at solving complex problems and navigating ambiguity—crucial for career growth and leadership. Those who misuse it create complicated processes that stall execution and overwhelm everyone involved.

Correlation analysis shows strong positive relationships between Complexity Preference and Decision Flexibility, Practical Intelligence, Personal Autonomy, and Career Flexibility. These synergies enable smart people to manage ambiguity, make thoughtful decisions, and apply complex thinking in ways that drive momentum—not stall it. When applied well, this combination helps them solve sophisticated problems and generate deep insights that others miss. But when complexity is mismanaged, smart people either overcomplicate or oversimplify—limiting their impact and missing key opportunities for growth.

Reflection: Have you ever over-complicated a task or decision? What was the impact?

Enabling & Disabling Aspects of Complexity Preference

Enabling Aspects:
When applied well, Complexity Preference empowers smart people to excel where others get overwhelmed. It helps them:

1. Spot patterns and connections others miss—especially in fast-moving or high-pressure situations.
2. Work confidently in ambiguity, making sense of incomplete or uncertain information.
3. Generate breakthrough ideas by exploring multiple angles of a problem.
4. Solve problems with nuance, balancing short-term demands with long-term impact.

Smart people who channel Complexity Preference effectively can see the forest and the trees—navigating chaos with clarity and precision.

Reflection: When you face a complex challenge, do you lean in—or get bogged down?

Checklist to Harness the Positive Aspects

1. Identify when complexity adds real value—and when it's just noise.
2. Break down complicated problems into clear, actionable steps.
3. Regularly step back to check if your solution is becoming harder than the problem.
4. Limit the number of variables you manage at once to maintain clarity.
5. Test ideas quickly to avoid getting stuck in endless planning.

Disabling Aspects of Complexity Preference

When Complexity Preference becomes imbalanced:

Too much Complexity Preference:

1. Overthinking leads to overengineering—turning clear solutions into convoluted frameworks.
2. Smart people get lost in analysis, delaying decisions or exhausting their teams.
3. They complicate processes to feel in control, even when simplicity would serve better.
4. They lose sight of the goal, prioritizing intellectual satisfaction over real results.
5. Overcomplication drains energy, making everything feel harder than it needs to be.

Too little Complexity Preference:

1. Smart people oversimplify problems, missing key variables that lead to failure.
2. They rely on surface-level analysis when deeper understanding is needed.
3. They dismiss nuance, which leads to rigid thinking and poor adaptation.
4. Avoiding complexity becomes a habit, weakening their ability to lead in uncertain or evolving environments.
5. Simplistic thinking breaks down in complex systems—creating avoidable risks and strategic missteps.

Reflection: *Do you tend to overcomplicate problems—or avoid complexity altogether? What does it cost you?*

Checklist to Mitigate the Disabling Aspects

To reduce overcomplication:

1. Force clarity—summarize your solution in three sentences. If you can't, it's not clear.
2. Set deadlines to prevent endless tweaking or overthinking.
3. Use constraints intentionally—to simplify choices and focus decisions.

To prevent oversimplification:

4. Ask: What variables am I ignoring that might matter later?
5. Slow down when things seem too easy—check for hidden layers.

To stay balanced:

1. Match the level of complexity to the actual needs of the problem—not your workload, stress level, or environment.
2. Step back periodically to assess whether your approach is driving clarity and results, not just speed or intellectual showmanship.

Smartness in Action

Rina was known for building elegant, layered solutions—until her team burned out from the constant complexity. She thought complexity showed depth, but it slowed them down. Once she started simplifying just enough to act, her team gained momentum and performance improved.

In contrast, Jordan oversimplified every challenge. He skimmed over important data, missed key dependencies, and delivered quick fixes that didn't hold. After several setbacks, he learned to pause and consider variables he was ignoring. His work became more thoughtful—and more trusted.

Smart people don't need to choose between complexity and clarity. When they strike the right balance, they move fast and think deep. Complexity Preference becomes a tool—not a trap.

Smartness is seeing what others don't—without making it harder than it needs to be.

> *"Smartness is knowing when complexity adds value—and when simplicity is the smarter move."*

Smart people tend to love layered thinking and intricate models. But complexity often becomes intellectual comfort food—an excuse to delay action. To become more successful, smart people should break big problems into parts, use plain language to explain ideas, and ask others, "Is this making sense?" If not, simplify. Clarity isn't dumbing it down—it's sharpening the insight.

For Deeper Insights

How does your Complexity Preference influence your problem-solving, decision-making, and career success? Do your mindset, behaviors, and habits reflect a strength or a hurdle? Take the Complexity Preference Assessment (*www.MySmartness.com/Assessments*) to identify your behavioral tendencies—whether you are a *Depth Seeker, Overcomplicator, Simplifier,* or *Balancer.* Get insights on what's driving your success, what's getting in your way, and how you could become more successful.

Reflection: Be honest—are you building complexity to impress others, avoid action, or feel in control? Or are you oversimplifying because you're afraid to face what the real problem demands? What truth are you avoiding under the guise of being "smart"?

CHAPTER 28

DECISION FLEXIBILITY

"A tree that is unbending is easily broken."
~ Tao Te Ching

Decision Flexibility is the ability to shift your thinking, update your conclusions, and change direction when new evidence or circumstances demand it. It's essential in real-life situations, especially in fast-changing or high-stakes environments.

Smart people often assume their intelligence guarantees good decisions. But in complex situations, rigid thinking becomes a trap. Decision Flexibility is the *Smartness Factor* that allows smart people to shift gears, adapt their choices, and reconsider their assumptions—without feeling like they're compromising who they are. It separates those who keep moving forward from those who stall, even when they know better.

In a Bengaluru tech firm, Sanjay made a bold strategy call early in a new product development project. As new data came in, his team flagged risks—but Sanjay refused to change course. He feared looking weak or wrong. The project faltered, and the client moved on. Months later, Sanjay admitted, "My smartest decision would've been to change my decision."

For many smart individuals, the drive to maintain consistency—rooted in intelligence, status, or societal expectations—can become a liability. Holding on to past choices to protect their reputation or validate their intelligence often blocks better options from emerging.

As the African proverb says, *"You cannot change the wind, but you can adjust the sails,"* underscoring the power of adaptability. Being flexible doesn't mean being indecisive. It means making informed decisions—and then adjusting them as new information emerges. Smart people with strong Decision Flexibility avoid the trap of clinging to a plan that no longer works. Instead, they reassess, reframe, and re-engage.

Reflection: When you've made decisions in the past, how often have you changed course when new facts emerged? Was that easy or hard for you?

Smartness Assessment Data Analysis

Decision Flexibility emerged as a top enabler for successful smart people. In the *Smartness Assessment*, 82% of highly successful participants identified Decision Flexibility as a key enabler. Among less successful participants, only 41% identified it as a strength.

That means smart people who struggle often get stuck not because they lack intelligence, but because they're unwilling to shift direction once they've made a decision. They over-identify with being "right," and fear that changing their mind will make them seem inconsistent, weak, or indecisive.

The gap between the two groups is one of the strongest in the data. Smart people who succeed tend to treat decisions as working hypotheses—not final answers. That mindset helps them adapt faster, correct course earlier, and seize emerging opportunities that others miss.

The correlation analysis shows that Decision Flexibility has strong positive relationships with Practical Intelligence, Complexity Preference, Situational Judgment, and Career Flexibility. Smart people who excel at these interconnected factors tend to update their views, learn from feedback, and stay open to better options. Rigid decision-makers, by contrast, get stuck defending old choices—even when the world has moved on.

Enabling Aspects of Decision Flexibility

Smart people who apply Decision Flexibility effectively:

1. Adapt quickly to changing circumstances, recognizing when a situation demands a shift.
2. Incorporate new data into their thinking without ego getting in the way.
3. Make iterative decisions, treating early choices as pilots, not permanent.
4. Remain open to input from others and use diverse perspectives to refine their thinking.
5. Let go of sunk costs and pivot when the evidence supports it—even if it means admitting they were wrong.

Reflection: When has flexible thinking helped you seize a better opportunity or avoid a costly mistake?

Checklist to Harness Enabling Aspects of Decision Flexibility

1. Treat early decisions as hypotheses that can be refined.
2. Ask: What new data would cause me to change course?
3. Use decision journals to track why you chose a path—and when to reassess.
4. Build psychological safety into your team so that changes aren't seen as failures.
5. Praise updates and pivots as signs of intelligence, not inconsistency.

Disabling Aspects of Decision Flexibility

Too little flexibility:

1. Smart people double down on bad decisions to avoid looking inconsistent.
2. They ignore new evidence, fearing it undermines their prior judgment.

Decision Flexibility 161

3. They miss emerging opportunities because they're too committed to old plans.
4. Their teams suffer because changing direction feels forbidden or shameful.
5. They lose trust, not because they changed course, but because they refused to.

Too much flexibility:

1. Smart people over-value on new inputs and constantly shift strategies.
2. They struggle to commit—second-guessing themselves into inaction.
3. Their decisions lack conviction, confusing peers and teams.
4. They chase every new trend, never building mastery.
5. They appear unmoored—smart but unreliable.

Checklist to Mitigate Disabling Aspects of Decision Flexibility

To avoid rigidity:

1. Reframe course changes as learning, not failure.
2. Use "presumed valid until proven otherwise" for decisions—not dogma.

To avoid over-flexibility:

3. Commit to minimum timeframes before reassessing.
4. Limit major changes to those backed by significant data or stakeholder input.

To stay balanced:

5. Track your major decisions—and how often you revise them.

Reflection: *Do you pride yourself on consistency? Could that be stopping you from adjusting when it matters most?*

Smartness in Action

Nathan, a rising leader in a healthcare tech company, was known for his rapid execution. But he had a blind spot: once he made a decision, he rarely revisited it. After a product launch flopped due to unmet user needs, he learned to incorporate more feedback loops and checkpoints. That shift helped his team build better solutions and hit bigger milestones.

On the flip side, Tanya, a brilliant analyst, changed her mind constantly—chasing new ideas before finishing the last. Her brilliance was undeniable, but her peers stopped trusting her judgment. When she learned to anchor her decisions for a set period, her credibility grew—and so did her influence.

Smart people who master Decision Flexibility remain grounded in purpose, open to new data, and unafraid to course-correct. In the *Achievement Cycle*, Decision Flexibility sustains momentum without derailing progress. *Smartness* isn't being rigid—it's knowing when to hold firm and when to shift.

> *"Smartness is knowing when to stick with what works—and when to pivot fast before it stops working."*

Smart people tend to stick with their first decision—believing consistency is strength. But conditions change. To become more successful, smart people should test decisions over time, ask others what's changed since the original call, and give themselves permission to pivot without guilt. Strength lies in adjusting—not in sticking for the sake of it.

For Deeper Insights

True success stems from balancing the stability of predictability with the growth potential of adaptability. Do your mindset, behaviors, and habits reflect a strength or a hurdle? Take the *Decision Flexibility Assessment* to identify your behavioral tendencies—whether you are an *Agile Strategist, a Steady Optimizer, a Routine Navigator,* or a *Stubborn Mule* at www.MySmartness.com/Assessments. Get insights on what's driving your success, what's getting in your way, and how you could become more successful.

Reflection: *Are you sticking to familiar decision patterns because they've worked before—or constantly switching strategies to dodge the unknown? When was the last time your need for certainty held you back from something bigger?*

CHAPTER 29

Thinking & Feeling

"The heart has its reasons, which reason knows not."
~ Blaise Pascal, French Mathematician and Philosopher

Thinking & Feeling is the *Smartness Factor* that enables smart people to integrate logic and emotion when making decisions, solving problems, and relating to others. Smart people who develop this factor are able to combine analytical thinking with emotional awareness to improve judgment, communication, and influence. Without it, they risk becoming either cold and disconnected or overly emotional and unclear.

In a busy Los Angeles emergency room, Demetri, a highly skilled doctor, faced a challenge that had nothing to do with medicine. His diagnosis was complete, but he struggled to communicate with the anxious patient and their family. His words were factual, precise, and technically correct—but cold. The patient became agitated and so did his family. They didn't just hear what he said—they felt dismissed. Another doctor, Ana, less experienced but warm and empathetic, stepped in, calmed the patient, and delivered the same information in a way that was well-received. Demetri's intelligence was undeniable, but his inability to connect emotionally made him less effective in that moment.

For smart people, the ability to balance Thinking & Feeling isn't optional—it's essential. This chapter explores how combining the two enhances decision-making, strengthens relationships, and fuels creativity—while preventing disablers like miscommunication or indecision.

Reflection: Do you tend to lean more towards logical reasoning like Demetri or balance logic with Emotional Intelligence like Ana? How can you adjust your approach to achieve greater success in your profession?

Smartness Assessment Data Analysis

In the *Smartness Assessment* of 1200+ participants, 52% reported difficulty balancing logic and emotion in decision-making. The gender gap is notable: 58% of men struggle with integrating emotional input compared to 46% of women. This data suggests a tendency among smart men to default to logic, sometimes at the expense of relational awareness, while women tend to integrate emotional cues more consistently—though challenges exist across both groups.

The performance gap is significant. Smart people who successfully balance Thinking & Feeling report stronger career progression and more effective leadership outcomes. They make decisions that blend rigorous analysis with emotional intelligence, enhancing both judgment and influence. Those who rely solely on logic often miss key emotional and relational signals, weakening their ability to lead, collaborate, and adapt under pressure. Conversely, over-reliance on feelings can lead to impulsive, inconsistent decisions that erode credibility.

Correlation analysis reveals high positive relationships between Thinking & Feeling and Emotional Intelligence, Interpersonal Skills, Situational Judgment, and Belief Reinforcement. Smart people who excel in these interconnected areas navigate complex situations with both clarity and connection, improving their ability to make nuanced decisions and sustain productive relationships. Mastering this balance is a key differentiator in achieving consistent, high-level performance.

Enabling Aspects of Thinking & Feeling

1. Strengthens decision-making by integrating logic with emotional awareness.
2. Enhances leadership by balancing analytical judgment with empathy.
3. Improves communication by reading emotional cues and responding appropriately.
4. Increases adaptability through a better understanding of both rational and emotional dynamics.
5. Builds trust and influence by aligning clear thinking with genuine connection.

Checklist to Harness Positive Aspects of Thinking & Feeling:

1. Practice active listening to grasp both logical content and emotional context.
2. Reflect regularly on decisions, considering rational analysis and emotional impact.
3. Engage in activities blending logic and creativity, like problem-solving and art.
4. Build Emotional Intelligence through mindfulness, empathy exercises, and feedback.
5. Apply logic-based theories to understand and manage emotions, like identifying triggers.

Reflection: *Can you recall a situation where balancing logical thinking and emotional insight led to a successful outcome? How did this balance contribute to your success?*

Disabling Aspects of Thinking & Feeling

While balancing Thinking & Feeling offers benefits, an imbalance can create challenges.

Thinking & Feeling

Too much Thinking:

1. Decision Paralysis: Over-analysis or intense emotions can lead to inaction, causing missed opportunities—common among highly driven individuals.
2. Miscommunication: Imbalance may make logical individuals seem detached or emotional ones appear irrational, straining relationships.
3. Creativity Block: Over-reliance on logic stifles creativity as it lacks emotional spark.
4. Poor Stress Management: Logical thinkers risk burnout by ignoring emotions.

Too much Feeling:

1. Impulsive Decisions – Acting without analysis (thinking).
2. Inconsistency – Emotion-driven swings.
3. Escalated Conflicts – Reacting emotionally without control.
4. Hindered Growth – Lacking self-awareness and clarity.

Checklist to Mitigate Negative Aspects of Thinking & Feeling:

To prevent too much Thinking:

1. Pause and check emotional signals before deciding.
2. Invite empathetic feedback to balance logic.

To prevent too much Feeling:

3. Slow down decisions with structured analysis.
4. Review facts objectively before acting.
5. Use a 'cool-off' window before high-stakes decisions.

To maintain balance:

6. Practice mindfulness to stay present with both logic and emotion.
7. When making decisions, consciously balance logical analysis with your gut feelings to avoid over-reliance on either.
8. Incorporate stress management techniques, such as mindfulness and structured problem-solving, that address both your emotional and logical needs.
9. Actively seek feedback and perspectives from others who may have different thinking and emotional styles to ensure a more balanced approach.

Smartness in Action

Max was a senior consultant at a firm known for pushing high performers hard. He wasn't the most technically gifted analyst, but he mastered one essential habit: when priorities shifted, he adapted quickly. Max could sense when a project needed more speed, when the client was confused, or when leadership needed a quick turnaround—and he delivered. He wasn't rigid about sticking to his original plan. He adapted without drama, stayed action-oriented, and showed up where it counted. Within two years, he was promoted twice and trusted with the firm's most volatile clients.

Dana, on the other hand, was brilliant—and stuck. Her slide decks were flawless. Her analysis was airtight. But she resisted changing course, even when it was obvious the situation had changed. She clung to her original plan and worked late into the night refining it, long after the project's scope had shifted. When her ideas were challenged, she doubled down. When things went sideways, she blamed unclear expectations. She wasn't wrong—she just wasn't adapting. Her results lagged, her reputation faded, and her once-bright future dimmed. Max applied Smartness and succeeded while Dana did not.

Smart people tend to trust logic above all and often overlook emotional signals. This can lead to sound reasoning but emotionally disconnected outcomes. To become more successful, smart people should check how others feel before deciding, pause to name their own emotions, and explore how facts and feelings can co-exist in their process. Emotion, when acknowledged, sharpens—not weakens—thinking.

For Deeper Insights

The Thinking & Feeling Assessment helps you identify your behavioral tendencies—find out if you are a *Logical Strategist, a Considered Decision-Maker, an Emotional Thinker,* or an *Instinctual Decision-Maker.* Get insights on what's driving your success, what's getting in your way, and how you could become more successful. You can take the *Thinking & Feeling Assessment* at: *www.MySmartness.com/Assessments.*

Balancing Thinking & Feeling empowers smart people to integrate emotional intelligence with analytical rigor, making better decisions that consider both data and human dynamics. Over time, this balance enhances their leadership and influence, strengthening relationships and decision quality. In the *Achievement Cycle,* mastering Thinking & Feeling creates well-rounded judgment that drives success in both technical and relational arenas.

> *"Smartness is knowing when logic leads best—and when empathy is the key that opens the door."*

Balancing Thinking & Feeling strengthens decision quality and relationships. But smart people also need to adapt their approach based on context. The next *Smartness Fact*or—Situational Judgment—shows how they read the moment and adjust their decisions and actions to fit the situation.

Reflection: Are you using logic as armor to avoid emotional messiness—or letting feelings run the show when clear thinking is what's needed? What would it take for you to make decisions that are both sharp and human?

CHAPTER 30

SITUATIONAL JUDGMENT

"Intelligence and knowledge without the smarts to use them are like a load of books on the back of an ass."
Japanese Proverb

Situational Judgment is the ability to read a situation accurately and adapt your behavior to fit the context, enabling smarter decisions and better outcomes.

It's what turns knowledge into action when the rules aren't clear. It helps smart people adapt in fast-changing environments, solve problems in real time, and avoid blindly applying old solutions to new situations. Without it, intelligence stalls in rigid thinking, poor choices, and missed opportunities.

In a Palo Alto coffee shop on University Avenue, Alan, a startup founder, faced a dilemma his advanced education hadn't prepared him for. His grandmother's voice echoed: "Books teach you a lot about the world, but the streets teach you about living." Despite his intelligence, Alan struggled to navigate the unpredictable realities of running a business. He had book smarts—but lacked street smarts.

In contrast, Akila, an entrepreneur, combined formal education with hands-on learning in the hustle and bustle of her hometown, Chennai. She read people well, spotted opportunities others missed, and adapted quickly. Her success didn't come from being the smartest in the room—it came from reading the room well.

Many smart people assume their intellect, credentials, or some other advantage will guarantee success. Yet Situational Judgment—often referred to as 'street smarts'—could be a real differentiator. It determines how well someone applies their intelligence in fluid, real-world scenarios. Without it, even the smartest individuals struggle, making poor decisions, missing opportunities, and failing to adapt.

Reflection: *Reflect on a time when you faced a real-world challenge that your formal education, power, position, or wealth hadn't prepared you for. How did you navigate that situation, and what role did Situational Judgment play in your approach?*

Smartness Assessment Data Analysis

In the *Smartness Assessment* of 1,200+ participants, Situational Judgment ranked as the third most significant differentiator between successful and struggling smart people. 65% of less successful individuals reported it as a disabler, compared to 51% of successful ones—a sharp 14% gap.

The performance gap on this factor is clear. Smart people who master Situational Judgment are better able to navigate complex, ambiguous situations with agility and accuracy. They apply their intelligence in practical, real-world contexts, making informed decisions that fit the moment. Those who struggle often misapply their knowledge, relying too heavily on theoretical understanding or rigid frameworks. This leads to poor decisions, missed opportunities, and an inability to adapt as circumstances shift.

Correlation analysis shows that Situational Judgment has strong positive relationships with Career Flexibility, Decision Flexibility, Interpersonal Skills, and Emotional Intelligence. Smart people who excel in these areas combine sharp situational reading with the flexibility to adjust, the social awareness to influence, and the emotional intelligence to build trust. However, there's a risk of over-reliance on situational factors—those who lean too heavily on experience may dismiss new information that contradicts prior knowledge, limiting their adaptability over time. The best performers balance consistency with flexibility, using Situational Judgment to make timely, effective decisions.

Reflection: *Have you ever summarily dismissed new information because it contradicted your experience? What was the impact?*

Enabling Aspects of Situational Judgment

When harnessed effectively, Situational Judgment can greatly contribute to one's success. Key enabling aspects include:

1. Resourcefulness: Maximizing limited resources and finding creative solutions.
2. Adaptability: Quickly adjusting to new environments and challenges.
3. Decision-Making: Applying knowledge pragmatically to assess options and make sound choices.
4. Social Awareness: Navigating relationships effectively and building strong networks.
5. Resilience: Handling setbacks, learning from failures, and staying composed under pressure.
6. Leadership: Inspiring teams, making informed decisions, and adjusting to change.

Reflection: *How can you leverage Situational Judgment to drive greater success in your career?*

Checklist to Harness Enabling Aspects of Situational Judgment:

1. Seek real-world challenges that force adaptive thinking.
2. Apply theory actively—don't just analyze, experiment.
3. Sharpen social radar by asking how others experience you.
4. Build resilience through failure reflection, not avoidance.
5. Lead in ambiguous projects to build judgment under pressure.

Situational Judgment

Reflection: Can you recall a situation where your Situational Judgment helped you solve a problem or achieve a goal? How did it make a difference in the outcome?

Disabling Aspects of Situational Judgment

When Situational Judgment becomes imbalanced:

Too much Situational Judgment:

1. Overanalyzing every situation, delaying decisions.
2. Adjusting constantly to please others, losing direction.
3. Second-guessing effective strategies.
4. Avoiding action by obsessing over nuance.

Too little Situational Judgment:

1. Applying the same approach to every problem.
2. Missing cues that signal change is needed.
3. Relying on rigid rules, even when they don't fit.
4. Acting without reading the situation—creating avoidable errors.

Checklist to Mitigate Disabling Aspects of Situational Judgment

If You Tend to Overdo It:

- Set decision deadlines to limit endless analysis.
- Anchor your behavior in strategy—don't chase every shift.
- Avoid second-guessing effective patterns just to stay flexible.

If You Tend to Underdo It:

- Pause and assess context before taking action.
- Read the room—pay attention to nonverbal cues and dynamics.
- Avoid autopilot—challenge your default approaches regularly.

To Maintain Balance:

- Ask for feedback on how well you adapt to the moment.
- Track when your adjustments improved—or hurt—outcomes.

Reflection: Reflect on a time when you over-relied on your experience and made a bad decision. What could you have done differently?

Smartness in Action

David excelled in structured settings but stumbled in ambiguity. He clung to routines even as circumstances shifted. After a failed project, he learned to "read the room," adapt his tone, and time his decisions better. As his situational awareness grew, so did his leadership credibility.

Leila, on the other hand, flexed constantly to fit every new scenario. But without consistent principles, her team got confused. Once she clarified her core values and made selective, strategic adaptations, she became a steady, trusted decision-maker.

Mastering Situational Judgment is about knowing when to adapt—and when to stand firm. It's how smart people move confidently in uncertainty, and how they earn trust without losing clarity.

Smart people tend to rely on logic or past models—but context evolves. What worked before may now miss the moment. To become more successful, smart people should observe social cues, seek input from those closest to the situation, and test smaller decisions before making large moves. The best answer is not always the most logical one—it's the one that fits the context.

Reading situations accurately helps smart people make better decisions in the moment. But without expanding their Thinking Range, they risk limiting themselves to familiar patterns and narrow perspectives. The next *Smartness Factor*—Thinking Range—shows how they broaden their thinking to explore more possibilities and generate better solutions.

> *"Smartness is knowing when to adapt to the moment—and when to anchor yourself in principle."*

For Deeper Insights

The Situational Judgment Assessment helps you identify your behavioral tendencies—find out if you are a *Situational Expert, Situationally Competent, Uncertain Evaluator,* or an *Oblivious Reactionary.* Get insights on what's driving your success, what's getting in your way, and how you could become more successful. You can take the *Thinking & Feeling Assessment* at: *www.MySmartness.com/Assessments.*

Reflection: Are you blindly trusting your instincts and experience—or constantly shifting your decisions to fit every moment? When's the last time your gut reaction or over-adjustment cost you clarity, credibility, or results?

CHAPTER 31

Thinking Range

"Smart people don't fall short because they lack intelligence, but rather because they fail to intelligently expand their thinking."
~ Ram V. Iyer

Thinking Range is the ability to think broadly, shift perspectives, and explore alternatives, allowing smart people to move beyond familiar patterns and generate better decisions.

Many highly intelligent people get stuck running the same mental playbook, applying old solutions to new problems until they hit a wall. Thinking Range is what separates those who adapt from those who stall. It helps smart people widen their lens, ask better questions, and consider different strategies. Without it, they risk tunnel vision, missed insights, and poor problem-solving.

In the fast-paced world of money management, Maya, a seasoned financial advisor, prided herself on quickly labeling investments as either safe or risky. But her black-and-white thinking led her to dismiss a fast-growing opportunity in an emerging market. Her colleague, Doru, took a broader view. He considered multiple angles, weighed risk and reward, and presented a conditional investment plan. His clients made strong gains—while Maya had to explain why they missed out.

This kind of real-world contrast underscores why Thinking Range matters. Narrow thinkers default to either/or choices. Wide thinkers explore the spectrum. It is especially valuable in complex decision-making roles, where oversimplification can hinder success. This chapter explores how expansive thinking drives growth and why limited thinking can hold it back.

Reflection: Think about a recent decision you made. Did you consider a range of options, or did you only consider the two extreme options? How could a broader thinking range have improved your decision and its outcome?

Smartness Assessment Data Analysis

In our *Smartness Assessment* data, Thinking Range showed up as the fifth largest differentiator between more and less successful smart people, with a 12% gap. Only 28% of unsuccessful respondents identified it as a disabler—meaning most didn't even realize it was limiting them. Men struggled with this factor more than women by 5%.

Smart people who excel here demonstrate cognitive flexibility. They shift between strategic, creative, analytical, and tactical modes as the moment requires.

Those who struggle often recycle the same solutions and ignore possibilities outside their mental habits.

Correlation analysis shows strong positive relationships between Thinking Range and Outward Confidence, Teamwork, and Self-Competence Views. But when overextended, it correlates negatively with Detail Focus, Need for Variety, and Action Orientation. Smart people who overextend their Thinking Range risk becoming scattered, neglecting important details, or delaying decisions in pursuit of too many ideas—and stall progress. Achieving balance is critical—broad thinking must be paired with focus and disciplined execution to translate ideas into results.

Enabling Aspects of a Broad Thinking Range

A broad Thinking Range empowers individuals to handle complexity, innovate, and make informed decisions. They can:

1. Shift perspectives easily to view problems from multiple angles.
2. Connect diverse ideas to generate innovative solutions.
3. Balance exploration and focus, knowing when to broaden and when to narrow.
4. Adapt thinking styles depending on the situation's complexity.
5. Challenge assumptions to uncover overlooked options.

Checklist to Harness the Benefits of a Broad Thinking Range:

1. Diversify information sources—look outside your field.
2. Engage in cross-disciplinary learning to expand thinking modes.
3. Reframe problems to challenge your assumptions.
4. Encourage idea generation before narrowing your focus.
5. Experiment and reflect—test multiple options, then refine.

Reflection: Can you recall a situation where your broad Thinking Range helped you to achieve a goal? What factors contributed to this outcome?

Disabling Aspects of Not Having a Broad Thinking Range

Thinking range can have two extreme disabling aspects to it:

Too much Thinking Range:

1. Overcomplicating simple decisions by considering too many options.
2. Getting lost in endless idea generation without moving to execution.
3. Struggling to prioritize or commit, or jumping between unrelated concepts.
4. Confusing others by constantly shifting direction or focus.

Too little Thinking Range:

1. Applying the same solutions to every problem, regardless of context.
2. Dismissing unfamiliar ideas without proper consideration.
3. Relying on rigid thinking even when situations change.
4. Overcommitting to one path without exploring alternatives.

Checklist to Mitigate Disabling Aspects

To prevent too much Thinking Range:

1. Set clear criteria to limit options and streamline decisions.
2. Define boundaries for exploration and stick to them.

To prevent too little Thinking Range:

3. Actively seek out opposing viewpoints before deciding.
4. Regularly expose yourself to unfamiliar fields and ideas.
5. Ask yourself, *"What else could work?"* before committing.

To maintain balance:

6. Timebox your idea generation before acting.
7. Review past decisions to check if narrow thinking limited better options.

Thinking Range is essential—but it must be balanced. *Smartness* means finding the right balance: knowing when to think broadly—or narrowly—and always aligning thinking with your objectives.

Reflection: *Recall a situation where your narrow Thinking Range hindered you from achieving a goal. How could a broader Thinking Range have changed the outcome?*

Smartness in Action

Fatima was known for her analytical sharpness, but she hit a ceiling when leadership demanded creativity and big-picture thinking. By pushing herself to explore divergent ideas and engage in strategic planning, she became a more adaptable leader with broader impact. Raj, on the other hand, was brimming with creative energy—but lacked the ability to drill down into details or apply rigorous analysis. His ideas were exciting but often impractical, and they fizzled before results materialized. When he learned to anchor his vision in structure and clear analysis, his projects finally gained traction—and began delivering measurable results that elevated his credibility and career momentum.

> *"Smartness is knowing when to expand your frame—and when to commit to what matters."*

Developing a broad Thinking Range gives smart people the flexibility to shift between strategic, tactical, creative, and analytical modes—based on what the situation demands. This versatility enables them to solve complex problems, lead diverse initiatives, tackle uncertainty, and connect insight to action across multiple domains.

Smart people tend to default to their favorite thinking style, applying it everywhere. But different problems require different tools. To become more successful, smart people should practice using opposite approaches (creative vs analytical), experiment with new frames, and evaluate which style fits the problem—not their preference.

But without strong Belief Reinforcement, that same flexibility can result in distractions or indecision. The next *Smartness Factor*—Belief Reinforcement—shows how smart people can stay grounded in conviction while staying open to new insights.

For Deeper Insights

How does this factor show up in your life? Do your mindset, behaviors, and habits reflect a strength or a hurdle? Take the Thinking Range Assessment (*www.MySmartness.com/Assessments*) to identify your behavioral tendencies—whether you are a *Wide-Frame Explorer, Focused Expert, Idea Weaver,* or *Linear Executo*r. Get insights on what's driving your success, what's getting in your way, and how you could become more successful.

Reflection: *Are you recycling the same tired solutions—or spinning in circles with too many ideas and no action? What shift in your thinking range would actually move you forward instead of keeping you stuck?*

CHAPTER 32

BELIEF REINFORCEMENT

Some smart people mistake intelligence for being right, believing their ideas are correct just because they're smart.

Belief Reinforcement is the ability to solidify and sustain conviction in the face of uncertainty, pressure, or challenge—without becoming rigid or closed off to learning.

It gives smart people the strength to stand by well-reasoned views, resist social pressure, and maintain clarity when facing complexity. Without it, intelligence often collapses into over-analysis, self-doubt, or reactive thinking.

As the ancient Indian proverb says, "The eyes do not see what the mind does not believe." This captures the heart of Belief Reinforcement, where people favor information that supports their existing views while ignoring what differs. This can quietly become a serious problem—especially for smart people, who may do it better (!)—because they can build compelling arguments for what they already believe. Over time, flexible thinking hardens into rigid certainty. But Belief Reinforcement isn't just a risk—it can also be a strength. When applied well, it helps smart people stay focused, make confident decisions, and lead others with clarity.

Beliefs shape how we interpret the world and drive our actions. They can create powerful momentum, but when left unchecked, they narrow options, block innovation, and trap smart people in patterns that limit success. Belief Reinforcement can be both a powerful advantage and a hidden obstacle. This chapter shows how to keep it working for you—without letting it take over.

Shivani, a young urban planner, had a bold vision for revitalizing a struggling neighborhood with green space, housing, and community hubs. Her data was solid, her plan carefully vetted—but senior leaders kept pushing her to water it down. At first, she caved. But the compromises made the project worse, not better. After nearly quitting, she doubled down on what she believed in—and began winning allies by explaining not just her plan, but the purpose behind it. Eventually, her vision became a city pilot.

In contrast, Donald had a history of digging in hard on his views. He prided himself on sticking to his guns, but often refused to revise his thinking—even when evidence proved him wrong. He wasn't grounded in conviction; he was trapped by his ego. Many smart people hold strong beliefs about how the world works. Those who understand how to use Belief Reinforcement to their advantage behave like Shivani while those who don't risk ending up like Donald.

This chapter explores how Belief Reinforcement can either drive your success or undermine it—and how to make it work in your favor.

Reflection: *Where have your strongest beliefs helped you succeed—and where might they be quietly steering you off course?*

Smartness Assessment Data Analysis

In the *Smartness Assessment* of 1,200+ smart people, Belief Reinforcement emerged as a barrier for 50% of participants who considered themselves less successful. This challenge showed up in two key forms: holding too tightly to outdated beliefs, or lacking confidence and wavering under pressure. Gender differences were minimal—men showed slightly higher resistance to updating beliefs, while women were slightly more prone to second-guessing themselves.

The performance gap driven by Belief Reinforcement is substantial. Smart people who master this factor demonstrate strong commitment to their guiding principles, enabling them to make confident decisions, stay focused on long-term objectives, and inspire others with clarity of purpose. In contrast, those who misuse Belief Reinforcement become rigid, ignoring contradictory evidence and resisting necessary change. On the other extreme, those with weak Belief Reinforcement abandon productive strategies too quickly, becoming indecisive and reactive.

Correlation analysis shows exceptionally strong positive relationships between Belief Reinforcement and Career Flexibility, Decision Flexibility, Interpersonal Skills, Emotional Intelligence, and Practical Intelligence. These synergies help smart people to maintain conviction while staying adaptable and socially attuned. Moderate positive correlations with Personal Autonomy, Complexity Preference, Outward Confidence, Thinking Range, Teamwork, Need for Variety, and Detail Focus indicate that effective Belief Reinforcement works best when it's grounded in independent thought, balanced perspectives, and collaboration. When well-managed, Belief Reinforcement creates stability in uncertainty. When misapplied, it traps smart people in outdated patterns that limit their growth and success.

Enabling Aspect of Belief Reinforcement

When applied well, Belief Reinforcement can be a powerful enabler. It gives smart people:

1. Clarity of conviction that builds confidence and focus.
2. The ability to inspire others by leading with purpose and clarity.
3. Resilient self-trust under pressure.
4. Capacity to act without full certainty.
5. Courage to take unpopular stands.
6. Resistance to groupthink.
7. Stability during uncertainty—keeping themselves and others grounded.

8. Protection of mental energy—by filtering noise and staying committed to what works.

Checklist to Harness Enabling Aspects

1. Define your core beliefs and revisit them regularly.
2. Test your ideas under pressure to build durable conviction.
3. Build feedback loops that sharpen confidence, not weaken it.
4. Clarify the why behind your decisions.
5. Practice confident humility—own your stance while staying open.

Reflection: Think of a recent decision you made with complete confidence—how much of that confidence came from evidence, and how much came from reinforcing what you already believed?

Disabling Aspects of Belief Reinforcement

When Belief Reinforcement becomes imbalanced:

With too much Belief Reinforcement:

1. Ignoring evidence that contradicts your existing views.
2. Becoming overconfident and resistant to feedback.
3. Dismissing new ideas before fully considering them.
4. Defending outdated strategies long after they've stopped working.

With too little Belief Reinforcement:

1. Constantly second-guessing yourself and your decisions.
2. Abandoning useful ideas too quickly under pressure.
3. Struggling to maintain focus without clear guiding beliefs.
4. Being easily swayed by others' opinions, even when they lack merit.

Checklist to Mitigate the Disabling Aspects of Belief Reinforcement

If you tend to overdo it:

- Pause when challenged—ask if pride is in the driver's seat.
- Look for disconfirming evidence before defending your stance.
- Invite trusted critics to poke holes in your logic.

If You Tend to Underdo It:

- Revisit past wins—what made you trust your thinking then?
- Define red lines—what will you stand for even under pressure?
- Role-play resistance to prepare for pushback.

To Maintain Balance:

- Distinguish conviction from rigidity.
- Build a conviction checklist—facts, reasoning, purpose.

Reflection: Are you open to being wrong—or just afraid to be?

Smartness in Action

Liam had great instincts but often lacked follow-through. He changed direction or folded too quickly when he faced pushback. When he started reinforcing his beliefs—revisiting his purpose and focusing on his long-term vision—he became more resilient, building habits of confident persistence. His credibility grew, and so did his results.

Conversely, Yara was so locked into her beliefs that she ignored valid feedback and warning signs. Her rigidity hurt collaboration and caused major delays. Once she re-examined her convictions, using fresh data and active listening, her leadership shifted—from intimidating to inspiring, and started delivering better outcomes.

Belief Reinforcement enables smart people to stay committed to their long-term goals, especially when faced with setbacks or ambiguity. Over time, this internal alignment strengthens their resilience and keeps them focused on high-impact outcomes. In the *Achievement Cycle*, mastering Belief Reinforcement sustains motivation and persistence, which are critical for long-term success. However, Belief Reinforcement must be strongly tied to another *Smartness Factor*, Action Orientation, in order to turn their beliefs into consistent action, driving real-world results. We'll discuss that factor in the next chapter.

> *"Smartness is knowing when to hold firm to your beliefs—and when to let new evidence reshape them."*

Smart people tend to cling to their beliefs, especially when those beliefs are tied to identity or reputation. New evidence gets filtered or dismissed. To become more successful, smart people should actively seek contrary data, revisit their assumptions regularly, and ask themselves: "Would I still believe this if I didn't invent it?" Updating beliefs is not a loss of self—it's the evolution of self.

Reflection: When was the last time you either clung too tightly to a belief—or gave up on one too quickly—and what were the consequences?

For Deeper Insights

How does this factor show up in your life? Do your mindset, behaviors, and habits reflect a strength or a hurdle? Take the *Belief Reinforcement Assessment* (www.MySmartness.com/Assessments) to identify your behavioral tendencies—whether you are a *Confident Driver, Open-Minded Evaluator, Stubborn Defender,* or *Cautious Doubter*. Get insights on what's driving your success, what's getting in your way, and how you could become more successful.

Reflection: Are your beliefs fueling momentum—or quietly blinding you or breaking your focus? When's the last time you doubled down when you should've adapted—or bailed when you should've held the line?

ACTION SMARTNESS FACTORS

CHAPTER 33

ACTION ORIENTATION

"Many smart people don't stall from lack of ideas; they stall because they overthink—and don't act."
~ Ram V. Iyer

It's not intelligence that holds smart people back—it's when they act too late, too fast, or not at all. Action Orientation is what turns intelligence into results. Without it, smart people get stuck refining theories and overanalyzing details—living in their heads—and waiting for perfect conditions (I know, I've been there many times!). The smarter you are, the easier it becomes to convince yourself that thinking is progress, that more analysis will solve the problem, and that waiting "just a little longer" will give you the clarity you need. But all of that thinking leads nowhere without action. Action breeds confidence and courage; inaction only makes your doubts and fears grow. If you want to conquer fear, do not just think about acting—act!

Consider Ravi, who consistently moves projects forward, even when the path isn't clear. His bias for action helps him build momentum, learn from mistakes, and seize opportunities. Contrast that with Aihan, who delays decisions while searching for the perfect plan. Weeks pass. Then months. While Ravi's results build on themselves, Aihan's hesitations leave her stuck, watching opportunities pass by and wondering why others keep pulling ahead.

This is how smart people quietly sabotage themselves. They lean on their intelligence, their expertise, or their influence, believing those advantages alone will carry them forward.

Many smart people hesitate to act because they assume knowing and understanding something is the same as executing on it. This mindset creates a dangerous blind spot—where thinking replaces doing. That because they're intelligent, they'll know what to do when the time comes. But the truth is, most success does not come from brilliance—but from bold, consistent follow-through. But none of that matters without Action Orientation. Success doesn't come from ideas. It comes from doing something with them. This chapter will show you how to stop overthinking, start moving, and make sure your intelligence actually creates results

Reflection: *Do you often regret not acting, even when you knew what to do? What held you back?*

Action Orientation

Smartness Assessment Data Analysis

In a survey of 1200+ smart people, Action Orientation emerged as the single most common barrier to greater success. A staggering 96% of participants who described themselves as less successful identified Action Orientation as a challenge. Half of them considered it a major obstacle, while another 45% cited it as a moderate one. This overwhelming figure highlights a pervasive issue among highly intelligent people—the knowing-doing gap—knowing what to do but failing to take effective action.

The performance gap here is dramatic. Smart people who master Action Orientation transform ideas into execution, take timely action, and sustain momentum even when conditions aren't perfect. Those who struggle with Action Orientation get stuck in overthinking, excessive planning, and hesitation. They delay decisions, miss opportunities, and often watch others move ahead while they remain stalled by their own analysis paralysis.

Correlation analysis underscores Action Orientation's critical role in achievement. It shows strong positive correlations with Practical Intelligence, Career Flexibility, Risk Tolerance, and Decision Flexibility. These factors collectively enable smart people to act decisively, pivot when necessary, and take calculated risks rather than remaining trapped in endless deliberation. However, low Action Orientation often coincides with difficulties in Teamwork, Thinking Range, and Outward Confidence—making it harder for smart people to collaborate, adapt, and demonstrate leadership. Strengthening Action Orientation is the essential first step to turning intelligence into results and overcoming the inertia that holds so many smart people back.

Enabling Aspect of a Strong Action Orientation

When smart people apply Action Orientation effectively, they:

1. Quickly move ideas into execution without waiting for perfect conditions.
2. Build momentum through consistent action, allowing progress to compound.
3. Learn by doing, using feedback from real-world results to refine their approach.
4. Balance risk with forward movement, knowing that overplanning can become its own risk.
5. Stay focused on outcomes, ensuring that tasks and decisions align with meaningful goals.

Checklist to Harness Enabling Aspects

To strengthen your Action Orientation:

1. Set short deadlines to force movement, even when you're not fully ready.
2. Break large projects into small, immediate actions to create momentum.

3. Prioritize progress over perfection, accepting that mistakes are part of the process.
4. Review daily what you've executed, not just what you've thought about.
5. Align actions to outcomes, ensuring every step directly supports a result you want.

By leveraging a strong Action Orientation, you can significantly enhance your ability to navigate challenges, achieve goals, lead others, and turn your aspirations into achievements.

Reflection: *Where has taking quick, decisive action created success for you—and how can you apply that same approach to what you're working on now?*

Disabling Aspects of Action Orientation

When Action Orientation becomes imbalanced:

Too much Action Orientation:

1. Rushing into decisions, leading to superficial solutions that overlook root problems.
2. Burning out from constant activity without rest or reflection.
3. Becoming inflexible, sticking to quick decisions even when new information suggests a better path.
4. Straining relationships by pushing ahead without considering others' input, sometimes coming across as dismissive or condescending.

Too little Action Orientation:

1. Overanalyzing every option, causing delays that kill momentum.
2. Waiting endlessly for perfect conditions, which rarely arrive.
3. Focusing on planning and preparation while avoiding actual execution.
4. Missing opportunities because of hesitation and fear of making the wrong move.

Highly intelligent people often fall into the trap of overthinking, assuming that more analysis will eventually create the perfect answer. But clarity comes from action, not endless reflection.

Reflection: *Where has overthinking kept you stuck—and what small action could you take right now to move forward?*

Checklist to Mitigate Disabling Aspects

To prevent too much Action Orientation:

1. Pause to evaluate potential consequences before making decisions to avoid impulsiveness.
2. Incorporate regular breaks and reflection to prevent burnout and keep your actions intentional.

To prevent too little Action Orientation:
3. Set clear deadlines to push yourself out of overthinking and into action.
4. Focus on progress over perfection to keep moving forward, even if conditions aren't ideal.

To maintain balance:
5. Actively seek input from others to avoid blind spots and strengthen relationships.
6. Regularly review results to adjust your approach, making sure your actions are creating real impact.

Both the enabling and disabling powers of Action Orientation underscore the importance of exercising good personal judgment when choosing to act. Act as appropriate and achieve greater success.

Reflection: *When have you pushed ahead too quickly—or waited too long—and how did either extreme affect your results? Which one or two checklist items could you regularly practice to mitigate the disablers?*

Smartness in Action

Emily had sharp insights and deep expertise but often hesitated to act, waiting for the perfect plan. Opportunities passed her by as she overanalyzed her options. When she committed to taking action sooner—accepting that adjustments could be made along the way—she gained momentum and delivered real results, building a reputation for getting things done.

On the other side, Marc acted too quickly without thinking through consequences. His impulsiveness led to rushed decisions and costly mistakes. Once he learned to pause just long enough to evaluate key risks, his actions became more targeted and effective. His team gained confidence in his leadership, knowing he could act decisively without unnecessary risk.

Developing Action Orientation ensures that smart people consistently translate insight into decisive action. Over time, this habit of execution builds momentum and drives tangible progress toward their goals. In the *Achievement Cycle*, strong Action Orientation bridges the gap between potential and achievement, accelerating results through consistent follow-through.

Smart people tend to plan more than they act - or act so fast they lose sight of their strategy. To become more successful, smart people should set action deadlines, test small ideas quickly, and evaluate outcomes—not just intentions. Intelligence plus action builds momentum. Start sooner. Reflect smarter. Act faster.

Consistent action drives progress, but smart people also need the right level of Risk Tolerance to navigate uncertainty. The next *Smartness Factor*—Risk Tolerance—shows how they balance bold moves with thoughtful risk management to achieve greater success.

> *"Smartness is knowing when to pause and think—and when to move before the moment passes."*

For Deeper Insights

How does this factor show up in your life? Do your mindset, behaviors, and habits reflect a strength or a hurdle? Take the Action Orientation Assessment (*www.MySmartness.com/Assessments*) to identify your behavioral tendencies—whether you are a *Decisive Doer*, *Thoughtful Planner*, *Hesitant Analyzer*, or *Deer in the Headlights*. Get insights on what's driving your success, what's getting in your way, and how you could become more successful.

Reflection: *Are you still convincing yourself that thinking is progress—or finally ready to take effective action before the moment passes? What's one thing you know you should've done by now—but didn't?*

CHAPTER 34

RISK TOLERANCE

"The greatest risk is taking no risk at all, but the worst is risking everything recklessly. The wisest approach lies in taking calculated risks."
~ Ram V. Iyer

Risk Tolerance is the ability to take bold but informed action despite uncertainty, balancing courage with caution to create opportunity without courting disaster.

Many smart people don't fall short because they lack opportunities—they fall short because they avoid the risks that could unlock them. In the Chinese language, the word for challenge, '危机' (wēijī), combines 'danger' (危) and 'opportunity' (机), suggesting that every crisis holds both risk and the potential for advantage. This concept captures the dual nature of challenges.

What happens when the fear of failing outweighs the possibility of succeeding? For some smart people, risk doesn't just mean possible loss—they may hesitate because they don't want to look bad, make the wrong call, or risk damaging their reputation. When you're expected to be right, stepping into uncertain territory can feel like too much to gamble. So instead of moving forward, you wait. You play it safe. You protect what you have—while others take the chances that lead to something more.

Consider Jordi, who weighed the downside and launched a new product line, knowing the risks. It wasn't guaranteed, but he acted—and it paid off. Now contrast that with Maya, who turned down a high-profile opportunity because the uncertainty made her uncomfortable. Years later, she's still in the same role, wondering if that was her shot—and if she missed it by playing it too safe.

Of course, not every smart person hesitates. Some jump too fast, underestimating the dangers. Some others push too hard, assuming boldness always wins. But for some smart people, the challenge is balancing the fear of failure with the need for growth. Risk Tolerance isn't about taking every chance—it's about knowing which ones matter and acting decisively.

Risk Tolerance doesn't operate alone. In the *Achievement Cycle*, it works alongside Emotional Intelligence and Situational Judgment to help you evaluate risks thoughtfully and stay resilient when outcomes are uncertain. This chapter will help you find that balance, so you don't let hesitation hold you back from what's next.

Reflection: *When was the last time you played it safe—and what might have happened if you'd taken the risk?*

Smartness Assessment Data Analysis

In the *Smartness Assessment* of 1200+ smart people, Risk Tolerance emerged as a major barrier to success. Among less successful respondents, 87% cited Risk Tolerance as a disabler, with 7% calling it a severe obstacle. This means that 80% of unsuccessful individuals experience hesitation that results in inaction or ineffective action. Gender differences were minor, though women showed slightly higher risk aversion than men. While both groups face challenges, smart people often allow the fear of loss to outweigh the potential for gain—waiting instead of seizing high-potential opportunities.

The performance gap driven by Risk Tolerance is critical. Smart people who manage this factor well are able to make calculated decisions under uncertainty, leading to breakthrough innovations and growth opportunities. Those who struggle with Risk Tolerance frequently avoid high-stakes situations, overanalyze potential downsides, or delay decisions until opportunities pass them by. On the flip side, those who have too much Risk Tolerance can make reckless decisions that undermine credibility and waste resources.

Correlation analysis shows strong links between Risk Tolerance and Outward Confidence, Career Flexibility, and Action Orientation. These connections indicate that when smart people balance risk with confidence and adaptability, they are better equipped to navigate uncertainty and seize opportunities. Without these balancing factors, low Risk Tolerance limits Thinking Range and hinders collaboration—particularly in environments where uncertainty is unavoidable. Managing risk wisely turns hesitation into momentum—and recklessness into resilience.

> *"For smart people, the fear of losing is much worse than the excitement of winning."*

Enabling Aspects of Risk Tolerance

When smart people manage Risk Tolerance effectively, they:

1. Pursue opportunities others avoid, gaining an edge.
2. Adapt quickly in uncertain environments.
3. Balance boldness with caution, maximizing upside and minimizing loss.
4. Decide with confidence under pressure.
5. Stretch outside their comfort zones, sparking growth.

Checklist to Harness Enabling Aspects of Risk Tolerance

1. Identify calculated risks that align with your goals.
2. Review past wins that came from bold moves.
3. Set boundaries for acceptable risk—and act inside them.
4. Surround yourself with challengers and advisors.
5. Take smaller risks to build toward bigger ones.

6. View failure as data.
7. Ground your risks in real trends and data.
8. Practice antifragility—use every outcome to get stronger, whether you succeed or fail.

Reflection: *Recall a time when taking a calculated risk paid off. What factors contributed to your success?*

Disabling Aspects of Risk Tolerance

When **Risk Tolerance** becomes imbalanced:

Too much Risk Tolerance:

1. Acting before understanding consequences.
2. Taking risky bets to prove confidence.
3. Ignoring red flags.
4. Wasting resources on long-shot ideas.

Too little Risk Tolerance:

5. Avoiding opportunities out of fear of failure or looking bad.
6. Overanalyzing every risk until momentum is lost.
7. Settling for safe, familiar options that limit growth.
8. Deflecting responsibility—Avoiding ownership of hard decisions.

Checklist to Mitigate Disabling Aspects

To reduce excessive risk-taking:

1. Pause to assess potential downsides before making major decisions.
2. Ask trusted advisors for input.

To reduce risk avoidance:

3. Identify what you're avoiding and try to understand why.
4. Set decision deadlines to push yourself beyond hesitation and into action.

To stay balanced:

5. Regularly review both your wins and misses to spot risk patterns.
6. Define your personal risk threshold.

Reflection: *Where are you playing it too safe—and what's one calculated risk you're ready to take to push your success forward?*

Smartness in Action

Ravi avoided risky projects, missing high-impact opportunities. When he started evaluating risks more strategically and making thoughtful bets, his career surged. He led breakthrough initiatives and became known as a high-impact leader. Leena, on the other hand, was overly bold. She rushed into decisions and suffered costly failures. Once she began balancing her gut instincts with analysis, her projects became more successful, and her reputation as a bold *and* responsible leader grew.

Smart people tend to avoid risk unless success seems certain—or they take wild chances to prove boldness. Both extremes limit long-term gains. To become more successful, smart people should define acceptable risk thresholds, commit to small risks with high learning potential, and review the outcomes of previous bold decisions. Risk becomes smart when it's intentional—not reactive.

Mastering Risk Tolerance allows smart people to make calculated bets that lead to breakthrough opportunities. Over time, this comfort with risk-taking sharpens their ability to innovate and lead change. In the *Achievement Cycle*, healthy Risk Tolerance enables smart people to seize high-reward opportunities while managing downside exposure.

Comfort with risk is crucial, but smart people also need an accurate view of their own competence to make sound decisions and recover from setbacks. The next *Smartness Factor*—Self-Competence Views—shows how they balance confidence with self-awareness to sustain growth and success.

> *"Smartness is knowing when to bet big—and when to protect what really matters."*

For Deeper Insights

How does this factor show up in your life? Do your mindset, behaviors, and habits reflect a strength or a hurdle? Take the Risk Tolerance Assessment (*www.MySmartness.com/Assessments*) to identify your behavioral tendencies—whether you are a *Strategic Risk-Taker*, *Cautious Optimizer*, *Risk-Averse Avoider*, or *Reckless Gambler*. Get insights on what's driving your success, what's getting in your way, and how you could become more successful.

Reflection: *Are you playing it so safe you're passing on real opportunities—or acting too fast and sabotaging your own progress? What's one bold but calculated risk you've been avoiding that could change everything?*

CHAPTER 35

SELF-COMPETENCE VIEWS

"Believing you can is the first step to doing. Doubting yourself is the first step to hesitation or inaction."
~ Ram V. Iyer

Self-Competence Views reflect how accurately and confidently smart people assess their own ability to succeed—neither inflating nor minimizing their potential. Many doubt themselves despite repeated wins. Others assume they're always right because of intelligence or past successes. Their intelligence and track record may suggest they should succeed—but their self-competence may tell a different story.

These distorted judgments affect more than confidence—they shape decisions, actions, and outcomes. Self-Competence Views act as a hidden filter through which opportunities are evaluated. When misaligned with reality, progress stalls. At its core, this factor is about the Earned Mindset—a grounded belief in one's capability, developed through achievement, shaped by honest feedback, and strengthened through deliberate action.

Mastering this factor means seeing yourself clearly—knowing what you can do, where you're strong, and where you need to grow. Too much doubt leads to hesitation. Too much certainty breeds complacency. The goal is calibrated confidence—earned through effort and good judgment, not assumed just through intellect or past successes.

Christian had the credentials, a strong track record, and was promoted to a high-visibility position. But privately, he wondered if he could really perform at that level. His doubts led to hesitation, and within months, he was demoted to his old role. By contrast, Marianna had similar doubts—but she pushed through and reminded herself of past successes. She prepared deliberately and gave herself permission to learn on the job. Today, she leads a global team and is considered a fast-tracker.

> *"Many smart people don't fall short because they lack ability—they fall short because they misjudge their competence or fail to leverage their own competence."*

Reflection: *Reflect on a time when self-doubt affected your performance. How did it impact the outcome, and what steps could you have taken to build more positive views of your personal competence?*

Smartness Assessment Data Analysis

In the *Smartness Assessment* of 1200+ participants, Self-Competence Views ranked among the top five disablers. Among those who considered themselves less successful, 41% reported struggling with their Self-Competence views—13% more than those who described themselves as successful. Additionally, women were 7% more likely than men to doubt their own competence, highlighting an important demographic trend that impacts confidence and decision-making.

The performance gap on this factor is profound. Smart people with strong, realistic Self-Competence Views are more likely to take on high-stakes projects, lead effectively, and recover from setbacks with resilience. In contrast, those who misjudge their abilities—whether through chronic self-doubt or inflated confidence—either hold themselves back unnecessarily or make unforced errors by overestimating their capability. Both extremes erode trust, stall personal growth, and limit leadership potential.

Correlation analysis shows high positive relationships between Self-Competence Views and Outward Confidence, Belief Reinforcement, Teamwork, Thinking Range, and Thinking & Feeling. Smart people who maintain accurate Self-Competence Views are not only confident in their abilities but also more adaptable, collaborative, and insightful in complex situations. However, weak Self-Competence Views undermine these strengths, creating ripple effects that diminish both personal and team performance. An earned, realistic sense of competence acts as a stabilizing force—bridging the gap between intelligence and achievement.

> *"Self-confidence is essential for success. If you think you can't, you won't. If you think you can, you might."*

Reflection: *Where do you tend to misjudge yourself—by doubting your abilities or by assuming you're always right? How has that shaped your success?*

Enabling Aspects of Accurate Self-Competence Views

Smart people who maintain a realistic view of their own competence know what they can do—and what they can't. This clarity drives better decisions, stronger execution, and consistent results.

1. Assess themselves honestly and regularly.
2. Trust their ability to figure things out—even in uncertainty.
3. Bounce back from failure, using it as fuel for growth.
4. Seek and apply feedback without defensiveness.
5. Lead when ready, and grow into stretch roles.

Reflection: *How well do you understand your real strengths? What's one skill you should trust yourself to use more?*

Self-Competence Views   191

Checklist to Harness Accurate Self-Competence Views:
1. Audit your strengths and gaps.
2. Take on challenges that reveal your true ability.
3. Ask trusted peers for candid feedback.
4. Track your results—do they match your self-view?
5. Step up when you're ready; step back when you're not.

Reflection: *When has an accurate view of your capabilities helped you succeed?*

Disabling Aspects of Inaccurate Self-Competence Views

When your self-perception is off—too high or too low—it distorts your decisions.

When you overestimate your competence:
1. You overlook limitations and take reckless risks.
2. You ignore feedback and dismiss red flags.
3. Risky decisions based on inflated self-belief.
4. You misjudge the complexity of challenges.

When you underestimate your competence:
1. You hesitate, doubt, and miss key opportunities.
2. You rely too much on others for reassurance.
3. You struggle to recognize your real strengths.

Checklist to Mitigate Inaccurate Self-Competence Views:

To prevent overestimating your competence:
1. Ask for feedback before making high-stakes decisions.
2. Ground your decisions in real data.

To prevent underestimating your competence:
3. Track successes to build evidence of your abilities.
4. Take on challenges—even small ones—that prove your abilities (to yourself).

To maintain balance:
5. Regularly review both wins and mistakes to maintain perspective.
6. Compare your self-view with actual outcomes.

Reflection: *Where are you misjudging your capabilities—and how's it affecting your growth?*

Smartness in Action

Sophia had deep expertise but doubted her ability to lead complex projects. She often hesitated to volunteer for high-stakes roles, believing she wasn't ready.

After receiving feedback and reflecting on her skills, she redefined her view of competence—understanding that readiness comes from action, not waiting for perfection. She began stepping up, took on bigger challenges, and her success reinforced her growing confidence. Hugo, by contrast, assumed he was always the smartest in the room. He dismissed feedback and overpromised. His projects underdelivered—resulting in failed projects and negative feedback. He reframed his self-view. He started seeking input and preparing more thoroughly, resulting in improved performance.

Smartness means seeing yourself clearly—neither smaller nor larger than you are—and taking action from that place of clarity.

Smart people tend to may quietly doubt themselves—or assume past wins guarantee future success. Either way, they misread their current capability. To become more successful, smart people should compare self-assessments to real-world results, ask trusted peers for reality checks, and track growth with objective markers. Real confidence is calibrated—not just declared.

Mastering Self-Competence Views helps smart people take ownership of their growth without getting stuck in self-doubt or blinded by ego. In the *Achievement Cycle*, this factor supports confident action, real-time learning, and continuous improvement.

But seeing yourself clearly isn't enough. Others need to see it, too. The next *Smartness Factor*—Outward Confidence—shows how to project competence authentically, build credibility and earn trust.

| *"Smartness is knowing what you're good at—and what still needs work."*

For Deeper Insights

How does this factor show up in your life? Do your mindset, behaviors, and habits reflect a strength or a hurdle? Take the Self-Competence Views Assessment (*www.MySmartness.com/Assessments*) to identify your behavioral tendencies—whether you are a *Balanced Believer*, *Underconfident Doubter*, *Overconfident Booster*, or *Cautious Improver*. Get insights on what's driving your success, what's getting in your way, and how you could become more successful.

Reflection: *Are you quietly playing small because you underestimate your abilities—or stumbling into setbacks because you think you're better than you are? What would change if you saw yourself exactly as you are—no more, no less?*

CHAPTER 36

Outward Confidence

"When you believe in yourself, others are more likely to believe in you. When you don't, they rarely will."
~ Ram V. Iyer

Outward Confidence is the ability to project credible self-belief—without slipping into arrogance or insecurity. It's how smart people earn trust, inspire action, and get taken seriously.

Many smart people know they're capable—but others can't see it. Why? Because they fail to project the confidence that inspires belief. Outward Confidence isn't about faking it or bragging—it's about showing up in a way that signals credibility.

When smart people under-project, their ideas get overlooked. When they over-project, they come across as arrogant. The key is balanced visibility: projecting belief in your abilities without tipping into arrogance.

Satya, a respected business leader, was known for his calm presence and steady confidence. People trusted his judgment and followed his lead. Jessica, a brilliant Ivy League lawyer, often let confidence blur into arrogance. Her dismissive tone and tendency to talk over colleagues created tension. Despite her intellect, people quietly avoided working with her—as she was viewed as pompous and difficult to work with.

Confidence isn't just what you project—it's also how others perceive. You can try tactics—like striking power poses or dressing the part—but if others don't actually perceive confidence, it won't land. Outward Confidence is what makes competence visible. And when smart people learn to project it well, doors open.

This chapter explores the dual nature of Outward Confidence, showing how it can be a powerful strength when handled well or a stumbling block when it tips into arrogance. By recognizing this difference, you can maximize confidence's positive impact while avoiding its potential downsides.

Reflection: How does your Outward Confidence influence the way others perceive and interact with you? Are there moments when you might come across as arrogant?

Smartness Assessment Data Analysis

In the *Smartness Assessment*, Outward Confidence was reported as an enabler by 65% of successful respondents and 60% of those who were less successful. This suggests that most smart people display a high degree of outward confidence—and that it isn't a major differentiator between high and low performers.

However, it was cited as a disabler by 35–40% of both groups. While only 4% said it severely disabled them, roughly 30% experience moderate misfires with this factor. These are often easier to address than deep-seated blockers.

Gender differences were minimal: men were slightly more likely to come across as overconfident, while women were somewhat more likely to underplay their strengths.

Outward Confidence showed strong positive correlations with Interpersonal Skills, Teamwork, Self-Competence Views, and Thinking Range—suggesting that smart performers use it to enhance collaboration and influence. However, unchecked confidence negatively correlates with Action Orientation and Need for Variety. This implies that some overconfident individuals may avoid action or dismiss diverse perspectives.

Balancing confidence with humility allows smart people to unlock the upsides of this factor—without shutting others out.

Reflection: Do people like and respect you, or do they see you as being arrogant? What behaviors are causing people to see you that way?

Enabling Aspects of Healthy Outward Confidence

Outward Confidence can be a powerful asset when it's grounded in credibility and self-awareness. Here's how smart people can use it to their advantage:

1. Project authority and credibility, making others more likely to trust and follow.
2. Present ideas clearly and convincingly, increasing influence in decisions.
3. Stay composed under pressure, even in high-stakes situations.
4. Step into visible roles, raising their professional profile.
5. Assert needs and boundaries, avoiding burnout or invisibility.
6. Radiate capable, grounded presence, opening doors to new opportunities.

Checklist to Harness Outward Confidence:

7. Evaluate whether your confidence reflects real skills and experience.
8. Practice presenting ideas with clarity and conviction.
9. Ask for feedback on how your confidence is perceived.
10. Take on visible roles that stretch and showcase your leadership.
11. Balance assertiveness with humility to avoid coming across as dismissive.

Reflection: Who is the most strikingly confident person you know, and how could emulating that person's Outward Confidence enable your success?

Disabling Aspects of Overconfidence

Outward Confidence becomes a liability when smart people lose balance, either becoming overconfident or underconfident.

When Outward Confidence Becomes Excessive

1. You speak and act with too much certainty—even when unsure.
2. You dismiss feedback or constantly interrupt others.
3. You tend to dominate discussions and push your ideas without paying attention to the resistance.
4. You often inflate your accomplishments.
5. You rely on credentials, affiliations, or status to inflate your importance.
6. You undermine collaboration by insisting on having the final say.
7. You tend to overpromise and underdeliver.
8. You alienate peers and leaders who see you as arrogant or self-absorbed.

When Outward Confidence Is Too Low

1. You hesitate to speak up—even when you have something valuable to contribute.
2. You downplay your successes, reinforcing doubts about your value.
3. You defer decisions to others—even when you may be the most qualified.
4. You come across as uncertain or fade into the background.
5. You allow more assertive voices to overshadow your contributions.
6. You avoid leadership or visible roles, fearing you'll be exposed as unqualified (impostor syndrome).
7. You miss opportunities because you hesitate to step forward.

In either extreme, smart people lose the ability to convert intelligence into influence. Arrogance drives people away, while insecurity keeps them unseen.

Checklist to Mitigate Disabling Aspects of Factor

To prevent excessive Outward Confidence:

1. Seek honest feedback to stay grounded and avoid overestimating your abilities.
2. Ask for feedback on how your confidence comes across.
3. Pause before interrupting or pushing your ideas.
4. Monitor conversations to ensure you are inviting input, not dominating the room.

To prevent insufficient Outward Confidence:

5. Step into small leadership roles to build visible presence and reinforce your capabilities.
6. Remind yourself of past achievements to counter self-doubt and hesitation.
7. Track your wins and remind yourself of real value.
8. Practice presenting with presence and authority.

To maintain balance:

9. Regularly assess whether your confidence aligns with real outcomes and feedback from others.
10. Pair assertiveness with humility to strengthen relationships and sustain long-term influence.
11. Lead with curiosity—not just conviction.

Reflection: *When has either arrogance or insecurity in your outward confidence hurt your success, and what can you do to correct it?*

> *History is more likely to remember your faults and failings than your virtues and successes.*

That's why Outward Confidence matters. It amplifies your strengths before others can misinterpret your silence—or your swagger. Sustained success depends projecting confidence that is real, grounded, and inviting to others.

Smartness in Action:

Victor had a solid track record but kept getting overlooked for bigger opportunities. After getting feedback, he realized he rarely voiced ideas with conviction or took the lead in meetings. He worked on projecting his thinking more confidently—without changing the content, just the tone and presence. Within a year, he was promoted to lead a major initiative. Monica, by contrast, was brilliant but often let others dominate the room. Her colleagues respected her insights—but she rarely spoke up. Even when she had better ideas, her hesitation made others doubt her readiness. Eventually, she missed a key leadership role simply because people couldn't imagine letting her lead.

Outward Confidence is how your capability becomes visible to others. When you show up with grounded belief, people believe in your competence and reliability., and that could open new doors. Mastering Outward Confidence helps smart people project credibility without tipping into ego. Arrogance can isolate you from valuable allies; hesitation could cause you to be overlooked. In both cases, your potential remains untapped because others struggle to connect with you.

Smart people tend to present a confident front—but it can sometimes come off as rigid, guarded, or dismissive. To become more successful, smart people should check their tone and body language for signs of openness, admit when they don't know, and accept visibility as part of leadership. Confidence isn't projection—it's presence.

In the *Achievement Cycle*, it builds trust, creates visibility, and opens doors. But projecting confidence isn't enough on its own. Smart people also need to take responsibility for what they deliver. The next *Smartness Factor*—Self-Reliance—explores how to take full ownership of outcomes, even under pressure.

> *"Smartness is knowing when to project strength—and when to show you're grounded in reality, not ego."*

Reflection: *When have you relied on your intelligence to 'prove' yourself, and how might balancing that with others' ideas and engagement have changed the outcome?*

For Deeper Insights

How does Outward Confidence show up in your life? Do your mindset, behaviors, and habits reflect healthy confidence or something that holds you back? Take the Outward Confidence Assessment (*www.MySmartness.com/Assessments*) to identify your behavioral tendencies—whether you are *Magnetically Confident, Mostly Confident, Unsteady in Your Confidence,* or *Living in the Shadows*. Get insights on what's driving your success, what's getting in your way, and how you could become more successful.

Reflection: *Do you lead with real confidence—or are you just faking it? How often are you projecting strength to gain respect... but overbearingly pushing people away without realizing it? What would change if your confidence invited people in instead of keeping them at a distance?*

CHAPTER 37

SELF-RELIANCE

"The smartest people know when to do it alone—and when doing it alone is the dumbest thing they can do."
~ Ram V. Iyer

Self-Reliance is the ability to act independently and take full ownership of outcomes—while knowing when to involve others to achieve better results.

Many smart people pride themselves on being independent. They get things done without hand-holding—and often prefer to work alone. For some, Self-Reliance feels like the most reliable strategy. When you consider yourself the smartest or most capable person in the room, why wouldn't you handle everything yourself? And many do! But how far can that really take you?

When taken too far, Self-Reliance turns into isolation. Smart people become islands unto themselves. Those who don't ask for help—or who try to carry everything—limit their impact. Silent struggle and rejected input lead to missed insights and weaker results. Even solo practitioners can't afford to rely only on themselves—being the only employee doesn't mean going it alone. At what point does independence stop being strength—and start becoming self-sabotage?

Christine consistently delivered high-quality work and expected others to do the same. But she rarely asked for input and pushed through obstacles solo—even when stuck. Over time, her team disengaged. Steve, on the other hand, knew when to seek support. He stayed accountable but brought others in when needed. His team got stronger—and so did his outcomes. Self-Reliance matters, but lasting success depends on knowing when to lean on others. No achievement happens alone.

This chapter explores how Self-Reliance helps and hurts—and how smart people manage it to thrive within the systems they depend on.

Reflection: *When has relying only on yourself limited your success, and what might change if you involved others more often?*

Smartness Assessment Data Analysis

The *Smartness Assessment* data shows that Self-Reliance was the biggest differentiator between successful and unsuccessful respondents – by a whopping 19%. 63% of the unsuccessful respondents were disabled by this factor whereas only 44% of the successful ones were. It is a severe disabler for only 8% of the respondents, indicating that for many unsuccessful people, it affects them to varying degrees – more fixable than for the ones who are acutely disabled by it.

The primary issue wasn't a lack of ability but an overreliance on themselves—leading to isolation, bottlenecks, and missed opportunities for collaboration. Gender differences were minimal, though men were slightly more likely to report struggles with overreliance.

Correlation analysis reveals high positive relationships between Self-Reliance and Career Flexibility, Personal Autonomy, Practical Intelligence, Complexity Preference, and Decision Flexibility. These factors enable smart people to navigate complexity independently and make confident decisions. However, Self-Reliance also shows negative correlations with Teamwork and Outward Confidence, confirming that overuse of this factor can limit collaboration and visibility. The highest achievers master the balance—leading with independence while building strong systems of support.

Reflection: *How has your approach to Self-Reliance influenced your ability to collaborate and lead? What changes could enhance your balance of independence and Teamwork?*

Enabling Aspects of Healthy Self-Reliance

1. You take initiative and move projects forward without waiting for direction.
2. You solve problems independently, reducing bottlenecks and delays.
3. You build trust by following through on responsibilities.
4. You adapt quickly to new situations without needing constant input.
5. You deliver results that demonstrate reliability and capability.
6. You hold yourself accountable without blaming others.
7. You act without waiting to be told.
8. You protect your autonomy while still collaborating.
9. You know when to bring others in to get a better outcome.

Checklist to Harness Healthy Self-Reliance:

1. Recognize situations where independent action will drive progress.
2. Set a limit for how long you'll work alone before asking for input.
3. Build peer relationships before you need them.
4. Take initiative—but invite insight.
5. Set clear priorities to avoid getting stuck in tasks that others can handle.
6. Reflect on recent successes to reinforce confidence in handling challenges.
7. Balance self-initiative with regular check-ins to stay aligned with the team.

Reflection: *Can you recall a situation where your ability to balance Self-Reliance with leveraging the strengths of others helped you to achieve a goal?*

Disabling Aspects of Poorly Balanced Self-Reliance

When Self-Reliance is overused or distorted, it becomes a liability—limiting impact, damaging relationships, and exhausting your capacity.

When Self-Reliance is excessive:

1. You avoid asking for help—even when it's clearly needed.
2. You micromanage or refuse to delegate.
3. You dismiss feedback that could improve your work.
4. You assume your way is best and shut down alternatives.
5. You struggle to trust others or collaborate effectively.
6. You isolate yourself and miss better outcomes.
7. You reject collaboration, convinced others can't meet your standards.
8. You take on too much—leading to burnout and missed deadlines.
9. You alienate potential allies by making them feel shut out or unvalued.

When Self-Reliance Is Poor:

1. You rely too heavily on others for direction.
2. You avoid taking initiative or full ownership.
3. You wait to be told what to do—even when capable.
4. You deflect blame when things go wrong.
5. You expect others to lead, even when you could.
6. You hesitate to decide independently, slowing progress.
7. You avoid responsibility—hoping someone else will step in.
8. You miss chances to show competence and initiative.

Sustainable success requires knowing when to take charge—and when to invite others in.

Checklist to Mitigate Poorly Balanced Self-Reliance:

To prevent excessive Self-Reliance:

1. Seek feedback early—don't assume your way is best.
2. Identify what others can take on—and delegate it.

To prevent poor Self-Reliance:

3. Take ownership of projects instead of waiting for direction.
4. Practice making independent decisions to build confidence.

To maintain balance:

5. Regularly assess when to act alone and when to involve others.
6. Combine personal responsibility with collaboration to improve results.

Reflection: *Recall a situation where your lack of balance in Self-Reliance prevented you from achieving a goal. How could you have changed your approach and succeeded?*

Smartness in Action

Nia constantly second-guessed herself, leaning on others for validation before making decisions. It slowed her down and made her seem unsure. When she began trusting her expertise and making independent calls, her speed and confidence grew. Taking ownership boosted her credibility and presence as a leader.

Omar, on the other hand, prided himself on doing everything alone. He refused input and avoided delegation. This slowed progress and isolated him from his team. When he finally balanced independence with collaboration, his efficiency soared—and so did his team's respect. His leadership impact multiplied.

Self-Reliance helps smart people move fast, solve problems, and make confident decisions without waiting for permission. Over time, this builds efficiency—and trust in their ability to deliver. Within the *Achievement Cycle*, Self-Reliance keeps things moving by reducing bottlenecks and hesitation.

Smart people tend to take pride in doing it all. But extreme independence limits scale and slows growth. To become more successful, smart people should identify where they can delegate, ask for help before it's critical, and share ownership without losing control. Self-reliance is powerful when paired with selective collaboration.

Operating independently gives smart people control—but without Career Flexibility, they risk staying stuck on paths that no longer serve them. The next *Smartness Factor*—Career Flexibility—shows how successful people adapt, pivot, and seize new opportunities.

> *"Smartness is knowing when to stand tall on your own—and when to stand stronger with the right people beside you."*

For Deeper Insights

How does Self-Reliance show up in your life? Do your mindset, behaviors, and habits reflect healthy independence or something that holds you back? Take the Self-Reliance Assessment (*www.MySmartness.com/Assessments*) to identify your behavioral tendencies—whether you are an *Independent Powerhouse, Mostly Independent, Need Constant Guidance,* or the *Dependent Puppet*. Get insights on what's driving your success, what's getting in your way, and how you could become more successful.

Reflection: *Are you calling it independence when it's really control? How often does your need to "do it right" stop others from helping you go further? What would happen if you stopped trying to prove you can do it alone—and started letting the right people in?*

CHAPTER 38

CAREER FLEXIBILITY

"Smart people get stuck when they see careers as destiny rather than choices—forgetting that even the best paths can become obsolete, and only career flexibility keeps them growing and relevant."
~ Ram V. Iyer

Career Flexibility is the ability to pivot—adapting your direction, approach, or strategy to stay aligned with your career goals in a changing world. It doesn't mean bouncing around aimlessly. It means adjusting your path when the one you're on no longer fits your current reality—or the future you want.

Smart people often build careers on early strengths, passions, or plans. But what happens when those plans become traps? When they outgrow the role, lose interest, or hit a ceiling—but keep going through the motions? That's when intelligence becomes inertia. Career Flexibility keeps you relevant, energized, and strategically positioned—no matter how things change.

Why do so many smart people end up dissatisfied with their careers? The biggest reason is simple: they neither take the time to find a career they love nor learn to love the one they have. Instead, they follow what's popular—the paths their peers admire, the roles that sound impressive, the industries everyone else is rushing into. Why question it? If it works for others, shouldn't it work for them?

But what happens when the industry shifts, the work turns dull, or their interests evolve? Why do so many stay stuck in careers that no longer interest or excite them—telling themselves they've invested too much to leave? That their intelligence, credentials, and years of effort would all go to waste if they walked away now?

It's the sunk cost fallacy in action: clinging to what's familiar, not because it's still right—but because they've already spent so much getting there. And the longer they wait to make a change, the heavier the loss feels—and the harder it becomes to pivot. They feel trapped and unhappy, often for the rest of their career.

Avi was a brilliant software engineer who quickly climbed the ranks at a top tech company. But after ten years, the thrill was gone—and the trappings of seniority were seductive, hard to walk away from. He felt trapped—too successful to leave, too restless to stay. Friends said he was lucky, but he felt stuck and unseen.

When a smaller startup offered him a leadership role, he hesitated—afraid to give up his stability. After months of wrestling with it, he said yes. The first year was rocky, but he found renewed purpose—and soon became COO. His leap wasn't reckless—it was aligned with his evolving interests and passions. He didn't quit; he pivoted.

We spend more of our waking time in our careers than we do with most people in our personal lives. So, what do smart people want from their careers? Career Flexibility challenges the traditional idea of locking into a single path and instead invites exploration. For those stuck in unsatisfying careers—or staying in roles because someone else thinks they should—experimentation is essential. Smart people must use their personal judgment to decide whether to stay the course or take a different path. After all, why settle for being trapped in work that no longer fits when the goal is to build a career that is both successful and fulfilling?

Careers are not destinies but choices. Even once-excellent paths can become obsolete as industries shift, the world changes and opportunities disappear. What made sense five years ago can become a dead end. Without career flexibility, smart people can be stuck in place while the world moves on. The only question is whether they will pivot to a new career or unhappily remain stuck in their current career.

Reflection: *Given where you are in your career, are you happy with your current career path or would you rather be doing something else? Be honest with yourself.*

Smartness Assessment Data Analysis

Among 1,200+ smart people who completed the *Smartness Assessment*, 59% of the unsuccessful respondents identified Career Flexibility as a challenge or disabler. These are people unhappy in their careers—in line with broader surveys showing that more than half of professionals feel the same. There's a 17% gap between unsuccessful and successful respondents on this factor. If you feel unsuccessful or dissatisfied, pay close attention to this *Smartness Factor*—and start mitigating its disablers, whether subtle or severe. Gender differences on this factor were negligible.

Correlation analysis shows strong positive links between Career Flexibility and Practical Intelligence, Action Orientation, and Risk Tolerance. Smart people who pivot well apply intelligence in practical, results-driven ways, take decisive action, and tolerate uncertainty better than peers. There's also a moderate correlation with Personal Autonomy, underscoring the role of self-direction in career shifts. Mastering Career Flexibility alongside these traits expands a smart person's ability to lead in dynamic environments. Those who fail to develop it—especially when paired with low Risk Tolerance and poor Action Orientation—face higher risks of stagnation and irrelevance.

Reflection: *Does your current career make you feel good about yourself? If not, what changes might improve your professional satisfaction?*

Enabling Aspects of Career Flexibility

When you build Career Flexibility, you stay ahead of change instead of getting trapped by it. You don't cling to outdated plans—you recognize when something no longer fits and take action before stagnation sets in.

1. You embrace unfamiliar challenges to stay sharp and expand your perspective.
2. You take ownership of your growth and pursue new paths without waiting to be pushed.
3. You build diverse networks to uncover opportunities beyond your current role or field.
4. You adapt without ego, adjusting direction without viewing it as failure.

You also understand your own abilities—deeply. You don't just hope you're competent—you track it. Keeping a "Brag Sheet" of wins and reviewing it regularly builds real self-trust based on evidence, not ego.

Checklist to Harness Enabling Aspects of Career Flexibility:

1. Regularly assess whether your current work still fits your skills, interests, and opportunities.
2. Proactively take initiative when it's time to shift—don't wait for signs or permission.
3. Grow your network beyond your current role, team, or industry.
4. Seek out new challenges to stay engaged and evolving.
5. Adjust your career path when things change—without framing it as failure.

Reflection: *When was the last time you made a move that brought unexpected growth, energy, or momentum?*

Disabling Aspects of Career Rigidity

Smart people struggle with Career Flexibility when falling into either of two extremes:

Too Little Career Flexibility:

1. You cling to outdated career paths long after they stop providing growth or meaning.
2. You overvalue past achievements or prestige, convincing yourself staying put is smarter than starting over.
3. You delay necessary shifts, waiting for perfect certainty—letting opportunities slip by.

Career Flexibility

Too Much Career Flexibility:

4. You jump roles or industries too often, never building connections, expertise or results.
5. You bail at the first sign of boredom or difficulty, avoiding the focused effort required to achieve real success.
6. You make it harder to establish credibility or long-term impact.

Both extremes limit smart people. Too little flexibility leads to stagnation. Too much creates chaos. Career success depends on knowing when to hold steady—and when to move on.

Checklist to Mitigate Disabling Aspects of Career Rigidity:

To prevent too little Career Flexibility:

1. Regularly assess whether your current career path still offers growth, challenge, and satisfaction.
2. Let go of the belief that past success, credentials, or prestige guarantee future fulfillment.
3. Take proactive steps to explore new opportunities before reaching a crisis point.

To prevent too much Career Flexibility:

4. Commit to roles long enough to develop meaningful expertise and deliver real results.
5. Resist abandoning a career path at the first sign of boredom or difficulty.
6. Create stability and depth in your work history to support credibility and long-term progress.

To maintain balance:

7. Build enough stability to support lasting success while staying ready to pivot as industries, opportunities, and personal interests evolve.

Reflection: *Where are you at risk of having too little or too much Career Flexibility—and what specific adjustments could you make to create a healthier balance?*

A Personal Career Narrative Approach

Over time, I've found that developing a Personal Career Narrative is one of the most effective tools for building Career Flexibility. I use it with clients to help them align their work with long-term goals and values—and avoid getting stuck in roles that no longer fit. Career satisfaction isn't just about enjoying daily work. It's about building a career that stays fulfilling over time.

For smart people, it comes from progress—growing skills, stepping into bigger roles, hitting milestones like promotions or compensation growth. A

Personal Career Narrative helps you connect the story behind your career—not just titles, but why you made certain moves, what you learned, and how your skills and values have evolved. It helps you spot patterns, clarify what drives your success, and make smarter decisions about what's next.

I advise clients to structure their narrative across three time horizons:

- Short-Term (1 year): Build key skills or test a new role.
- Medium-Term (3–5 years): Hit major milestones—stepping into leadership or entering a new field.
- Long-Term (10 years): Define big-picture goals—leading an organization, mastering a niche, or balancing work and life on your terms.

Your narrative is dynamic—it evolves as you do. It keeps you clear on goals and gaps—whether in skills, experience, or relationships.

Many smart people either stay stuck in roles that no longer fit or keep jumping jobs hoping something will click. A Personal Career Narrative offers a better path: clear goals, a connected story, and a proactive way to build a career that's both successful and satisfying.

Reflection: *If you were to design your ideal career, what would it look like? What are your one-year, five-year, and long-term professional goals? What steps can you take now to move closer to that vision?*

Smartness in Action

Ariella built a reputation as a brilliant strategist in a prestigious firm. But after years of success, her work started to feel repetitive and disconnected from what she cared about. She felt restless but told herself she'd be foolish to leave such a respected position – the good old 'sunk cost fallacy'—the unwillingness to lose the investment already made. The longer she waited, the more stuck she felt. Eventually, she left—but only after burnout forced her hand. It took two years to rebuild her confidence and reenter a career path that actually energized her.

Aisha, on the other hand, had a strong track record in tech product management but sensed she was outgrowing the work. Rather than wait for burnout or drift, she used her Personal Career Narrative to explore what kind of leadership role she wanted next. She identified a mission-driven health tech company that aligned with her values and pitched a hybrid role they hadn't considered. Within months, she was leading a new vertical—and felt more energized than she had in years.

Career Flexibility helps smart people stay energized and effective by adjusting course before frustration turns to stagnation. It's not about quitting—it's about redirecting. *Smartness* means knowing when to evolve—and having the courage to do it before you're forced. In the *Achievement Cycle*, Career Flexibility ensures they stay relevant and positioned for growth, no matter how the landscape shifts.

Smart people tend to get attached to plans that made sense once—but no longer do. They equate change with failure. To become more successful, smart

Career Flexibility

people should regularly ask, "Is this still right for me?", explore paths quietly before leaping, and see reinvention as progress—not retreat.

Adapting to new opportunities keeps smart people relevant, but without Self-Advocacy, they risk being overlooked or undervalued in their careers. The next *Smartness Factor*—Self-Advocacy—shows how they actively promote their value and secure the opportunities and recognition they've earned.

> *"Smartness is knowing when to double down—and when to walk away before it's too late."*

For Deeper Insights

How does Career Flexibility show up in your life? Do your mindset, behaviors, and habits reflect a strength or a hurdle? Take the Career Flexibility Assessment (*www.MySmartness.com/Assessments*) to identify your behavioral tendencies—whether you are a *Strategic Shifter*, *Stable Navigator*, *Restless Jumper*, or *Reluctant Resister*. Get insights on what's driving your success, what's getting in your way, and how you could become more successful.

Reflection: *Are you holding on to a career that no longer fits—just because it once made sense? When was the last time you asked what you want, instead of what looks impressive or "smart" on paper? What would open up if you stopped chasing status signals and started pursuing a career that will excite you and achieve your aspirations?*

CHAPTER 39

SELF-ADVOCACY

"Smart people don't just know their own value—they make sure others do, too."
~ Ram V. Iyer

Self-Advocacy is the ability to clearly communicate your value, needs, and ambitions in ways that earn respect, visibility, and opportunity. It's not about arrogance or blatant self-promotion—it's about making sure your contributions are seen, understood, and rewarded.

Smart people often believe their intelligence and results should speak for themselves. They assume that delivering high-quality work, solving complex problems, or holding impressive credentials will naturally earn them recognition and advancement. But in the real world, that's rarely how it works.

Consider two of history's most brilliant minds: Thomas Edison and Nikola Tesla. Both were smart people. Both were extraordinary inventors. But only one became a household name. Why? Edison didn't just invent; he made sure the world knew what he invented. He promoted his work, secured financial backing, and kept his name in the spotlight. Tesla, on the other hand, was equally brilliant but struggled with self-advocacy. He assumed the quality of his ideas would be enough. They weren't. Without effectively championing himself, Tesla's influence diminished, leaving him under-recognized and undercompensated for his genius.

This is the self-advocacy trap many smart people fall into: they rely on intellectual strength but neglect the skill of promoting their value. Some of them wait to be noticed—only to watch less capable people advance by making their achievements visible. While they perfect the work, someone else has made the sale.

As Dr. Marshall Goldsmith writes in *The Earned Life*, credibility must be earned twice. First, by delivering real value—through competence, expertise, or impact. Second, by ensuring others recognize that value. Results alone aren't enough—smart people must communicate their contributions and value clearly and visibly.

Marshall warns that many talented people focus only on the first step, assuming their work will speak for itself. But without the second step—making sure the right people know—opportunities remain limited. This chapter is about that second step. Satya Nadella, the CEO of Microsoft, famously advised employees to focus only on step one and let the managers take care of step two. Bad advice!

Self-advocacy isn't about ego or empty promotion. It's about making sure your ideas, insights, and results are seen, heard, and acted on. It's about using

Self-Advocacy

intelligence to navigate competitive environments and earn the roles, recognition, and influence you deserve. Without self-advocacy, intelligence stalls. Smartness—the real-world application of intelligence—requires the courage to speak up, take credit, and ensure your value is known. Otherwise, you become the invisible genius: doing exceptional work while others lead the conversation.

For smart people who want more success, self-advocacy isn't optional. It's essential.

Reflection: *Where have you assumed your intelligence alone would get you noticed—and how might stronger self-advocacy change your results?*

Smartness Assessment Data Analysis

Self-advocacy emerged as a key factor for success only after we conducted the initial 1,200+ *Smartness Assessments*. Through research, reflection, and conversations with participants, we recognized the importance of this skill in driving achievement. Future versions of the *Smartness Assessment* will include this factor to explore its impact across different areas of life and career. As new data comes in, we'll share updated insights on our website: www.MySmartness.com/books.

Enabling Aspects of Self-Advocacy

When used wisely, self-advocacy becomes a powerful career accelerator. It helps smart people make their value visible—without arrogance, and without waiting for others to do it for them.

1. Increased visibility – You ensure your ideas and achievements are seen, earning the recognition you deserve.
2. Stronger negotiation outcomes – By clearly communicating your value, you secure better roles, compensation, and opportunities.
3. Confidence reinforcement – Each act of advocacy builds self-belief and makes it easier to take on bigger challenges.
4. Opportunity generation – Speaking up opens doors to advancement, collaboration, and leadership.
5. Credibility expansion – Controlling your narrative strengthens your influence within your field.
6. Network amplification – Visible contributions attract support from mentors, sponsors, and allies who elevate your success.

Checklist to Leverage Enabling Aspects of Self-advocacy

1. Identify where your contributions have been overlooked—and plan how to make them visible.
2. Regularly share your ideas and wins in meetings, reports, or conversations.
3. Seek allies who can echo and amplify your impact in key settings.

4. Practice self-promotion in low-stakes environments to build confidence.
5. Align your self-advocacy with genuine contributions—don't promote without delivering.

Smart people don't just need to recognize their own value—they need to make sure others do too. Effective self-advocacy isn't about overshadowing others. It's about making your impact visible so you can shape outcomes, champion your ideas, and open the door to bigger opportunities.

Reflection: What's one specific strength you can make more visible this week to advance your success?

Disabling Aspects of Self-Advocacy

Smart people struggle with Self-Advocacy when falling into either of two extremes:

Too Little Self-Advocacy:

1. You believe intelligence and results should speak for themselves, so you stay silent instead of visible.
2. You avoid self-promotion out of fear of sounding arrogant or being rejected.
3. You miss key moments to share your value—hesitating when it matters most.

Too Much Self-Advocacy:

4. You dominate conversations with self-promotion, making others feel unseen or undervalued.
5. You overplay confidence, tipping into arrogance that creates resistance.
6. You chase personal visibility so hard that it damages relationships and team trust.

Both extremes limit smart people. Too little self-advocacy leads to invisibility and missed opportunities. Too much creates friction and alienation. Long-term success depends on knowing when—and how—to make your value known without overwhelming the room.

Checklist to Avoid Disabling Aspects of Self-Advocacy:

To prevent too little Self-Advocacy:

1. Recognize when you're staying silent—and choose to speak up.
2. Reframe self- promotion as a way to ensure your work has real impact.
3. Build comfort by practicing in low-stakes settings.

To prevent too much Self-Advocacy:

4. Promote yourself only when it adds value to the moment.
5. Make space to acknowledge and elevate the contributions of others.
6. Watch for signs of resistance—and adjust your approach.

To maintain balance:

7. Pair clear communication of your value with genuine listening and curiosity.

Reflection: *Where have you let either under-advocacy or over-advocacy limit your success. What was the impact, and how could you approach it differently next time?*

Practical Applications of Self-Advocacy Across Different Environments

Self-advocacy isn't one-size-fits-all. You'll need to adapt your approach depending on the setting:

- At work: Make your achievements visible to decision-makers—but always connect them to real outcomes. Don't seek attention without delivering results.
- As an entrepreneur: Communicate your vision clearly to investors, clients, and partners. Balance confidence with openness to feedback.
- At networking events: Confidently introduce yourself and share your goals. Build your personal brand without dominating the room.

Smartness in Action

Amara was smart, skilled, and deeply committed to her work—but rarely spoke up about her accomplishments. She believed her results would speak for themselves. They didn't. When promotions came around, she was passed over—again. Managers praised her execution but couldn't recall the full scope of her impact. After one too many disappointments, she realized her silence had cost her. She began sharing her wins in team settings and offering input during leadership meetings. Within a year, she was tapped to lead a high-visibility project—and finally promoted.

Kenji, on the other hand, leaned hard into self-advocacy, but pushed too far. He dominated meetings, constantly referenced his achievements, and frequently took credit in group settings. While no one doubted his talent, people stopped wanting to collaborate with him. His reputation shifted from "rising star" to a "self-centered show off." A trusted mentor pulled him aside and challenged him to start elevating others alongside himself. Once he made that shift, his influence improved—and so did new opportunities.

Self-advocacy isn't about chasing the spotlight. It's about owning your value—and sharing it in ways that build trust, not tension. *Smartness* is knowing when to speak up—and how to do it so others actually want to listen. In the *Achievement Cycle*, Self-Advocacy is key to securing the roles and support necessary for sustained advancement.

Smart people often assume that good work speaks for itself. But visibility isn't automatic. To achieve greater success, you need to clearly name your contributions, ask for recognition when appropriate, and frame your impact as leadership—not self-promotion. Being seen isn't always egotistical—it's sometimes effectiveness.

Mastering Self-Advocacy enables smart people to communicate their value and negotiate for opportunities, recognition, and resources. Over time, this proactive behavior ensures they are not overlooked and that their contributions are rewarded. But greater visibility brings more opportunities. And if they don't manage their Need for Variety, they risk chasing too many things—losing focus, burning out, or leaving things half-finished. The next *Smartness Factor*—Need for Variety—shows how smart people stay engaged and energized without losing focus, depth, or follow-through.

Advocating for themselves opens doors for smart people, but without managing their Need for Variety, they risk losing focus and spreading themselves too thin. The next *Smartness Factor*—Need for Variety—shows how they stay engaged and energized without sacrificing consistency or follow-through.

> *"Smartness is knowing when to let your work speak, and when to speak up so people actually hear it."*

For Deeper Insights

How does Self-Advocacy show up in your life? Do your mindset, behaviors, and habits reflect a strength or a hurdle? Take the Self-Advocacy Assessment (*www.MySmartness.com/Assessments*) to identify your behavioral tendencies—whether you are an *Assertive Advocate, Steady Self-Promoter, Passive Speaker,* or *Silent Spectator*. Get insights on what's driving your success, what's getting in your way, and how you could become more successful.

Reflection: Are you quietly hoping someone will notice your value—or making sure people actually see it? When has downplaying your contributions held you back? What might open up if you made your value clear, visible, and impossible to overlook?

CHAPTER 40

NEED FOR VARIETY

> *"Greater success rarely comes from constantly chasing variety or completely avoiding it; neither extreme results in consistent success."*
> ~ Ram V. Iyer

Need for Variety is the desire for stimulation, novelty, and diverse experiences to stay engaged and motivated. Smart people often crave variety, but without managing it well, they risk sacrificing focus, follow-through, and long-term progress.

Smart people often thrive on intellectual stimulation, new challenges, and diverse experiences. But when the need for variety goes unchecked, it becomes a hidden trap—pulling them away from focus, consistency, and sustained success. Too little variety leaves smart people bored, stagnant, and disengaged, while too much scatters their attention and drains their energy.

> *"Variety fuels creativity until it kills momentum."*

Consider Adam, Lena, and Carlos: three smart people managing their work very differently. Adam constantly chases new projects, jumping from idea to idea without finishing anything. Lena sticks rigidly to the same routines, resisting any new approaches, and her results have stalled. Carlos finds the balance: he focuses on his big project but then helps other colleagues on the side, keeping both his mind engaged and his outcomes strong.

For smart people, the challenge isn't whether they crave variety—it's how they manage it. The smartest people know how to bring fresh energy into their work without losing focus and how to explore new possibilities without abandoning what matters. This chapter shows how they do it.

Reflection: *Given your personal and professional life, how does the* Need for Variety *influence your motivation and performance?*

Smartness Assessment Data Analysis

Among 1,200+ smart people who completed the *Smartness Assessment*, 63% identified Need for Variety as a challenge or disabler. Smart people often have fast minds and deep curiosity—but what begins as agility often becomes distraction. They struggle to stay focused on a single goal, constantly chasing novelty instead of follow-through. This pattern is often rationalized as "learning" or "exploring options," but it leads to scattered efforts and unfinished work.

There's a 10% difference in this factor between unsuccessful and successful people. Focus and follow-through are obviously important to achieve successful outcomes. There was a negligible difference between the genders.

Correlation analysis shows strong positive relationships between Need for Variety and Risk Tolerance, Career Flexibility, and Thinking Range. Smart people who balance variety with focus use that flexibility and risk appetite to pursue new opportunities strategically—without losing momentum. There's also a moderate correlation with Action Orientation, suggesting that focused doers can convert variety into outcomes. But when high variety-seeking combines with low action, the result is chronic distraction and little real progress—regardless of intelligence.

The data is clear: smart people succeed when they balance variety—keeping work engaging and creative without losing sight of the outcomes that matter.

> *"Smartness stems from either bringing more discipline to your variety or more variety to your discipline."*

Enabling Aspects of the Need for Variety

For smart people, embracing variety fuels success by:

1. Stimulating creativity through diverse experiences that spark fresh ideas. Steve Jobs credited a calligraphy course with inspiring Apple's typography.
2. Enhancing problem-solving by applying insights across fields, like using marketing strategies to improve product design.
3. Building resilience through new challenges that strengthen adaptability and push beyond comfort zones.
4. Broadening social perspective by engaging with different people and cultures, improving empathy and teamwork.
5. Driving lifelong learning by keeping curiosity active and skills sharp in a constantly changing world.

Checklist to Harness Positive Aspects of Factor

1. Seek out new experiences that complement and enhance your existing work.
2. Apply lessons from unrelated fields to bring fresh solutions to familiar problems.
3. Balance new projects with the disciplined completion of current priorities.
4. Regularly engage with people outside your usual circles to expand your thinking.
5. Build time into your schedule for exploration, learning, and creative pursuits.

Reflection: *How can you introduce meaningful variety into your work without losing focus?*

Disabling Aspects of the Factor

Smart people struggle with the Need for Variety when falling into either of two extremes:

Too Little Variety:

1. Clinging to familiar routines, even when they no longer provide challenge or growth.
2. Avoiding new ideas, methods, or experiences that could improve results.
3. Becoming mentally stagnant, leading to disengagement and missed opportunities.

Too Much Variety:

1. Jumping between projects without finishing, leaving a trail of incomplete work.
2. Seeking constant stimulation at the expense of consistency and follow-through.
3. Overcomplicating tasks by adding unnecessary elements just to make them feel new.

Both extremes limit smart people. Too little variety leads to boredom and decline. Too much creates chaos and burnout. Success depends on finding the right rhythm between novelty and stability.

Checklist to Mitigate Disabling Aspects of the Need for Variety

To prevent too little variety:

1. Challenge yourself to experiment with new methods or perspectives regularly.
2. Rotate responsibilities or seek out projects that push you beyond routine tasks.
3. Connect with people who introduce fresh ideas and ways of thinking.

To prevent too much variety:

4. Finish existing projects before committing to new ones.
5. Set clear boundaries on how much change you introduce at once.
6. Prioritize depth and mastery over constant reinvention.

To maintain balance:

7. Combine steady, long-term goals with periodic bursts of exploration to keep your work both grounded and engaging.

The *Achievement Cycle* shows that lasting success comes from balancing the drive for variety with focused goals. For smart people drawn to novelty, the key is using variety to fuel creativity and adaptability—while staying anchored to one's goals. This balance ensures that the excitement of variety contributes to achievement rather than distracting from it.

Reflection: Where are you overindulging—or underusing—variety, and how is it affecting your results?

Smartness in Action

Mateo, a product designer from Manila, thrived on new challenges but became restless when projects turned routine. He often left roles too soon, missing the chance to develop deeper expertise. After learning to balance his need for variety with a commitment to seeing initiatives through, he found greater fulfillment and earned recognition for delivering innovative products with long-term impact.

On the other hand, Zhang Wei, a financial analyst from Nanjing, China, avoided change and stuck to familiar tasks for years. While dependable, his career stagnated. When he embraced opportunities to work on cross-functional projects and explore new skills, his creativity and career prospects expanded significantly.

Smart people who embrace their Need for Variety maintain high levels of engagement and creativity by seeking out new challenges and experiences. Over time, this drives innovation and prevents stagnation in their careers. In the *Achievement Cycle*, harnessing the Need for Variety sustains energy and enthusiasm, accelerating ongoing personal and professional growth.

Smart people tend to crave stimulation and change—often jumping to the next new thing too early or resisting the consistency success requires. To become more successful, smart people should finish before switching, bring curiosity into repetition, and ask themselves, "Am I running toward purpose or away from discomfort?" Variety should be used as a tool for growth, not a distraction from completion.

Staying engaged through variety fuels creativity and growth, but without Emotional Intelligence, smart people risk missing the interpersonal signals that drive collaboration and influence. The next *Smartness Factor*—Emotional Intelligence—shows how they navigate emotions and relationships to build stronger connections and achieve better outcomes.

> "Smartness is knowing when to expand your curiosity—and when to rein it in to stay focused."

For Deeper Insights

How does the Need for Variety show up in your life? Do your mindset, behaviors, and habits reflect a strength or a hurdle? Take the Need for Variety Assessment (www.MySmartness.com/Assessments) to identify your behavioral tendencies—whether you are a *Thrill Seeker, Balanced Explorer, Steady Navigator,* or *Comfort*

Need for Variety 217

Zone Guardian. Get insights on what's driving your success, what's getting in your way, and how you could become more successful.

Reflection: *Are you stuck in routines that no longer challenge you—or constantly chasing new things without finishing what matters? How often does your curiosity distract you instead of drive you? What could shift if you brought more discipline to your variety—or more variety to your discipline?*

RELATIONAL FACTORS

CHAPTER 41

EMOTIONAL INTELLIGENCE

"Emotions are the language of the soul. Understand them, and you'll unlock the doors to greater success."
- Adapted from a Chinese Proverb

Emotional Intelligence is the ability to recognize, manage, and respond effectively to your own emotions—and the emotions of others. For smart people, it's what turns intellect into influence.

Smart people often rely on logic, analysis, and problem-solving to drive success. But when they neglect emotional intelligence, it becomes a liability—undermining relationships, decisions, and leadership. It leaves them disconnected, reactive, and prone to misunderstanding others. Too much unchecked emotion causes the opposite problem—over-empathizing, poor boundaries, and decisions clouded by feelings. Emotional Intelligence complements intelligence, credentials, and experience—helping smart people navigate complex relationships, manage stress, and make better decisions over time.

Consider Sarah and Alphonso—two smart people navigating work very differently. Sarah, a highly skilled developer in Austin, can't manage her reactions. When a colleague points out an error, she explodes with anger and embarrassment, damaging team engagement. Alphonso, leading an AI startup in Cambridge, reads the room effortlessly—adjusting his tone to engage people in meetings. His emotional intelligence turns interactions into better engagement.

The challenge isn't whether emotions matter—they do. The real question is how well smart people manage their own emotions and respond to others. The smartest use emotional intelligence to guide thinking, actions, and relationships—without letting feelings take over. They stay composed under pressure, connect with others, and use empathy to drive results—not derail them. This chapter shows how.

Reflection: *Reflecting on your career and experiences, are you satisfied with your emotional intelligence? How would you like to improve it?*

Smartness Assessment Data Analysis

Among 1,200+ smart people who completed the *Smartness Assessment*, 67% of the unsuccessful respondents identified Emotional Intelligence as a challenge—compared to 60% of successful ones. For both groups, it's a significant issue. Women scored 12% higher than men—but they struggle here too. 59% of the women struggle with this whereas 71% of men do. Relationships are driven by emotion, so this is a critical factor for all of us to improve.

Correlation analysis shows strong positive relationships between Emotional Intelligence (EI) and Decision Flexibility, Interpersonal Skills, and Thinking and Feeling. Smart people with high EI balance logic with empathy, making decisions that account for both data and human dynamics. There's also a medium correlation with Career Flexibility, suggesting that greater emotional awareness supports career transitions and leadership abilities. Failing to develop EI—especially alongside low Interpersonal Skills—leads to isolation, strained relationships, and missed opportunities, regardless of intellect.

For smart people, EI isn't just an advantage—it's a foundational skill that powers other *Smartness Factors* and drives real-world success.

Reflection: *How do your emotions influence your decision-making under stress? How can you better manage this influence to improve outcomes?*

Enabling Aspects of Emotional Intelligence

For smart people, Emotional Intelligence (EI) turns raw intellect into sustained influence. High EI helps you manage relationships, adapt under pressure, and guide thinking and actions with clarity. The smartest performers don't let emotions run the show—but they don't ignore them either. Here's what strong Emotional Intelligence looks like in action:

1. Empathy helps you read and respond to others' emotions, building trust and collaboration.
2. Self-regulation keeps you calm and focused under pressure—when others lose control, you stay grounded.
3. Motivation fuels sustained effort through challenges, driven by purpose—not external rewards.
4. Social skills help you build relationships, influence others, and align people toward shared goals.
5. Self-awareness gives you insight into your patterns and blind spots—so you can adjust instead of repeat.

When you actively apply these traits, you lead better, adapt faster, and execute more effectively—even in high-stakes environments.

Checklist to harness the enabling aspects of EI:

1. Track your emotional triggers—and how you typically respond.
2. Observe others closely during conversations—what are they not saying?
3. Set goals driven by personal values—not just external metrics.
4. Use stress management tools to stay grounded when tension spikes.
5. Sharpen your communication to build deeper connection and influence.

Reflection: *Which of these enabling aspects of Emotional Intelligence have contributed most to your success? How can you use it to your advantage further?*

Disabling Aspects of Emotional Intelligence

Smart people struggle with Emotional Intelligence when falling into either of two extremes:

Too Little Emotional Intelligence:

1. Misread emotional cues, leading to poor communication and strained relationships.
2. Avoid feedback, which blocks growth and damages trust.
3. React impulsively, letting frustration or defensiveness derail progress.

Too Emotional:

1. Over-empathize, prioritizing others' emotions over your own goals.
2. Seek constant harmony, avoiding necessary conflict and honest feedback.
3. Rely on external validation, weakening your independence and slowing decisions.

Both extremes limit smart people. Too little EI creates blind spots and isolation. Too much drains energy and focus. *Smartness* means staying emotionally attuned—without letting emotions take control.

Checklist to mitigate disabling aspects of Emotional Intelligence

Too little Emotional Intelligence:

1. Slow down and double-check your interpretations of others' emotions before reacting.
2. Consider how your emotional responses could affect those around you.
3. Develop routines to pause and reset when emotions run high.

Too much Emotion:

4. Clarify personal goals to stay grounded in what matters.
5. Welcome honest conflict when it helps drive progress.
6. Strengthen your confidence—make decisions without chasing approval.

To maintain balance:

7. Pair empathy with action—use emotional insight to drive clarity, not confusion.

Smart people succeed when they use emotion as a guide—not a leash or a crutch. The *Achievement Cycle* shows that lasting success comes from managing EI as both a tool and a boundary—used to engage others effectively without letting unchecked empathy derail progress. For smart people, the goal isn't just to feel more or understand others better—it's to leverage emotion to drive achievement without losing clarity, direction, or results.

Reflection: *Where are you allowing either too little or too much Emotional Intelligence to affect your success, and how can you bring it back into balance?*

Smartness in Action

Thabo, a regional manager from Johannesburg, was known for his technical brilliance—but struggled to manage his team's emotions. His blunt feedback and lack of empathy led to high turnover. After improving his EI—listening more and responding with empathy—team engagement rose, and performance dramatically improved. Pinky, a software engineering leader in Bengaluru, was so focused on keeping everyone happy that she avoided giving honest feedback. Problems went unaddressed, and performance slipped. Once she balanced empathy with direct communication, her team respected her more—and results followed.

Mastering Emotional Intelligence helps smart people manage their own emotions and respond to others effectively. It strengthens leadership, improves conflict resolution, and builds strong teams. In the *Achievement Cycle*, EI amplifies influence and creates collaborative environments that sustain success.

Smart people tend to understand emotional theory but may react impulsively or shut down under pressure. Their EQ is analytical, not lived. To become more successful, smart people should pause before reacting, label emotions clearly, and ask others how their emotional presence affects the room. Influence grows when people feel understood—not just managed.

EI helps smart people understand emotions—but without strong Interpersonal Skills, they risk missing opportunities to connect, collaborate, and lead. The next *Smartness Factor*—Interpersonal Skills—shows how they build trust, communicate clearly, and achieve results with others.

> *"Smartness is knowing when emotions need space—and when they need boundaries."*

For Deeper Insights

How does Emotional Intelligence show up in your life? Do your mindset, behaviors, and habits reflect a strength or a hurdle? Take the Emotional Intelligence Assessment (www.MySmartness.com/Assessments) to identify your behavioral tendencies—whether you are *Emotionally Successful, Emotionally Attuned, Emotionally Reactive,* or *Emotionally Unaware.* Get insights on what's driving your success, what's getting in your way, and how you could become more successful.

Reflection: *Do you manage your emotions—or do they manage you? Are you avoiding emotional discomfort and missing what people really need from you? What would improve if you used emotional insight to lead more powerfully instead of just reacting or retreating?*

CHAPTER 42

INTERPERSONAL SKILLS

"The most important ingredient in the formula of success is knowing how to get along with people."
~ Theodore Roosevelt

Interpersonal Skills are the ability to build relationships, communicate clearly, and navigate social dynamics in ways that generate trust, alignment, and collaboration.

We are not recluses. We live, work, and build with other humans. Our success comes from doing things with others, and our impact depends on what we contribute to others or society at large. Building and leveraging relationships is one of the most important ways to make intelligence more relevant—and success more likely.

African wild dogs succeed in nearly 9 out of 10 hunts because they operate as a team. Cheetahs, despite being the fastest land animals in the world, succeed less than half the time—because they hunt alone. What sets wild dogs apart isn't just teamwork—it's their ability to communicate, coordinate, and quickly adjust their actions to work in harmony. In other words, they have remarkable interpersonal skills.

Some smart people become self-absorbed in their own intelligence, abilities, ideas, and execution. They underestimate the human dynamics that create leverage, multiply outcomes, and drive trust, influence, and collaboration. Their impact isn't limited by intelligence—but by how well they connect with the people around them.

Consider Kwame, a highly skilled software engineer at a top tech company in Cambridge. His coding was flawless—but projects consistently stumbled. Miscommunications, stalled collaborations, and growing frustration with colleagues began to overshadow his talent. Without strong interpersonal skills, Kwame's intelligence couldn't drive results. Contrast that with Anushka, a Wharton grad thriving in a biomedical incubator in Philadelphia. Her technical expertise—combined with clear communication and emotional attunement—made her indispensable to the team. By listening actively, managing conflict, and building strong relationships, Anushka didn't just contribute to her team's success—she elevated it.

For smart people, interpersonal skills aren't optional. Every meaningful achievement depends on working with, through, and alongside others. This chapter explores how smart people build, strengthen, and apply interpersonal skills to turn intelligence into sustained success.

Reflection: Think about a time when your interpersonal skills (or lack thereof) significantly impacted a project or relationship. How did it influence the outcome, and what could you have done differently?

Smartness Assessment Data Analysis

Among 1,200+ smart people who completed the *Smartness Assessment*, 63% of unsuccessful people identified Interpersonal Skills as a challenge or disabler. In comparison, it affected only 53% of the successful people. The difference between genders is just 3%, with women being a bit more challenged on this factor. This is not an acute disabler for either, meaning a majority of smart people have good interpersonal skills—just that most of them are challenged by this to some extent.

Correlation analysis shows strong positive relationships between Interpersonal Skills and Emotional Intelligence, Thinking and Feeling, and Decision Flexibility. Smart people who excel here manage complex dynamics while maintaining clarity and empathy. There's also a medium correlation with Career Flexibility, reinforcing how relationships fuel career advancement. Interestingly, there's a medium correlation in teamwork, offering a very interesting insight - Interpersonal Skills help you connect—both one-to-one and one-to-many. Teamwork helps you deliver—together, requiring many-to-many interaction. Interpersonal skills and Teamwork support each other, but they're not the same. That's why they correlate—but not strongly. Failing to develop Interpersonal Skills—especially when paired with low Emotional Intelligence—creates many barriers to success. For smart people, Interpersonal Skills aren't optional—they're essential to turning intelligence into lasting results.

Reflection: How do your interpersonal skills influence the way others perceive and respond to you in professional or personal settings? Have any of your Interpersonal Skills limited your success, and how can you strengthen them to better support your goals?

Enabling Aspects of Good Interpersonal Skills

For smart people, strong Interpersonal Skills turn intelligence into sustained influence and results. These skills help you connect, collaborate, and lead—so your strengths move people and outcomes forward.

1. Clear communication lets you express complex ideas simply, listen actively, and ensure your insights are understood and usable.
2. Empathy and understanding help you relate to others' perspectives, building trust and strengthening relationships.
3. Conflict resolution allows you to manage disagreements constructively, balancing needs without losing focus on shared goals.
4. Leadership and teamwork improve as you use interpersonal skills to align people, build trust, and drive collective success.

Interpersonal Skills

5. Adaptability and networking keep you connected across diverse settings, opening doors and expanding your influence.

Interpersonal Skills are a core *Smartness Factor*—connecting your personal strengths to shared success. Smart people who develop them consistently turn potential into meaningful, sustained achievement.

Checklist to harness the enabling aspects of Interpersonal Skills:

1. Prepare for key conversations to ensure clarity—and confirm your message is understood.
2. Listen actively by focusing fully, summarizing key points, and confirming alignment.
3. Approach conflict constructively with direct, respectful language and a shared-goal mindset.
4. Strengthen leadership by recognizing contributions and inviting open, honest dialogue.
5. Seek regular feedback to improve how others experience your communication.
6. Sustain key relationships through check-ins and genuine interest in others' goals.

Reflection: *Can you recall a situation where your interpersonal skills and strengths helped you achieve a goal?*

Disabling Aspects of Interpersonal Skills

Smart people struggle with Interpersonal Skills when they fall into either of two extremes—too little or too much interpersonal focus. Both create barriers to trust, collaboration, and influence.

With Weak Interpersonal Skills:

1. You communicate in ways that confuse or alienate others—losing clarity and connection.
2. You struggle to build rapport—focusing too much on tasks and not enough on the people behind them.
3. You avoid conflict—letting small issues fester into larger problems.

Too Much Interpersonal Focus:

4. You over-accommodate—diluting your priorities to please everyone.
5. You avoid hard truths—seeking harmony at the cost of honest feedback.
6. You over-network—scattering your energy and draining focus from real work.

Both extremes limit smart people. Too little interpersonal skill isolates them and weakens influence. Too much interpersonal focus scatters attention and weakens decision-making. Success comes from balancing clarity, empathy, and assertiveness—so that relationships support, not sabotage, results.

Checklist to mitigate disabling aspects of Interpersonal Skills:

To prevent too little interpersonal skill:

1. Simplify your language and confirm understanding in high-stakes conversations.
2. Practice active listening—fully focusing, paraphrasing, and checking for clarity.
3. Engage regularly with colleagues to build trust and connection.

To prevent too much interpersonal focus:

4. Set clear priorities so social obligations don't crowd out critical work.
5. Maintain boundaries—balancing empathy with your own direction.
6. Give honest feedback when needed, even if it disrupts short-term harmony.

To maintain balance:

7. Combine clear communication, empathy, and purposeful networking to support both relationships and results without losing focus.

Reflection: *Based on the insights gained from this chapter, what is one small but impactful change you can make to strengthen your interpersonal skills?*

Riko, a project coordinator in Osaka, excelled at her individual tasks but struggled to build strong relationships with colleagues. She often worked in isolation, missing key opportunities to collaborate. Once she focused on improving her interpersonal skills—joining team discussions, showing empathy, and building rapport—her projects ran more smoothly, and her visibility increased. Samuel, a marketing executive in Nairobi, was highly social but lacked the ability to build deeper connections. His networking felt superficial, limiting trust with key stakeholders. When he made an effort to listen more and invest in authentic relationships, he built stronger alliances that advanced his career. Most smart people cannot succeed alone. Interpersonal Skills turn intelligence into collaboration, connection, and long-term influence.

For smart people, the goal is to engage others without becoming either dependent on approval or spreading themselves too thin. In the *Achievement Cycle*, Interpersonal Skills accelerate success by enhancing cooperation and broadening access to resources and support.

Smart people tend to focus on tasks over trust. They collaborate to complete, not to connect. To become more successful, smart people should slow down, share more than just deliverables, and ask: "What would deepen this relationship?" Competence earns respect; connection builds loyalty.

Building strong relationships lays the groundwork for success, but without effective Teamwork, smart people risk struggling to align with others and

Interpersonal Skills achieve shared goals. The next *Smartness Factor*—Teamwork—shows how they collaborate to drive collective success without losing sight of personal accountability.

> *"Smartness is knowing when to listen deeply and when to speak impactfully—and how to stay connected the rest of the time."*

For Deeper Insights

How do your Interpersonal Skills show up in your life? Do your mindset, behaviors, and habits reflect a strength or a hurdle? Take the Interpersonal Skills Assessment (www.MySmartness.com/Assessments) to identify your behavioral tendencies—whether you are a *Charismatic Connector*, a *People-Savvy Navigator*, a *Social Struggler*, or an *Invisible Wallflower*. Get insights on what's driving your success, what's getting in your way, and how you could become more successful.

Reflection: *Do your conversations build connections—or create distance? Are you being clear, present, and engaged—or drifting into confusion and detachment? What would improve if you treated every interaction as a chance to build trust, influence, and collaboration to achieve your desired outcomes?*

CHAPTER 43

TEAMWORK

"Alone, we can do so little; together, we can do so much."
~ Helen Keller

Teamwork is the ability to collaborate effectively with others—aligning around shared goals, contributing reliably, and delivering results together. It is a many-to-many skill for the team—but a one-to-many skill for you. For smart people, it turns isolated talent into collective impact.

Teamwork builds on Interpersonal Skills—but goes a step further. It's not just about connecting with others—it's about aligning, committing, and delivering results together. Remember the wild dogs and the cheetah example? Their success wasn't just about good communication—it was about coordinated execution. The same is true for smart people: it's not enough to be smart and communicate well—you have to work well, together.

Smart people often assume that getting the answer right is all that matters. But when work involves others—and it almost always does—success depends on the ability to collaborate, communicate, and contribute as a part of a team. Teamwork turns intelligence into impact by aligning diverse skills, perspectives, and ideas around shared goals.

Consider Alex, a gifted researcher at a biotech firm, whose preference for working alone left his team disconnected. Withholding crucial updates led to project delays, missed opportunities, and failure. In contrast, Lena, a senior strategist at a marketing agency, created an environment where ideas flowed freely and everyone contributed. Her team delivered innovative solutions, and their success became a shared win.

For smart people, the challenge isn't whether they can work independently—it's whether they can work with others. The smartest performers know how to blend individual strengths into cohesive, high-performing teams. For those seeking greater success, mastering teamwork dynamics is essential. This chapter explores how they do it and how Teamwork's enabling and disabling aspects influence outcomes across different settings.

Reflection: *How do your personal strengths and weaknesses influence your teaming skills? What adjustments can you make to enhance teamwork?*

Smartness Assessment Data Analysis

Among 1,200+ smart people who completed the *Smartness Assessment*, 24% of unsuccessful respondents identified Teamwork as a disabler—compared to 15% of successful ones. That 9% difference is significant. Teamwork helps you deliver—together—and requires many-to-many interaction. Your ability to contribute depends on how well you operate one-to-many. This isn't one of the more acute disablers for smart people—most do reasonably well here. There's no significant gender difference on this factor.

Correlation analysis shows strong positive relationships between Teamwork and Interpersonal Skills, Emotional Intelligence, and Relational Adaptability. Smart people who excel at Teamwork adjust their approach to fit different personalities and group dynamics—without losing effectiveness. There's also a medium correlation with Situational Judgment, showing that success in teams often depends on reading the room and shifting strategies. Teamwork and Interpersonal Skills support each other—but they're not the same. Their correlation is moderate. Failing to develop Teamwork—especially when combined with low Interpersonal Skills—limits influence, weakens collaboration, and reduces leadership potential, no matter how intelligent you are.

Reflection: *How do your teamworking skills shape how others perceive and respond to you? Have those skills held you back—and how can strengthening them support your goals?*

Enabling Aspects of Teamwork

For smart people, strong teamwork is essential to translating individual talent into collective success. When fully developed, teamwork allows them to collaborate, innovate, and deliver results that go beyond what any one person could achieve alone.

1. Better problem-solving and decision-making come from combining diverse perspectives—leading to more creative, well-rounded solutions.
2. Higher productivity and efficiency emerge when work is divided by strengths, allowing smart people to focus where they add the most value.
3. Faster learning and development happen when teammates share knowledge and insight—improving both individual growth and team cohesion.
4. Stronger relationships foster trust, respect, and open communication—motivating smart people to contribute more fully.
5. Productive conflict resolution helps smart people address disagreements directly, keeping momentum and morale intact.

Teamwork amplifies *Smartness* by linking individual abilities into a system that drives lasting achievement. Smart people who master it consistently outperform those who work alone.

Checklist to harness the enabling aspects of Teamwork:

1. Communicate openly and clearly to keep everyone aligned.
2. Delegate based on strengths to maximize performance.

3. Invite diverse perspectives and value different viewpoints.
4. Set clear, shared goals to guide team focus.
5. Build trust and respect to create a strong team culture.
6. Resolve conflicts quickly and collaboratively.
7. Celebrate wins to boost morale and reinforce shared success.
8. Give regular feedback to support growth.
9. Stay flexible and adapt as conditions shift.
10. Promote learning to strengthen the team over time.

Reflection: *Where have your teamwork skills contributed most to your success, and what could you do to strengthen them further?*

Disabling Aspects of Teamwork

Smart people struggle with Teamwork when falling into either of two extremes:

Too Little Teamwork:

1. Working in silos and avoiding collaboration, leaving others disconnected from critical information.
2. Rejecting diverse perspectives, resulting in stagnant ideas and missed opportunities.
3. Prioritizing autonomy over shared goals, weakening relationships and eroding team trust.

Too Much Teamwork:

1. Over-collaborating—too many meetings and consensus decisions slow momentum.
2. Hiding behind group decisions to avoid personal accountability.
3. Letting constant input dilute focus, leading to scattered efforts and unclear priorities.

Both extremes limit smart people. Too little teamwork breeds isolation and inefficiency. Too much creates confusion and decision paralysis. Repeated success requires balancing independent contribution with collaborative execution.

Checklist to Mitigate the Disabling Effects of Poor or Absent Teamwork:

To prevent too little teamwork:

1. Share regular updates to keep communication flowing and projects aligned.
2. Seek input from colleagues with complementary skills to gain new insights.
3. Identify collaboration opportunities—even when you're working independently.

To prevent too much teamwork:
4. Set boundaries—collaborate only when it adds value.
5. Own your responsibilities, no matter the team's decisions.
6. Streamline processes—don't let group input overcomplicate things.

To maintain balance:
7. Align your personal goals with shared team objectives.
8. Assess if your team dynamics are fueling progress—or just activity.

The *Achievement Cycle* shows that lasting success comes from managing Teamwork as both a strength and a safeguard—building strong collaborations while ensuring clarity and accountability. For smart people, the goal isn't just to work well with others—it's to create environments where the efforts of smart people combine, multiply, and turn shared effort into meaningful results.

Reflection: *Where do you tend to fall—too little or too much teamwork—and how is that affecting your success?*

Smartness in Action

Deepthi, a data scientist in Mumbai, was highly independent and preferred working alone. She struggled to collaborate with cross-functional teams, which limited her influence on large projects. When she began engaging more in team discussions and aligning her work with group goals, her contributions had broader impact—and she was tapped to lead collaborative initiatives.

Anthony, a team leader in Toronto, was so focused on consensus that he delayed decisions waiting for everyone's input. His team grew frustrated by the lack of progress. When he learned to balance collaboration with decisiveness, their productivity increased—and they delivered on time without losing unity.

Mastering Teamwork allows smart people to contribute to and lead high-performing teams—leveraging collective strengths to achieve complex goals. Over time, this capacity to collaborate increases their impact and scales their contribution. In the *Achievement Cycle*, effective Teamwork accelerates success by fostering synergy and delivering better results.

> *"Smartness is knowing when to collaborate fully—and when to lead with clarity and conviction."*

Smart people tend to see teams as inefficient or frustrating—slowing them down. They jump in late or stay detached. To become more successful, smart people should engage early, clarify shared goals, and contribute actively before taking control. Teams are not obstacles—they're multipliers.

For Deeper Insights

How does Teamwork show up in your life? Do your mindset, behaviors, and habits reflect a strength or a hurdle? Take the Teamwork Orientation Assessment (www.MySmartness.com/Assessments) to identify your behavioral tendencies—whether you are a *Teamwork Guru, Reliable Contributor, Reluctant Teammate,* or *Lone Wolf.* Get insights on what's driving your success, what's getting in your way, and how you could become more successful.

Reflection: *Do you elevate your team—or drift toward isolation? Are you building synergy—or avoiding collaboration because it feels slower or messier? What would change if you treated teamwork as an impact multiplier instead of a threat to your independence?*

CHAPTER 44

PERSONAL AUTONOMY

"Independence is a great virtue, but the best results are achieved when you also have the wisdom to seek help when needed."
~ Ram V. Iyer

Personal Autonomy is the ability to make decisions and act independently—without waiting for permission, external validation, or consensus. For many smart people, it's a key driver of fulfillment, impact, and long-term success.

Many smart people take pride in working independently. They trust their own intelligence and judgment, confident they can find the best solutions without needing much from others. But when Personal Autonomy goes unchecked, it becomes a disabler—isolating smart people, cutting them off from valuable collaboration, and quietly limiting their success.

In Samsung's phone lab, Park Joon, a brilliant designer, often worked solo, immersed in his unconventional ideas. He rarely shared his concepts or collaborated, missing out on input that could improve his work and drive wider acceptance. His independence, once his edge, was holding him back. By contrast, Maria, an engineer at a top Silicon Valley tech firm, balanced her autonomy with collaboration. She led projects with confidence but engaged colleagues and delegated many tasks to tap into their complementary strengths, quickly creating market-ready products—and propelled her career.

For successful smart people, the challenge isn't about operating autonomously, rather learning when to collaborate to be more effective and productive.

Reflection: *Do you tend to work independently like Park Joon or balance autonomy with collaboration like Maria? How might adjusting your approach improve your success?*

Smartness Assessment Data Analysis

Among 1,200+ smart people who completed the *Smartness Assessment*, Personal Autonomy affects 83% of unsuccessful respondents and 76% of successful ones—it's a major disabler of smart people. There is no significant gender difference—this struggle cuts across both men and women.

Correlation analysis shows strong positive relationships between Personal Autonomy and Complexity Preference, Risk Tolerance, Need for Variety, and Practical Intelligence. Smart people who develop these traits make independent decisions, take calculated risks, pivot when needed, and trust their judgment.

There's also a mild negative correlation between Personal Autonomy and both Teamwork and Thinking Range—suggesting that strong autonomy may sometimes reduce openness to collaboration or expansive thinking.

For smart people, developing Personal Autonomy means taking control of their path—while still knowing when collaboration, feedback, and shared decisions can elevate the outcome.

Enabling Aspects of Personal Autonomy

When smart people harness Personal Autonomy effectively, they unlock greater success across both work and life. The most successful smart people don't just act independently—they do so in ways that drive results and strengthen their impact.

1. Boosts intrinsic motivation: Autonomy fuels self-driven engagement, productivity, and satisfaction by aligning work with personal values.
2. Improves decision-making: Acting independently builds confidence and supports higher-quality, values-based decisions.
3. Encourages creativity: Freedom from rigid constraints invites experimentation, risk-taking, and innovation.
4. Builds resilience: With more control, smart people adapt faster to challenges and change.
5. Reduces stress and increases happiness: Living and working by your own values improves well-being and fulfillment.

Smart people who apply Personal Autonomy effectively also strengthen collaboration. They respect others' autonomy, support shared ownership, and build teams where accountability and creativity thrive. Bridgewater Associates, founded by Ray Dalio, is a prime example: they hire highly autonomous people who also operate with full accountability—creating a culture in which independence and collaboration drive performance.

Checklist to Harness Positive Aspects of Personal Autonomy

1. Be clear about your values and goals to guide decisions and keep your work aligned.
2. Choose environments and relationships that support independent thinking.
3. Reflect regularly on whether your daily actions match your long-term goals.
4. Make decisions that reflect your priorities, then refine your approach accordingly.
5. Surround yourself with others who value both autonomy and accountability, so you're consistently growing without sacrificing independence.
6. Practice decision-making—it will help you refine your approach and re-examine your values.

Personal Autonomy 235

For smart people, Personal Autonomy is a powerful enabler of success and well-being. Long-term achievement where autonomy and accountability thrive together.

Reflection: Think of a situation in which you had autonomy as well as accountability that contributed to your success and well-being. What made it work for you?

Disabling Aspects of Personal Autonomy

Personal Autonomy becomes a disabler when it goes too far in either direction—too much or too little. Both extremes can quietly sabotage success.

Too much Personal Autonomy:

1. You isolate yourself from collaboration and teamwork—cutting off ideas and support that could sharpen your thinking. The life of a lone wolf is not an easy one.
2. You get overconfident and make risky decisions without enough input.
3. You resist feedback—stalling your own growth.
4. You put personal agendas ahead of shared goals—eroding alignment and trust.

Too little Personal Autonomy:

1. You constantly rely on others for decisions, slowing progress.
2. You avoid responsibility—waiting for direction instead of taking initiative.
3. You fear acting independently—limiting innovation and courage.
4. You suppress your ideas or values to avoid conflict or fit in.

Checklist to Mitigate Disabling Aspects of Personal Autonomy

To prevent too much Personal Autonomy:

1. Actively seek input—even when you feel certain—to pressure-test your thinking.
2. Align your goals with shared objectives so your independence supports the team, not works against it.

To prevent too little Personal Autonomy:

3. Take ownership of decisions that are yours to make.
4. Assert your ideas and values even when they're unpopular—especially when they matter.

To maintain balance:

5. Treat feedback as a growth tool—not a threat to your independence.
6. Recognize when you're burning out from doing everything alone—and ask for help.

7. Know which challenges need collaboration, and which demand decisive solo action.

Reflection: How has too much or too little Personal Autonomy held you back? How can you create better balance to achieve better outcomes?

Smartness in Action

Nanditha, a program manager in San Francisco, frequently allowed others' opinions to sway her decisions. She found herself taking on projects that didn't align with her long-term goals, leading to frustration and burnout. After clarifying her priorities and setting clear boundaries, she began making choices that reflected her values and aspirations. Her performance improved, and her career took off. In contrast, Deng, a technology consultant in Hanoi, was fiercely independent but resisted feedback and collaboration. His rigid autonomy isolated him and limited his opportunities for growth. When he learned to maintain his personal autonomy while remaining open to input, he became more adaptable and effective, building stronger partnerships along the way.

Personal Autonomy empowers smart people to act according to their values and priorities without being unduly influenced by external pressures. Over time, this independence supports consistent, purpose-driven decision-making. In the *Achievement Cycle,* Personal Autonomy ensures they stay aligned with their long-term goals, accelerating meaningful success on their terms.

Smart people often resist structure, direction, or collaboration—seeing it as interference. They define freedom as control. To become more successful, smart people should align personal freedom with shared vision, ask for input without giving up ownership, and focus on making decisions that connect independence with effectiveness. Real autonomy accelerates, it doesn't isolate.

Maintaining Personal Autonomy keeps smart people aligned with their values, but without Relational Adaptability, they risk struggling to adjust to different people and environments. The next *Smartness Factor*—Relational Adaptability—shows how they stay authentic while flexing their approach to build stronger, more effective relationships.

Reflection: Where have you sacrificed your own autonomy and judgment to fit in, and how could reclaiming your autonomy lead to greater success?

> "Smartness is knowing when to go it alone—and when to align with others to go further."

For Deeper Insights

How does this factor show up in your life? Do your mindset, behaviors, and habits reflect a strength or a hurdle? Take the Personal Autonomy Assessment to identify your behavioral tendencies—whether you are a *Fiercely Independent,*

Self-Sufficient Strategist, Approval-Seeker, or *Direction-Dependent.* Get insights on what's driving your success, what's getting in your way, and how you could become more successful.

Reflection: *When did you sacrifice your autonomy to fit in—and what did it cost you? How would your career or life be different if you reclaimed that control? What decision are you avoiding that's truly yours to make?*

CHAPTER 45

RELATIONAL ADAPTABILITY

"Success isn't just about your capabilities or resources. It's how well you work with the people who don't think like you."
~ Ram V. Iyer

Relational Adaptability is the ability to adjust how you engage with different people and situations—without compromising who you are. Some smart people apply the same communication style across all situations—confident their message will land with everyone. But when they fail to adapt to different personalities, roles, or expectations, their ideas don't land—or get resisted. That's where Relational Adaptability becomes essential. It's not just what you say—it's how you say it, and how well it fits the person or situation in front of you.

Consider White, a brilliant engineer who thought the strength of his logic would carry the day. In meetings, he over-explained details, argued minor points, and left his colleagues frustrated. Instead of leading with clarity and influence, he buried good ideas under unnecessary complexity. Now contrast that with Deepa, a sharp consultant who rose quickly by adapting her communication to every setting. With executives, she was brief and solution-focused. With peers, she co-created ideas. With clients, she listened first and advised second. Deepa's Smartness wasn't just in what she knew—but in how she brought others along to solve problems.

Relational Adaptability isn't about being fake. It's about being smart enough to know that different people and situations require different approaches. You could think, "That's obvious!" However, for many smart people, this is one of the hardest skills to master, because they often live in their own head.

Reflection: *When have you stuck with your usual approach to engaging people, even when it clearly wasn't working? How could you change your approach to achieve better results?*

Smartness Assessment Data Analysis

Relational Adaptability was recently added to the *Smartness Factors* during research for this book. While smart people consistently reported struggles with communication, collaboration, and interpersonal dynamics, this factor pulls those themes together into one clear focus.

Though we don't yet have direct survey data for this factor, the correlation patterns are strong. Future versions of the *Smartness Assessment* will include

Relational Adaptability to explore its impact across life and career. As data emerges, we'll publish updated insights at www.MySmartness.com/books.

The strongest correlations appear with Emotional Intelligence, Interpersonal Skills, and Situational Judgment. Smart people who excel in these areas are better able to adjust their relational style in real time—improving collaboration, influence, and leadership impact.

Enabling Aspects of Relational Adaptability

When smart people apply Relational Adaptability well, they expand their influence and get their ideas heard and acted upon by a broad range of people. Smart people who master this skill don't just sound smart—they engage others in ways that move things forward.

1. Improves Engagement and Collaboration – Adapting your style strengthens group problem-solving and makes teamwork more productive.
2. Increases Influence – When you flex your communication, you build trust and credibility with diverse audiences.
3. Enhances Problem-Solving – Flexibility helps you integrate different perspectives for better solutions.
4. Strengthens Leadership – Knowing when to lead, support, or collaborate keeps you effective in any role.
5. Reduces Misunderstandings – Adjusting to context lowers the risk of friction and communication breakdowns.

When you master Relational Adaptability, you engage others in ways that get them aligned, involved, and invested in bringing your ideas to life.

Checklist to Harness Enabling Aspects of Relational Adaptability

1. Observe how people respond to you—and adjust your style accordingly.
2. Switch between leading, collaborating, and supporting roles based on the situation.
3. Prepare differently for meetings with executives, peers, and clients—don't show up the same way for everyone.
4. Ask for feedback from people you trust: How well do you adapt in group settings?
5. Reflect after high-stakes interactions. Did your approach fit the person and the moment?

Reflection: *How intentional are you in choosing how you communicate and present yourself—and where could greater clarity and presence help you create more impact?*

Disabling Aspects of Relational Adaptability

When Relational Adaptability becomes imbalanced:

Too much Relational Adaptability:

1. Over-accommodating others and losing your own voice.
2. Constantly shifting styles to please everyone, creating confusion.
3. Diluting your core message to avoid conflict.
4. Prioritizing social harmony over necessary truth.

Too little Relational Adaptability:

1. Relying on the same communication style, no matter the audience.
2. Ignoring social and emotional cues.
3. Overusing logic when empathy is needed.
4. Rejecting feedback about how your communication lands.

Checklist to Mitigate Disabling Aspects of Relational Adaptability

To prevent too much Relational Adaptability:

1. Stay clear on your key message, even as you adjust your delivery.
2. Set boundaries to avoid over-accommodating others' preferences.

To prevent too little Relational Adaptability:

3. Pay attention to how people are reacting—and modify your approach when needed.
4. Balance logic with emotional awareness in conversations.

To maintain balance:

5. Regularly ask for feedback on how your communication is received.
6. Prepare for different audiences by planning not just what to say, but how to say it.

Reflection: *When have you overcommunicated or held back—and how could better judgment in communication and presentation help you be more effective?*

Smartness in Action

Matthias, a regional director for an international development organization, was known for driving initiatives forward. Originally from Germany, he was used to direct communication, strict timelines, and top-down decision-making. It worked well at home, but when he began leading projects across different countries, his approach met resistance. In some regions, his fast decisions came across as dismissive; in others, his focus on efficiency over relationships slowed progress. Once Matthias adjusted—taking time to build trust, listening more, and involving local leaders earlier—partnerships strengthened, and projects moved forward with less friction.

Developing Relational Adaptability enables smart people to adjust how they communicate and interact to fit different people and situations. Over time, this flexibility strengthens relationships and broadens their influence. In the *Achievement Cycle*, Relational Adaptability accelerates achievement by enhancing their ability to lead diverse teams and navigate complex social dynamics.

Smart people tend to use a single relational mode—usually direct, data-driven, or efficient. But not all people respond the same way. To become more successful, smart people should observe others' communication preferences, flex their tone and pacing, and use empathy to build bridges. Influence starts with adjustment.

Adapting to different people and situations builds connection, but without intentional Communication Choices, smart people risk sending mixed signals that weaken their influence. The next *Smartness Factor*—Communication Choices—shows how they deliver clear, effective messages that align with their goals and strengthen their impact.

> *"Smartness is knowing when to flex your style—and when to stand firm in your identity."*

For Deeper Insights

How does this factor show up in your life? Do your mindset, behaviors, and habits reflect a strength or a hurdle? Take the Relational Adaptability Assessment (www.MySmartness.com/Assessments) to identify your behavioral tendencies—whether you are a *Lone Expert, Over-Explainer, Challenger,* or *Social Harmonizer*. Get insights on what's driving your success, what's getting in your way, and how you could become more successful.

Reflection: *Where have you applied a one-size-fits-all approach to relationships—and how might adjusting your style result in stronger connections and better results? When has your usual communication helped—or hurt—your influence? What would change if you became more intentional about when to flex and when to stand firm?*

CHAPTER 46

COMMUNICATION & PRESENTATION CHOICES

"Communication and presentation are not decorations—they're how the world sees, hears, and experiences you."
~ Ram V. Iyer

Communication and Presentation Choices are how you share your ideas, represent yourself, and shape how others experience you and your value. For smart people, this isn't about polish—it's about impact. Smart people often assume their intelligence, credentials, or track record will speak for themselves. But they don't—unless communicated and presented wisely. Achieving greater success depends not just on what you know, but how, when, where, and what you choose to share—through writing, speaking, visual presentation, or visible signals like clothing, affiliations, or presence, across platforms from meetings to social media. It's about judgment: what to say, how to say it, and how to ensure it lands with the right audience. Every interaction becomes either an opportunity—or a risk—based on your choices.

Consider Toshi, a brilliant researcher who assumed his credentials and ability to analyze complex data would carry him through any presentation. Instead, his detailed and complex explanations bored the audience and buried his message. He forgot that it wasn't just the data—it was how he framed and presented the data, and whether his audience 'got it'. Contrast that with Lila, a sharp entrepreneur who understood that timing, tone, visuals, and audience engagement are critical. In investor meetings, she led with the problem and the opportunity, presenting data in clear visuals that emphasized outcomes—easy to understand and sufficient for the purpose. On social media, she shared insights that sparked excitement and conversations. Her *Smartness* wasn't just in her ideas—it was in how she delivered them.

For smart people, Communication and Presentation Choices are often the difference between ideas that sit unnoticed and ideas that create impact. It's not about talking more or dressing for effect. It's about knowing how to share and present what matters in ways that move things forward.

Reflection: *Think of a time your ideas landed with a thud and went nowhere—and how might better communication and presentation choices have made them take off?*

Smartness Assessment Data Analysis

Communication & Presentation Choices was added as a distinct *Smartness Factor* after the original *Smartness Assessment* was completed, based on research for this book. Future versions of the *Smartness Assessment* will include this factor to explore its impact across life and career. As data emerges, we'll publish updated insights at www.MySmartness.com/books. While there's no direct survey data yet, this factor surfaced through lived experience and consistent patterns—showing how smart people succeed or fail based on what they communicate, when they communicate it, and how they deliver the message.

Personal Experience in Communication & Presentation Choices

One of the hardest things I've had to learn as a smart person isn't what to say—but when to say it. I've said things like, "Do you know who I am?" to lean on my family lineage, or, "I know so-and-so," to establish connections, and yes, "I'm an MIT grad," when I thought it might open a door. Sometimes it worked. Sometimes it blew up spectacularly. The truth is, blanket advice like "Never say that" is useless. These are advantages. If I don't use them thoughtfully, I lose the edge they provide. If I use them carelessly, I risk sounding arrogant or totally off-key—and people shut down fast.

But it's not just about words. How I present myself has often spoken louder than anything I've said. I've walked into high-stakes meetings underdressed, thinking my ideas alone would win the room. They didn't. I could feel the attention drain out of the room before I started my first sentence. I've also shown up in a sharp suit, and the vibe was completely different. People took me seriously before I opened my mouth - they weren't glued to their phones! That's when I realized that presentation isn't vanity. It's strategy.

And sometimes it's subtle. I've worn my MIT cap at certain gatherings, especially when I knew I'd be in a room with Ivy League or elite school alumni. It wasn't just a hat—it was shorthand that said, "I'm one of you." And it worked. But I've also left it in my bag when I knew it would make me look like I was trying too hard, or worse, like I thought I was better than everyone else. The MIT cap that gave me credibility in one room could make me seem tone-deaf in another.

I've learned—sometimes the hard way—that communication and presentation aren't afterthoughts. They're the front door to how people experience me, my ideas, and what I have to offer - often before I say a single word or do a single thing. If I get it wrong, they won't take me seriously or pay attention. Communicating your advantages requires good personal judgment. That's why this *Smartness Factor* exists.

Enabling Aspects of Communication and Presentation Choices

1. Clarifies value – Communicating and presenting clearly helps others quickly understand what smart people bring to the table.
2. Builds credibility – Thoughtful choices in what to say and how to present themselves reinforce trust and authority.
3. Increases engagement – Adapting communication and presentation to the audience keeps people interested and invested.
4. Strengthens influence – The right words, tone, and presence move others to support and act on their ideas.
5. Protects advantages – Knowing when to speak up—or stay silent—preserves credibility and prevents overexposure.

Checklist to Harness Enabling Aspects of Communication and Presentation Choices

1. Think ahead about how you want to communicate and present yourself in a particular situation. Decide on the impression you want to create—and how you could do it.
2. Focus on your objectives and what matters most to your audience. Clarify the key messages you want to deliver, in your own mind.
3. Figure out how to adapt your delivery—words, tone, and presence—to fit the audience, timing, and setting.
4. Pay attention to what your appearance, affiliations, and non-verbal cues are communicating saying before you say or do anything.
5. After key interactions, reflect on whether you communicated and presented yourself in a way that reinforced your objectives, value and credibility.

Disabling Aspects of Bad Communication and Presentation Choices

When smart people mismanage how they communicate and present themselves, they weaken their influence and credibility. They either **overcommunicate** or **under-communicate**, and both extremes limit their success. Poor communication and presentation choices often stem from ignoring the audience, failing to adapt, or relying too much on credentials or status instead of substance.

Overcommunicating

1. Oversharing credentials, achievements, or affiliations to the point of seeming arrogant.
2. Dominating conversations and leaving little room for others to contribute.
3. Over-promoting on platforms leads to audience fatigue or disinterest.

Communication & Presentation Choices

4. Relying on signals like titles, affiliations, or name-dropping instead of adding real value.

Under-Communicating

1. Failing to communicate key strengths or insights when they could make a difference.
2. Staying silent in important discussions, missing opportunities to contribute, lead, or be visible.
3. Under-communicating achievements, leaving others unaware of their value.
4. Avoiding self-promotion entirely, which leads to being overlooked for opportunities.

Checklist to Mitigate Disabling Aspects of Communication and Presentation Choices

To avoid overcommunicating:

1. Focus on relevance. Share only what directly supports the conversation, decision, or objective.
2. Create space for others. Don't dominate conversations or make it all about you.
3. Limit self-promotion. Let your results and impact speak for themselves when possible.
4. Watch for audience fatigue. Don't overexplain, overshare, or overuse your credentials.

To avoid under-communicating:

5. Recognize key moments to speak up. Share your credentials or experience when it helps solve a problem or builds trust.
6. Push through the discomfort. Offer your insights even when self-promotion feels awkward.
7. Clarify your contributions. Don't assume others know what you've done—or what you're capable of.
8. Ask for feedback. Trusted peers can help you see if you're too invisible or missing key moments to communicate your value.

To maintain balance:

9. Match your message to the moment. Adjust what and how you share based on the audience and setting.
10. Be intentional about your signals. Use appearance, tone, and timing to reinforce—not distract from—your value.
11. Review your impact. After key interactions, ask yourself: Did I make my value clear—or muddy the message?

Smartness in Action

Olivia, an American operations manager at a British firm with a formal culture, struggled to connect with colleagues from different backgrounds. Her direct communication style often came across as blunt, and her presentation—showing up in casual clothes and delivering dense, data-heavy slides—created distance in an environment that valued polish, formality, and relationship-building. When she adjusted both how she communicated and how she presented herself—dressing more formally, simplifying her visuals, and leading with clear, relatable stories—her ideas gained traction. Cross-cultural collaborations improved, and her influence grew.

Developing Communication and Presentation Choices helps smart people manage how they are seen and heard. Over time, this sharpens credibility, strengthens influence, and ensures their ideas get the attention they deserve. In the *Achievement Cycle*, Communication and Presentation Choices accelerate achievement by ensuring clarity, alignment, and impact in every interaction.

> *"Smartness is knowing when to flex your style—and when to stand firm in your identity."*

Smart people tend to either take over conversations or fade into the background. Some dominate with too much detail or intensity, while others say too little and miss chances to influence. To become more successful, smart people should lead with what matters, match tone to context, and adapt their delivery to the audience. Communication and presentation should clarify, not overwhelm—and influence, not hide.

Mastering the *Smartness Factors* equips smart people with the mindsets, behaviors, and skills to turn intelligence into consistent success. But knowing the factors isn't enough. In Part 5, we explore how smart people apply the Achievement Cycle to bridge the gap between potential and real-world achievement—turning *Smartness* into greater success, again and again.

For Deeper Insights

How does Communication and Presentation Choices show up in your life? Do your mindset, behaviors, and habits reflect a strength or a hurdle? Take the Communication and Presentation Choices Assessment (www.MySmartness.com/Assessments) to identify your behavioral tendencies—whether you are a *Clear Communicator, Adaptive Presenter, Reluctant Communicator,* or *Misaligned Communicator*. Get insights on what's driving your success, what's getting in your way, and how you could improve your ability to communicate and present yourself for greater success.

Reflection: *Where have your communication or presentation choices worked against you—and how might refining them increase your influence and results?*

Communication & Presentation Choices

Now that you've learned how to communicate and present yourself effectively, it's time to apply those choices in a way that accelerates your results. In the next chapter, we'll bring it all together into a repeatable cycle that turns your smarts and potential into sustainable achievement. Smart people don't just think or talk about success—they act, and they strengthen their *Smartness* every time they do.

Reflection: *When have your communication or presentation choices amplified your impact—and when have they held you back? Are you clearly signaling your value and intention, or sending mixed messages that confuse or diminish your influence? What small shift could help your words, tone, or presence speak more powerfully on your behalf?*

PART 5

LEVERAGING SMARTNESS TO ACHIEVE SUCCESS

Now that you understand all the *Smartness Factors*, you know how critical it is to align your mindsets, behaviors, and skills in order to turn intelligence into consistent achievement. But knowing what to do isn't enough. This is where action matters—you need to apply *Smartness* systematically to close the gap between potential and lasting success.

Many smart people chase recognition—grades, titles, applause. But success isn't built on applause. It's built on impact. The moment you stop asking "What will they think?" and start asking "What will this change?" is when Smartness truly activates. Part 5 is about moving from idea to execution—from insight to action. This is where it counts.

Smart people often over-rely on their intelligence, credentials, or status—expecting results to follow. They don't. Success doesn't come from your advantages—it comes from how well you use them.

Leveraging *Smartness* means recognizing your advantages, using them intentionally, and consistently turning potential into real outcomes. This section focuses on how smart people use *Smartness* in their decisions, actions, and relationships to accelerate achievement.

> *"Success doesn't come from just being smarter. It comes from using Smartness effectively to achieve real-world results."*

CHAPTER 47

BRINGING IT ALL TOGETHER: THE ACHIEVEMENT CYCLE

"Greater success isn't achieved in a single step—it's an ongoing cycle of understanding yourself, taking action, learning, and adapting. That's how repeated success is achieved."
~ Ram V. Iyer

Over the years, I've heard countless claims about what drives success: the value of advantages like intelligence, elite credentials are a sure ticket to success (some smart people still think that), why street smarts are all you need to succeed, and how some individuals achieved repeated success by doing only 'one thing'. If those were true, wouldn't everyone already be highly successful?

Then, one day, I connected the dots and realized that *Smartness* is what separates intelligence from real-world success. Some smart people assume that intelligence alone will get them there, but without the ability to assess situations, adapt, and execute effectively, intelligence remains potential rather than progress. *Smartness* must be actively developed and applied. That's why some high school dropouts achieve more than Ivy League graduates—they use what they have and get smarter every time they act, reflect, and adapt.

I also realized that success doesn't follow a straight line—it's an iterative process. Smart people don't succeed because they get everything right the first time. They succeed because they keep learning, doing, and improving—again and again. The more you work at becoming successful—even if you fail several times—the more likely success becomes—not by chance, but by design.

But, what do you need to do, and what is the process?

We've covered the 'what' in the book already – understanding yourself, developing clarity of what you want to achieve, gathering the knowledge, learning how to use your enablers and mitigate your disablers, making decisions, and then taking action. That's most of it. In this chapter, we'll learn about a couple more steps and how these work as a cycle – the *Achievement Cycle*. Greater success doesn't come in a single step—it's a cycle.

The Success Triad

Before you dive into the cycle, check your Success Triad, which we covered in Chapter 1. No matter how smart you are, ask yourself:

1. Have I clearly defined my Aspirations—what success looks like for me?
2. Do I have the Knowledge required to move forward?

3. Am I taking Action toward my goals?

If you answered 'no' to any of these, return to the *Success Triad* before applying the *Achievement Cycle*. Without Aspiration, Knowledge, and Action in place, *Smartness* has nothing to optimize. In simple terms, the Success Triad is a prerequisite, and the *Achievement Cycle* is a method of applying *Smartness*.

> *"Smartness is what turns intelligent people into successful people."*

The Achievement Cycle: How Smart People Turn Potential into Results

The *Achievement Cycle* is the iterative, skill-driven process that ties together all the elements we've covered—advantages (like intelligence) and disadvantages, assessing situations, exercising judgment, taking action, and achieving. Each time you go through the cycle, you get sharper. And the smart use of your *Smartness Factors* enables even greater success.

Smartness enhances every step of the *Achievement Cycle*—and your *Smartness* improves every time you complete a cycle. The more you use the *Achievement Cycle*, the sharper your *Smartness* becomes. And the sharper your Smartness, the easier it is to move through each stage with confidence and clarity.

The Earned Mindset, which we covered earlier, is the foundation *Smartness* is built on—and *Smartness* powers every stage of the Achievement Cycle. Success is not granted. It must be earned—again and again. Smart people who apply the Achievement Cycle earn their success deliberately and consistently.

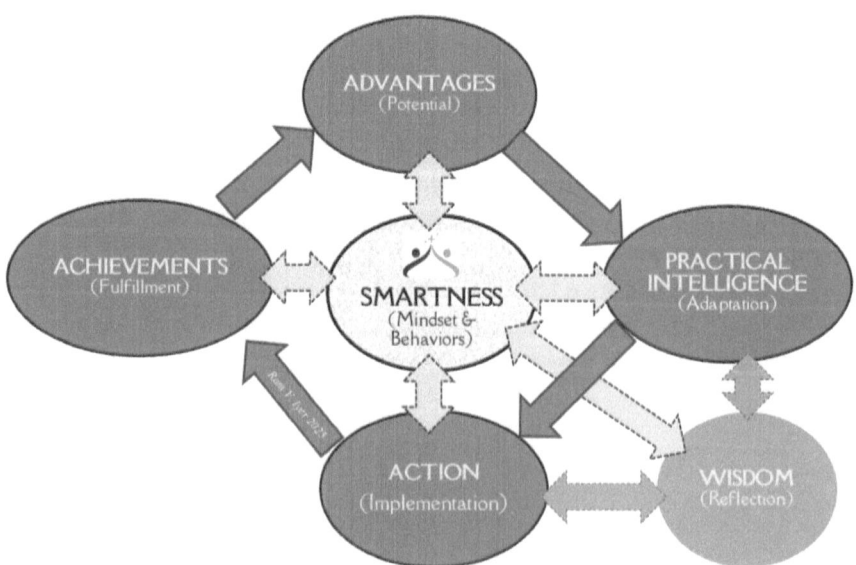

The Five Stages of the Achievement Cycle

Smartness strengthens every stage of the Achievement Cycle—and gets stronger every time you use it. Each pass makes you sharper, more adaptable, and more effective. The better your Smartness, the better you become at each of the five stages:

- You'll be more precise in identifying your Advantages.
- Sharper in applying Practical Intelligence.
- More decisive in taking Action.
- More insightful in gaining Wisdom.
- And more consistent in achieving real results.

Let's dig into each of the stages to understand them better:

1. Advantages (Potential)
What you have. Your raw materials—intelligence, skills, experience, networks, and resources. *Smartness* helps you recognize and use the full range of your advantages without over-relying on just one. You should also identify your disadvantages in the particular situation. When you actively identify and develop your advantages, and manage your disadvantages, you gain a clearer, more realistic view of what you're capable of. That makes it easier to make smart choices about when to act, how to adapt, and where to focus your energy.

2. Practical Intelligence (Adaptation)
It is about how you decide to use what you have. This is where you apply judgment, read situations, and adapt to what's happening in real time. *Smartness* sharpens your ability to assess situations and choose the best path forward. As your Situational Judgment improves, you get better at making smart, fast decisions that increase your chances of success.

3. Action (Implementation)
What you do. This is about moving from decision to action—and making it count. *Smartness* helps you break out of analysis mode and take decisive steps, even when the situation is uncertain. As your Action Orientation improves, your follow-through strengthens—and your results do too.

4. Wisdom (Reflection)
What you learn. Every experience teaches you something—if you're paying attention. Smartness helps you reflect on what worked and what didn't, and turn that insight into better decisions next time. For example, reflecting on how you handled a tough conversation might sharpen your Emotional Intelligence—helping you understand others more clearly and respond more effectively. The more you do this, the better you get at learning from experience—and the smarter you become over time.

5. Achievement (Fulfillment)
What you earn. This is the payoff. Smartness ensures your achievements aren't flukes—they're part of a process you can repeat. For example, as you deliver real results, you build greater Career Flexibility. More opportunities show up, and you're better equipped to take advantage of them. Achievement isn't about titles or trophies. It's about delivering results, sustaining success, and reaching the goals that matter to you.

The Cycle Reinforces Itself

The Achievement Cycle isn't a once-and-done model. It's a repeatable process that helps you keep learning, acting, and improving—building on itself. The more you use it, the better you get—and the more often you will succeed. That's how success compounds over time.

Without Smartness:

- Advantages will sit idle, wasting potential.
- Decisions will lack adaptability, making even smart people rigid in their thinking.
- Actions will become reactive, reducing the likelihood of success.
- Wisdom will plateau, causing people to repeat mistakes rather than improve.

Smartness turns the *Achievement Cycle* from theory into practice. It links every stage—and ensures your intelligence is actually put to work.

The Need to Be Right: A Barrier to Learning

The human desire to be right is a formidable obstacle to learning and achieving greater success. This need can prevent us from acknowledging mistakes, learning from them, and adapting —all critical steps in the Achievement Cycle. Ego overrides reflection and learning. In contrast, AI systems like ChatGPT—designed to perform tasks, learn from feedback, and improve over time—operate without ego, executing tasks, learning from feedback, and adjusting without needing to be right, or fear being wrong.

> *The biggest difference between humans and machines is not intelligence. It's ego.*

ChatGPT is a good example—it doesn't have ego, it adjusts based on feedback, and it keeps improving without defensiveness. It may come up with a wrong answer and you may call it "stupid," but it then apologizes and comes back with a better answer.

While many fear AI, few stop to ask why it works so well. It's not magic. It's process. AI systems were built by humans to do what we already know drives success: define goals, gather knowledge and insights, take action, reflect and learn, adapt, and repeat. They follow the Achievement Cycle—a framework originally developed by humans because it works. Ironically, AI applies this human-created process with more discipline and consistency than most people do. If you embrace the same process and apply it in your own life—with just as much discipline and commitment—you too can become more successful. If you want proof on the effectiveness of the Achievement Cycle, just look at how well AI platforms like ChatGPT and Claude work.

Like machines, the most successful people don't get stuck defending themselves—they act, learn, adapt, and move. Humans expect machine-like repeated success—without being consistently disciplined like machines. The Achievement Cycle helps you develop that discipline: to act, learn, adapt, and progress. As you repeatedly apply the Achievement Cycle, you develop your Smartness—and learn how to use it much more effectively.

> *If you want machine-like progress, you need ego-free learning —and the willingness to apply what you've learned and adapt.*

AI works because it follows a process we created—but often fail to follow ourselves. Imagine if we consistently did: not perfectly, not robotically, but with less ego and more consistent learning. Competence would build. Progress would accelerate. You'd start getting the results you want—by doing what you already know works. AI systems embody the very principles we advocate for: action, reflection, learning, and adaptation.

How Humans and AI Systems Apply the Achievement Cycle

Step	The Achievement Cycle (Humans)	AI Systems (Machines)
1. Aspiration	Define a meaningful goal or desired outcome	Set an objective or receive a user-defined task
2. Knowledge	Acquire the necessary skills, information, or insights	Access or retrieve data (memory, web, tools)
3. Action	Execute steps toward the goal—even imperfectly	Take structured steps—even if the answer might be wrong
4. Reflection	Evaluate progress, identify errors, extract learnings	Analyze results, detect failures or gaps – primarily from user feedback
5. Adaptation	Adjust mindset, strategy, or approach to improve	Rerun plan with user feedback and new context to improve
→ LOOP	Repeat with stronger execution and sharper insight	Repeat until task is completed or optimized

To truly harness our intelligence and become more successful, we must overcome the need to be right and embrace the continuous process of learning.

> *"The need to be right is the reason so many smart people never get better and struggle to achieve more."*

Smartness in Action: Real-World Examples of Success

Let's look at how extraordinary Smartness—not necessarily extraordinary intelligence—drives success. Richard Branson, the highly successful entrepreneur, is dyslexic and never seen as traditionally intelligent. Sam Walton, who built Walmart on relentless practicality, was not academically brilliant. Herb Kelleher, a lawyer with no aviation background, built Southwest into a highly successful airline through unconventional leadership. None of them were Ivy League grads or intellectual prodigies. Yet all three became world-famous—and were invited to speak at many elite universities. Not because of their intelligence—but because of their successes. What they share isn't raw IQ—it's extraordinary Smartness: the ability to assess, adapt, decide, and act effectively—again and again.

How to Use the Achievement Cycle to Accelerate Your Success

The Achievement Cycle turns intelligence into results—by removing hesitation, bottlenecks, and friction. Without Smartness, intelligence alone stalls. But with Smartness, your potential becomes performance.

You've completed your Smartness Assessment. You know your advantages. You see your enablers and disablers. Now it's time to act.

If you overthink, delay, or wait for better conditions, you're not alone. Most smart people hesitate—96% struggle with Action Orientation, to some extent (46%) little or a great extent (50%). Armed with the knowledge gained in this book, you can break that pattern.

The key is to act—deliberately and consistently. Success doesn't come from waiting. It comes from working the cycle. And you can start right now, from exactly where you are. As Matt Damon's character said in the movie, "We Bought a Zoo," – "It takes just 15 seconds of courage!"

Applying the Achievement Cycle

Smart people apply the *Achievement Cycle* intentionally and consistently to accelerate their success. Whether you're leading a team, navigating a transition, or growing personally, it adapts to your situation.

Bringing It All Together: The Achievement Cycle

Here's how to apply it in any context:

1. Take Inventory
   Identify your current Advantages. What do you have right now—skills, knowledge, relationships, resources—that can move you forward? Also be honest about your disadvantages—you need a clear view of both.
2. Assess the Situation
   Apply your Practical Intelligence. What's the current context? What's changing? What needs to change? What's the smartest next move?
3. Decide and Act
   Smart people don't stay stuck in analysis—they act. Decide on a clear next action that uses your advantages and fits the situation. Then move.
4. Reflect and Learn
   After action, take time to reflect. What worked? What didn't? What will you do differently next time? This is how you build Wisdom and sharpen *Smartness*.
5. Track Achievements and Restart the Cycle
   Recognize your results—whether success or lessons learned. Use that momentum to restart the cycle, with sharper *Smartness* and a clearer sense of direction.

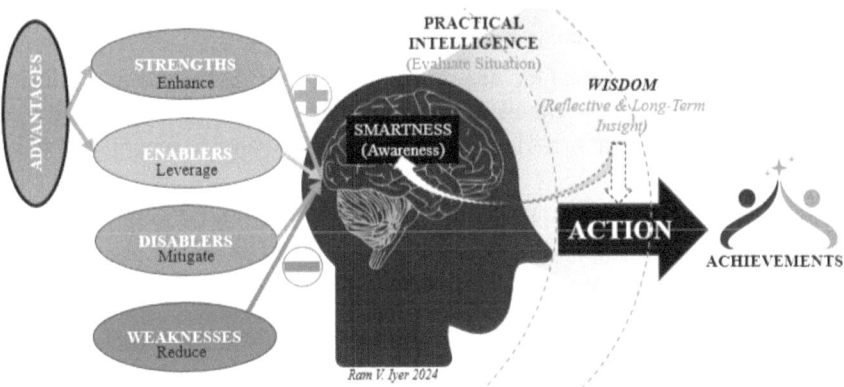

Where Are You in the Cycle Right Now?

Ask yourself:

- Which stage of the Achievement Cycle comes easily to you?
- Which one requires more attention or effort?
- If you're stalled, reassess your Advantages and act.
- If you're hesitating, make a decision and move.
- If you've acted, reflect on what worked and what didn't.
- If you're achieving, use that momentum to start the next cycle.

The smartest people don't wait. They work the cycle—again and again.

Example: Veronica's Achievement Cycle

Veronica was a brilliant data scientist—Ivy League educated, technically sharp, but stuck. Despite her credentials, she kept getting passed over for leadership roles.

1. When she took inventory of her Advantages, she realized she had more than just technical depth. She had a strong network, project leadership experience, and a calm presence under pressure.
2. She assessed the situation and saw that solving problems wasn't enough. The company needed leaders who could align teams and drive outcomes. She shifted focus—taking on visible, cross-functional projects.
3. Then she acted. She pitched a high-stakes initiative to leadership—outside her comfort zone, but high impact.
4. As the project rolled out, she reflected on what worked and what didn't. She improved how she communicated with stakeholders and handled resistance.

Then she did it again. Each cycle sharpened her Smartness and deepened her results. Veronica's success wasn't a one-off. It was built—step by step, cycle by cycle.

The result: a successful launch, measurable revenue growth, and expanded Career Flexibility. People now see her as a strategic leader—and she started getting recruited by other companies.

It's not just for careers. One person repaired a strained friendship by leaning into patience and timing—choosing the right moment, acting with honesty, and reflecting afterward. That experience shaped how they handled other relationships too.

No two smart people apply the cycle the same way. A CEO might use it to guide leadership decisions. A student might use it to choose a career path. The process stays the same—but how you apply it depends on your goals.

> *"Smart people who use the Achievement Cycle don't just succeed once—they succeed again and again. That's how they become truly successful people. "*

How Smartness Amplifies the Cycle

Smartness doesn't just power the Achievement Cycle—it grows through it. Each time you run the cycle, your judgment sharpens, your decisions improve, and your outcomes compound.

Smartness is shaped by time, experience, and situations. It's built through action—not theory. Every pass through the cycle makes you more effective at assessing, adapting, and acting in the real world. The Achievement Cycle functions as a feedback loop:

- The more effectively you apply your advantages, the stronger your judgment becomes. But if you misuse them, your judgment declines.
- The more experience you gain, the more wisdom and Smartness you develop.

Success builds through repetition. Smartness makes that repetition smarter.

> *"More big breakthroughs come from unlearning than from new learning; and from shedding bad habits than blindly developing new ones."*

Smart people often stay stuck not because they aren't smart, but because they stay wedded to their old ways of seeing the world, old ways of thinking, and old habits. That's where Inversion Thinking helps—it shows you what you need to let go of or change. The Achievement Cycle gives you a clear process to unlearn what's no longer working—or needs to change—and replace it with something better. And Smartness is what makes both possible. It gives you the ability to challenge outdated beliefs, break unhelpful habits, and build new patterns that actually lead to success. You don't need to become more intelligent—you need to get better at letting go, learning forward, and applying what matters most.

Focus on What You Control

Successful smart people focus on what they can control—not just the outcomes they want. Recognition, validation, and promotions are external. But effort, decisions, and relationships are in your hands.

The Achievement Cycle works when you manage the quality of your inputs: the work you do, the learning you apply, and how you show up. When that's deliberate, outcomes take care of themselves.

Don't over-rely on a single advantage. Wealth is useless if spent recklessly—and intelligence, if misapplied, leads to stagnation. Smartness is knowing what to use, when to adapt, and how to move forward.

> *"Achievement requires patience—often having to endure repeated failures."*

Success doesn't happen by chance. It's the result of repeated cycles of developing and applying one's *Smartness* intentionally. You now have the roadmap—use it. Success isn't guaranteed, no matter how smart you are. But by applying the Achievement Cycle—again and again—you can earn it.

How to Start Right Now

- *If you're stuck*, reassess your Advantages and take the next step.
- *If you're hesitating*, move forward—worst case, you'll learn from the experience.
- *If you've taken action*, reflect on what worked and what didn't.

- *If you're achieving*, use that momentum to begin the next cycle.

Smartness sharpens at every stage—but only if you move. Start where you are, and use what you have.

Reflection: *Where do you excel most in the Achievement Cycle right now? Which advantage do you tend to over-rely on—and how can you balance it? What's one action you can take today that moves you from potential to achievement?*

> "Intelligence is an advantage, but Smartness is what determines whether that intelligence leads to success or stagnation."

Nobody achieves their full potential alone. The next step is building a support system that accelerates your Smartness. That's what the next chapter is about. In that chapter, we explore how smart people find their tribe and mentors—people who challenge, support, and accelerate their growth.

Reflection: *What's really holding you back—hiding behind your advantages, stuck in overthinking, avoiding action, skipping reflection, or chasing wins without direction? When things get hard, which part of the cycle do you bail on first—deciding, doing, or learning from the fallout? What would change if you stopped hesitating and ran through that door like a bull?*

For a practical, step-by-step guide to implement the *Achievement Cycle*, get the companion *Smartness Playbook*. It's filled with hands-on tools and worksheets designed to help you build your personal roadmap, identify your enablers and disablers, and apply *Smartness* in your daily life with the *Achievement Cycle*.

CHAPTER 48

Find Your Tribe & Mentors

"Surround yourself with people who see your potential—even when you may not see it yourself"
~ Ram V. Iyer

You cannot become an achiever alone. Smart people often underestimate how much their success depends on who surrounds them. Early on, they rely on intelligence, credentials, and early wins. But as life and careers evolve, those advantages stop being enough. No one gets to the next level alone.

Smartness isn't just what you know or do—it's also who you surround yourself with. Who challenges you? Who holds you accountable for your commitments? Who helps you reflect? Who pushes you when you're stuck? If you're still relying on the same people who supported you early on—family, classmates, coworkers from your first job—you may already be behind. As you evolve, your tribe must evolve, too. The right people accelerate your growth. The wrong ones hold you back. That's why the smartest people build a Personal Support Ecosystem—a network of people who help them grow faster, deeper, and more consistently than they ever could alone.

You need three kinds of people: mentors (for perspective), tribe (for pressure), and accountability partners (to keep you honest).

> *"Who got you here can't get you there."*

The Role of Mentors vs. Tribe

Mentors and tribes serve different purposes in a smart person's journey—and you need both.

Mentors are typically more experienced. They've been there. Done that. Their wisdom helps you avoid costly mistakes. They offer guidance, perspective, and sharper thinking—based on walking the path ahead of you. They help you see around corners and accelerate your learning curve. Good mentors don't just tell you what to do—they challenge your assumptions and improve your thinking. They're not in the trenches. They don't see your day-to-day moves. Mentors provide perspective—and help you think better.

Your tribe is your peers—similarly driven, ambitious, and pushing for the next level. They're in it with you—facing similar challenges and sharing the same urgency. They hold you accountable, offer emotional support, and expand your thinking. Your tribe is both fuel and friction: they'll back you up—and call you out. Tribes raise the bar through collaboration, competition, and shared ambition. There's mutual respect—and neither side wants to fall behind.

Tribe brings pressure. They make sure you follow through. They're often the first to call you out when you stall or play small. The right tribe accelerates your Smartness—because they're committed to developing theirs, too. Smart people thrive in communities that challenge their thinking and push them beyond their comfort zones.

How to Identify a High-Value Tribe

A powerful tribe isn't just about who you like—it's about who can make you better. Seek people who:

- Expose you to new ways of thinking rather than simply reinforcing what you already know.
- Have strengths you lack—whether it's execution, networking, or risk-taking.
- Push you toward action, not just discussion.
- Hold you accountable to a higher standard than you set for yourself.

7 Ways to Build a Smarter Tribe

Now that we've explored the importance of having a tribe and mentors, let's look at how you can actively build your own network of like-minded individuals and supportive allies. Building a tribe isn't just about finding people—it's about cultivating meaningful relationships with those who align with your journey and values.

1. **Clarify your goals**
   Before building your tribe, be clear on what you're striving for and why. Don't chase prestigious names or status—look for people who genuinely care and will invest in your success.
2. **Make it a high priority**
   Don't leave it to chance. Building the right tribe is as strategic as building your skillset or business.
3. **Choose people with shared ambition—and high standards**
   Look for people who push themselves, not just talk a good game. They need to be as driven—or more driven—than you. Values matter, but so does urgency.
4. **Leverage existing networks**
   Tap into current circles—friends, colleagues, alumni groups, or professional communities. Most people overlook one of the easiest access points: alumni directories. If nothing fits, build your own.

5. **Look outside your current circle**
   Don't limit yourself to the familiar. Reach across industries, geographies, and stages of life. Growth rarely comes from comfort zones.
6. **Join strong communities**
   Get in rooms where excellence is the norm—masterminds, accelerators, high-performing groups. If it feels a little intimidating, that's a good sign. It means you're going to learn and grow.
7. **Join online communities**
   Use digital platforms—forums, social groups, or tools like LinkedIn and Doximity. Communities now form around everything: career stage, profession, industry, even mindset.
8. **Be intentional in how you connect**
   Don't wait for relationships to happen. Reach out. Follow up. Ask thoughtful questions. Connection is a practice, not a personality trait.
9. **Create value first**
   Share insight. Make introductions. Offer help. Givers build tribes. Takers burn bridges. Show them you're here to contribute.
10. **Ask for accountability**
    Invite people to hold you to your goals—and do the same for them. Don't just connect—commit.

Ditch the comfort crew of dinosaurs. Build a tribe of movers and shakers.

Reflection: *Who do you need more of—and less of—in your tribe to reach your next level? What bold move will you make to shift your circle?*

Accountability Partners

You also need somebody to hold you accountable. Even the smartest people procrastinate. Discipline is hard. We're wired to take the easy way out—mentally and physically. Without external accountability, most people drift.

If you're not crystal clear on your goals, have a compelling 'why,' and take intentional actions, you'll struggle to follow through consistently.

My good friend, world-renowned executive coach Dr. Marshall Goldsmith, has someone call him every single day to hold him accountable. If Marshall—one of the top coaches on the planet—needs this, what does that say about the rest of us?

An accountability partner complements—but doesn't replace—your tribe or mentors. They help you stay consistent on the daily grind, while your tribe expands your thinking and your mentors offer long-term guidance. You need all three to keep moving forward.

> *"Your mentors guide you, your tribe challenges you, and your accountability partner makes sure you follow through."*

Personal Example: My Journey with Mentors and Networks

I can relate to the importance of having the right tribe and mentors. When I got off the corporate track and sought to pursue an entrepreneurial venture, I was banking on my accomplishments, education, and existing tribe to continue propelling me.

For a while, they did... until they didn't.

I failed to sufficiently expand my tribe into the new field I was in. I had some successes in that venture, but not many. It got worse in my next venture when my old tribe—and the smallness of my expanded tribe—proved to be inadequate.

The problem was staring me in the face, but I didn't recognize it. I had mentors, but they were from the corporate world. They didn't fully understand the challenges I was facing as an entrepreneur and their well-intentioned advice was not helping.

I realized I couldn't break through without guidance and support. My close friends and family, though supportive, didn't truly understand the risks and pressures I was navigating.

Some thought I was infallible and needed no help. Others couldn't relate to my challenges as an entrepreneur.

It became clear that I needed guidance from those who had walked a similar path—mentors and peers who understood what I was going through and provide actionable advice, fresh perspectives, and encouragement. That realization was a rude awakening.

> *"Who got you here may not be able to get you there."*

I was reminded of a key insight from the book, *The Innovator's Dilemma*, written by one of my thesis advisors, the late Dr. Clayton Christensen of Harvard Business School. He argued that companies often struggle to adapt to the next stage of innovation because they rely too much on what made them successful in the past.

I realized that the same applies to people. My old mentors and tribe had helped me reach a certain level of success, but they weren't the right people to guide me into this next stage of my journey. To break through, I needed to step outside my existing network and actively seek out those who had already succeeded in the path I wanted to take. I also needed a tribe that understood the entrepreneurial game.

For my next venture, I made a conscious effort to seek out the right tribe and mentors who could guide me on the journey I was on, ones who had walked the entrepreneurial path before me. Their advice saved me from making costly mistakes. I also joined groups of like-minded individuals—fellow entrepreneurs navigating similar challenges. Sharing experiences with people who truly 'get it' was a game-changer. These networks not only provided guidance and feedback but also a sense of camaraderie and periodic confidence boosts.

Find Your Tribe & Mentors

Lesson learned: No matter how smart or knowledgeable you are, the right people can help you go further and faster than you might be able to on your own. And while one group may support you in some areas, it's unlikely they'll meet all your needs—you'll need to continually seek out different people and communities to support your growth in different ways.

Benefits of a Support System

If you're still wondering why, you should invest time in building your own support system, consider these key benefits:

1. **Perspective and Guidance**: No matter how skilled or knowledgeable you are, you can't see your own blind spots. Your tribe brings diverse perspectives, offering you feedback, insights, and wisdom you may not arrive at alone. They help you course-correct, spot opportunities, and avoid pitfalls.
2. **Support in Tough Times:** Success isn't a straight path—it's filled with challenges, failures, and setbacks. A strong tribe acts as your safety net, providing emotional support, encouragement, and constructive advice when you need it most. They help you stay grounded and resilient.
3. **Opportunities Through Connection:** Often, your next big break won't come solely from your talents but from the doors your tribe can open for you. They amplify your reach, connect you to influential people, and make introductions that lead to new opportunities.
4. **Accountability and Motivation:** Your tribe holds you accountable for your goals, helping you maintain focus and discipline. Knowing that people you respect are rooting for you—and expecting results—can be a powerful motivator.
5. **Accelerated Learning:** Learning doesn't only happen in isolation. Interacting with people who have walked different paths allows you to absorb their experiences and wisdom. This accelerates your growth in ways that self-study alone can't replicate.
6. **Inspiration and Energy:** Being part of a group that shares your values and ambitions fuels your own drive. Seeing others succeed pushes you to aim higher and reminds you that greater heights are achievable.

> *"The right tribe doesn't just support you—it makes you better!"*

Avoiding the Wrong Tribe

Not every group is worth joining. Some will pull you forward, while others will hold you back. The wrong tribe can reinforce bad habits, limit your thinking, or keep you stuck in an unproductive cycle. Smart people often assume that any intellectually stimulating group is beneficial—but if the group isn't pushing you toward action, it's just a distraction.

Here are three types of tribes to avoid:

- **The Comfort Zone Club.** If your tribe always agrees with you, validates your opinions, and never pushes you to grow, you're in the wrong room. The best groups challenge your thinking and force you to refine your ideas—not just cheerlead.
- **The Endless Debate Society.** Some groups are filled with brilliant talkers but poor executors. If your conversations are full of big ideas but nothing ever happens, you're stuck in an intellectual echo chamber that will slow you down.
- **The Stagnant Network.** If the people around you aren't learning, evolving, or actively pursuing bigger goals, they will keep you anchored in the past. A great tribe is full of people who are constantly leveling up—and expect you to do the same.

A strong tribe challenges you, helps you execute, and moves you forward. If your current network isn't doing that, it's time to upgrade.

The Smartness Community – A Tribe for Smart People

Smart people don't just need a network—they need a tribe that sharpens their *Smartness*. When you surround yourself with people who are equally committed to raising their own *Smartness*, it accelerates yours. That's the power of the right tribe: it multiplies your growth, sharpens your decision-making, and pushes you beyond what you could achieve alone.

Building a supportive tribe doesn't have to be daunting—you don't have to do it alone. There are established networks, communities, and platforms designed to bring like-minded individuals together.

For instance, the *Smartness Community* that we have built offers a space for those striving for greater success to connect, share experiences, and learn from each other. Whether you're looking for guidance, encouragement, or shared wisdom, being part of such a community can accelerate your journey toward achieving your goals.

Kudos to you for having found this book and the resources it provides. But you also need to find others who are on a similar journey—people who understand the challenges and opportunities you face.

I've had great difficulty finding such a tribe. That's why we built the *Smartness Community*—not just as a network, but as a tribe of smart people dedicated to sharpening each other's *Smartness* and pushing for greater success.

You can learn more about the community on the book's website – www.MySmartness.com.

Find Your Tribe & Mentors 265

Your Journey Ahead

As you finish this book, think about what you'll do next. Success is rarely a solo journey—it's built with the support and wisdom of others. But real growth happens when you act (or choose not to)—and when you have the right people in your corner.

Connect with resources and communities of like-minded achievers who support your ambitions. A strong tribe provides accountability, shared learning and mutual encouragement. Mentors bring experience and wisdom to help you avoid pitfalls and make smarter decisions.

The journey will be challenging, but with the right tools, mentors, and tribe, you can achieve your goals and grow into the person you're meant to be. As you grow, your goals will evolve—and so must your tribe.

Imagine a future where you're not just another average also-ran, but a true achiever, surrounded by a powerful tribe that helps you reach new heights.

Embrace your capabilities and advantages. Find your tribe. And, take the next step in your journey to lasting success.

Having the right tribe and mentors will certainly accelerate growth, but smart people still need to take ownership of their future. In the next chapter, we explore how they step into their next level of success by making bold decisions and taking decisive action—starting now, not later.

As you evolve, so should your tribe. Growth sometimes means outgrowing people—and that's not failure. That's movement. Don't cling to familiarity. Surround yourself with people who match who you're becoming—not just who you've been.

> *"How your tribe evolves is often a sign of your own growth."*

Reflection: *Who's really in your corner—pushing you to level up, or quietly keeping you small? When was the last time your tribe called you out—or pulled you up? What would change if you finally stopped trying to do it alone and built the support system your journey demands?*

Chapter 49

What Smartness Enables You to Do

"Intelligence is not who you are, it is what you can use."
~ Ram V. Iyer

Smartness isn't just the flexible application of your intelligence or advantages. It's the flexible embodiment of who you are.

Smart people often get stuck in "being smart." That's not Smartness—it's identity rigidity. Like a method actor clinging to one role, they build their entire identity around being smart, credentialed, talented, or connected—even when that role no longer fits the moment. What starts as an advantage becomes a trap. Many smart people struggle in life because they are wedded to their intelligence more than their desire to succeed. When the context shifts, they struggle—not because they lack intelligence, but because they're holding onto the wrong identity. They don't need to demonstrate intelligence. They need to use Smartness to assess the moment, choose who to be, how to act, or when to hold back.

> *"The key to achieving greater success for smart people is to loosen their embrace of being smart – as their prime identity."*

Smartness, as defined in this book, is the ability to recognize what needs to be done in a situation and to do it effectively using your intelligence, advantages, and judgment. It's practical. It's repeatable. It's not about who you are. It's about how you show up and what you do.

Being a great actor is a good metaphor. Unlike a method actor who is good at playing just one role, the great actor doesn't cling to a role—they step fully into whatever the scene demands. They shift with the context. That's what Smartness looks like in action: context-aware, role-flexible, and outcome-focused.

Here are the core differences:

Being Intelligent	Using Smartness
"This is who I am."	"What does this situation require?"
Identity-centered	Context-centered
Role rigidity	Role flexibility
Performing intelligence	Applying good judgment
Proving worth	Achieving desired outcomes

Story: Arun Breaks the Smart Identity

Many smart people over-rely on their analysis and insight, but underestimate the power of action. Smart people can be more successful by trusting their execution as much as they trust their thinking.

Arun was known as the strategist in every room. Polished. Sharp. Always with a model or a framework. Then he was asked to coach a struggling team going through emotional burnout.

His tools didn't work. The models fell flat. The frameworks didn't move anyone. His mentor said, "They don't need your brilliance. They need your presence." "The more you try to 'be' smart, the less you are free to do what Smartness demands in that moment."

So Arun stopped trying to be the strategist. He listened. He asked questions. He showed humility. That changed everything. Not because he was less smart, but because he used his Smartness.

How to Practice

- Reflect on whether "being smart" is part of how you define your worth.
- In your next meeting, don't focus on figuring out the most brilliant thing to say; instead, listen.
- In a domain outside work, be a learner. Let someone else take the lead.
- Ask yourself: What does this situation need you to be—and can you set aside the need to be impressive long enough to become it?
- In moments of doubt, act. Confidence builds through doing, not just thinking.

Pattern That Trips Up Smart People

Many smart people fail to succeed because they seek certainty with thought, whereas success comes from acting. Many fall into the trap of overusing their strengths. A person who's great at detailed analysis might keep analyzing even when quick judgment is needed. Someone with a talent for reframing complexity might resist simple, direct action. In these cases, what was once an advantage becomes a constraint.

> *"Many smart people fail because they fail to accept that their intelligence is a tool like a hammer, not the hand that wields it."*

They confuse consistency with capability. It's the classic hammer problem: when all you rely on is a hammer, everything starts to look like a nail. A strength used everywhere becomes a limitation. What worked before may not be what's needed next. Smartness isn't about repeating the same move—it's about recognizing what's required and using the right tools accordingly. Smartness is what helps you make decisions in the moment—especially when the situation is unclear, the stakes are high, or your default reactions may pull you in the wrong direction.

Smartness is not rigid. It is responsive. Success doesn't come from using the same tool repeatedly, but from knowing which tool to use—and when to set it down.

The Takeaway

Smartness is not about being a fixed type of person. It's about becoming what the situation requires. That requires humility, range, and identity flexibility.

In a changing world, success comes not from becoming smarter, but from adapting how you use what you already have to meet what the moment demands.

> *"Success comes to those who act—not to those who know but never act on their knowledge."*

That's what makes Smartness different. That's what makes it powerful.

Many aspects of Smartness can only be developed through observation, imitation, and deliberate practice. You can't just read your way into Smartness. You have to see it in others, notice what works in real situations, and try it for yourself. Judgment, adaptability, and timing—the very heart of Smartness—are refined through experience, not explanation. Some of your biggest shifts will come not from epiphanies, but from watching someone navigate a moment brilliantly and asking, "What did they just do—and why did it work?" And then asking yourself, "What would I do in such a situation?"

> *Smartness isn't who you are—it's a capability you can use whenever the moment calls for it.*

Want to See Smartness in Real Life?

Smartness isn't just learned by thinking harder. It's learned by watching others, noticing what works in real-world situations, and trying it for yourself. That's why we created mySmartness Stories—a space for people to share moments where Smartness made a difference.

These aren't polished success stories. They're real-life moments where someone paused, adapted, asked a better question, stayed silent when their ego wanted to speak, or changed course mid-stream. Sometimes it worked. Sometimes it didn't. Either way, the learning is gold.

Smartness isn't about success theater—it's about discovering what works, what doesn't, and why. You won't always get it right. And that's the point. We need to frame Action and Response not as "wins," but as learning moments—even when the action was flawed, the outcome disappointing, or the *Smartness* incomplete. That's where growth actually happens.

To make it easy to share, we've created a simple format:

myCAR: A Simple Way to Share Your Smartness Moment

- my Story – What happened to me?
  Describe the moment that triggered your Smartness response. What was going on?

- C – Context
  Why did this moment matter? What made it challenging, subtle, or emotionally loaded?

- A – Action
  What did you "see"? What did you do—and how did it reflect Smartness, whether in an enabling or disabling way in that moment?

- R – Response
  What happened next? What changed? What insight did you walk away with?

You can share your story—or read others—at www.mySmartness.com/stories. *Smartness* becomes real when it's seen, shared, and practiced. Let's build a collection of moments that help us all develop and use our *Smartness* better.

CHAPTER 50

WHAT IS A SUCCESSFUL LIFE?

Many people think success is a fixed destination. It's not—it's an evolving ideal. Everyone defines it differently. We all chase it, and sometimes fall short. That doesn't mean we stop trying.

It's like the ideal of always telling the truth. You might fall short once—but that doesn't mean you give up on being honest. You keep striving to be honest.

That's where the *Achievement Cycle* becomes your ally. Every time you reflect on your advantages, adapt your thinking to meet the moment, take meaningful action, and extract wisdom from the outcome to inform future actions, you become more capable of succeeding. Whether you hit your goal today or not, every loop increases your Smartness and your ability to succeed. Each pass through that cycle helps you close the gap between who you are and who you're striving to become.

A successful life isn't one big win—a home run, a touchdown, or a three-pointer.

Instead, it's progress. Getting to first base. Moving the ball down the field. Advancing up the court.

Life is a series of experimentations—loops in which you keep learning, adjusting, and moving forward.

> *"Success isn't about getting it perfect. It's about getting better every time—and striving until you attain the success you seek."*

Certainty, Doubt, and the Real World

Many smart people crave certainty before they act. But the real world doesn't work that way. The rules change. The answers shift. Feedback is slow or missing. The path ahead? Often unclear.

If you get addicted to certainty, you start waiting for it before taking action. You delay action, avoid risk, seek permission, or fear mistakes. You become dependent on guarantees: certainty, feedback, perfect timing, and someone else's validation.

Here's the truth: certainty never shows up when you need it most. And when it does, it's already in the past. Certainty is a backward-looking feeling. Doubt is what lives in the present. Progress comes from moving forward anyway.

What I have noticed is that the most successful people don't wait for perfect plans. They move with what they know, make thoughtful (often small) bets, and keep going. They fail, adjust, learn and retry. The Achievement Cycle helps you keep moving, even when things are unclear. It builds your capacity to learn, adapt, and improve—cycle by cycle. Over time, they build better judgment and stronger self-confidence—not by avoiding uncertainty, but by engaging with it.

That's how real success is earned.

> *"The most successful people are the ones who know how to thrive between the world's certainties."*

CHAPTER 51

STEP INTO YOUR FUTURE NOW

"Action is the bridge between knowing and doing. You will either succeed or learn by acting."
~ Ram V. Iyer

You didn't read this book to pass the time. You read it to become an achiever—to be more successful than average.

You've gained the knowledge. You've clarified your aspirations. What's left? Action. Not later. Not when it's convenient. Now.

Your future isn't waiting—it's happening right now. If you don't take action, you will have to settle for what comes to you!

If you're waiting for certainty before you act, you'll wait forever, and never act. The most successful people aren't necessarily the smartest. They're the ones who take calculated risks and take action. This book has equipped you with the knowledge and the tools.

I've seen insights from this book transform lives. For instance, an MIT grad challenged his whole perspective on strengths and weaknesses after attending one of my webinars, focusing on quickly reducing her biggest weakness. A third, a Berkeley alum, is re-examining his life based on how our weaknesses become more important to address in our mid-careers. So, it's not just theory; these concepts have real-world impact.

Reflection: *What is one belief you currently hold that might be holding you back? Could you challenge it based on what you've learned in this book?*

Implementing what you've learned about *Smartness* in your own life is the key to achieving greater success. You might feel fired up right now. But if you're like most people, this book will end up sitting on a shelf—its lessons forgotten as life pulls you back into the grind. If this pattern sounds familiar, this chapter is for you. It can help you bridge the gap between what you know and what to do, and turn your ambitions into tangible achievements—that is, take action.

You've heard the saying, "Knowledge is power," a mantra especially cherished by the intellectually inclined. However, many of us revel in the joy of learning and collecting wisdom, only to stumble when it comes to actual implementation. If that resonates with you, let me share a simple truth: success demands action.

Smartness Can Turn Knowledge and Advantages into Achievement.

> *"There are no hopeless situations in life. There are only failures to smartly use Smartness—and use one's advantages and manage the disadvantages—to achieve the successes one can achieve."*

Intelligence, credentials, and resources get you in the game—but *Smartness* determines how you play. That's why the *Achievement Cycle* matters. You've already seen how it helps smart people leverage their advantages, close their gaps, and take decisive action. Now it's time to apply it. Don't wait for certainty or perfection. Use what you've learned. Move forward with intention and execute. Smart people succeed when they act.

Your Path Forward: Turning Knowledge into True Achievement

Here you are at the close of this book, ready to step out and create the life you envision. If you've taken anything from these pages, let it be this: no matter how much intelligence, status, or advantage you start with, success doesn't come with guarantees. It's not an inheritance. It's built, bit by bit, by your choices, your grit, and your hunger to keep moving forward—even when it's tough. If you've been waiting for success to arrive on its own, it's time to change the game. Success won't come find you—you have to claim it, show it you mean business, and keep showing up to make it yours.

The insights you've gained here are more than ideas—they're tools you can pick up and use. So now, ask yourself: *What will I do next?* What steps can you take today, tomorrow, and next week to make sure you're shaping your own future? Because of those big ambitions of yours? They're not just dreams. They're possibilities, real things, waiting for you to bring them into the world. But it's only going to happen if you decide to make them real.

Nobody, without exception, will ever be as committed to your success as you can be. This book has given you the keys—knowledge, insights and tools. Now, it's up to you to turn on the ignition, press the pedal, and start steering toward those goals that drew you here in the first place.

As I said before: You're in the driver's seat. The question is whether you'll start the engine and move forward. Every single action you take, big or small, adds fuel to your journey. Today is the day to start. Remember this: Success isn't just about what you know, who you know, or what you've got. It's about how you choose to use them. It's about adding wisdom to every decision, meaning to every goal, and purpose to every effort. What turns potential into achievement? **Action.** Knowing how to use your intelligence, abilities, and resources—in ways that count—is how you turn ambition into something real, something lasting.

Becoming Your Future Self Starts Today

Who you will be in five years is shaped by the choices you make today.

> *"You can choose to be unhappy with where you are today or get excited about who you believe you can become. The choice is yours."*

Think about the smartest, most capable version of yourself. What will you do daily? What will you know? What risks will you take?

Now, ask yourself: What actions must you take now to become that person?

Instead of waiting for transformation to happen, make transformation happen—act like your future self today.

- If your future self is a successful entrepreneur, start taking calculated risks and making business decisions now.
- If your future self is an industry leader, start speaking up and taking leadership roles.
- If your future self is healthier, make healthy choices today.

Your future isn't something you arrive at—it's something you create, one action at a time.

To help you, with this book, *Smartness* gives you an edge—master it, and you'll thrive in the fast-changing world, seizing opportunities, outmaneuvering others, and achieving greater success. But if you don't strengthen and apply your *Smartness* while others do, you'll struggle to compete and be forced to settle for mediocrity - an also-ran in the race for greater success. Do you want to be an achiever or a nobody?

Don't Let Your Past Define Your Future

All of us are understandably proud of our past achievements. But don't let those successes be the only things that define you for the rest of your life. I applaud you for everything you've accomplished, but I urge you to see those achievements as stepping stones, not finish lines.

> *"If you only dwell on past achievements without striving for new ones, you've decided your best days are behind you—dooming yourself to a future of stagnation, decline, and regret."*

I tell myself every day, "The best days are ahead!". I encourage you to adopt this mindset and look at your life through that lens. If you feel like you have to start over, remember that you're not starting from scratch—you're starting with experience.

> *"Don't let your past define you; define your future."*

So here it is: Today is your day one. Step up. Embrace the journey. You'll be amazed at just how far you can go and how much you can achieve.

Bet on Yourself (and make it count)

Betting on yourself isn't a gamble—it's a smart decision. Not because you have all the answers, perfect timing, or guaranteed outcomes. You won't. You'll face hesitation, uncertainty, and maybe some failures. But you'll also build clarity, resilience, and momentum—things comfort never gives you. You'll grow wiser and sharpen your judgment. Growth doesn't come from standing still. It comes from taking calculated chances, even when things aren't certain. *Smartness* isn't about what you know—it's about the decisions you make and the actions you take, using what you know and adapting to the situation.

And that's the best bet you can make.

Your Journey Begins Now

If you've been waiting for the 'right time' to go after your dreams and take control, this is it. Right now. *This is your moment.*

> *Achieving greater success comes down to a simple choice: Will you wait until you find time, or will you make time to achieve greater success?*

As the old proverb says, "*The best time to plant a tree was 20 years ago. The second-best time is now.*" Today can be *day one* of your journey to greater success, if you want to become an achiever.

You're already smart. You're already capable. Being smart or capable isn't the goal—it's your starting point. What matters is making it count. This book has shown you how. What matters now is that you act. Smart people fail when they overthink. Achievers take the next step immediately. They act.

No more excuses. You've got the knowledge. You've got the tools. What's stopping you from becoming the kind of achiever others talk about?

ABOUT THE AUTHOR

Ram V. Iyer is an MIT-educated engineer, five-time entrepreneur, and former Fortune 100 executive and venture capitalist who has spent his life asking a simple but powerful question: Why do so many smart people underachieve? His journey from success to setback and back again has shaped a mission to help smart people everywhere become more successful—not by focusing on how smart they are, but by learning to use what they already have—their intelligence, assets, resources, and other advantages, more effectively.

Ram's voice is grounded in lived experience. He has worked at global corporations like Boeing and Lucent, been a venture capitalist in Silicon Valley, and launched startups on multiple continents. He has won, lost, and won again. *MONEY* magazine once called him "The Comeback Kid." The lessons he shares in this book are hard-earned, deeply personal, and designed to deliver real results.

He has been invited to speak at MIT, Harvard, Princeton, and over a dozen top-tier alumni organizations including Wharton, Ross, Booth, Kellogg, Dartmouth, and Berkeley. He served as President of the worldwide MIT South Asian Alumni Association and the MIT Club of Princeton. His work has been featured in *Money*, *Fortune*, *CIO*, *CFO*, and other major outlets.

Ram's turning point came when he realized that intelligence alone wasn't enough—not for him, and not for the thousands of smart professionals he's met. That insight led him to identify **The Advantage Illusion**—the false belief that intelligence or credentials alone guarantee success, and develop the **Smartness Assessment**, and the **Achievement Cycle**.

He defines **Smartness** as the ability to apply one's intelligence and other advantages adaptively to achieve real-world success. It is not a fixed trait but a capability anyone can develop and use at any age. His tools and ideas have now been used by over a thousand professionals globally to become more effective, more intentional, and more successful.

He founded **The Smartness Institute** (www.mySmartness.com) to make Smartness a lifelong capability people can build, use, and grow.

This book is the foundation of that mission—a practical, straight-talking guide for smart people ready to stop underachieving and start achieving more.

INTRODUCING THE SMARTNESS INSTITUTE

Helping Smart People Become More Successful—for Life

Smartness isn't just something you read about, it's something you build and use every day. It is behaviorally expressed and situationally applied. That's why I created **The Smartness Institute**: a global resource hub to help smart people like you develop the mindsets, behaviors, skills and capabilities that drive real-world achievement.

At The Smartness Institute, you'll find:

- Practical frameworks and micro-courses to grow your Smartness
- Deep dives into the Smartness Factors
- The *Smartness Assessment* and personalized development plans
- Tools for leaders, managers, and coaches to help others close their Smartness Gap
- A growing community of achievers who are getting unstuck—and moving forward
- The latest thinking and resources to develop and use your Smartness

If this book made you think differently, The Smartness Institute is your next step.

Visit www.mySmartness.com to start your Smartness journey today.

"Remember, being smart or capable isn't the goal. What matters is making it count."

~ Ram V. Iyer

APPENDIX

Resources to Sustain & Accelerate Your Success

"In the end, no one keeps score of how many resources you used—or didn't. What matters is whether you become an achiever. Use every resource purposefully to achieve what truly matters to you."
~ Ram V. Iyer

When I was working to reach the next level in my own success, I realized something: even with many advantages, skills, and experience, I wasn't moving fast enough. I needed more: more perspective, more tools, and more targeted support. That's often the difference between slow, incremental progress and accelerated achievement.

Smart people often face a unique challenge: their intelligence can lead to overthinking, hesitation, or waiting for perfect clarity before acting. The truth is, being smart doesn't guarantee success. What makes the difference is *Smartness*—the ability to apply your intelligence, advantages, and resources in ways that create real-world results. These resources are designed to help smart people like you move faster, act decisively, and translate potential into consistent achievement.

The question is: where do you find the right resources to help you move faster? Who can you trust to provide relevant guidance? How do you access tools and communities that help you focus, act, and sustain momentum?

These are easy questions to ask, but harder to answer. That's why I assembled this collection of resources. They're designed to help you accelerate your success. I'll keep adding to them as I discover more.

Here's the truth: many people resist seeking external help. They believe they should figure it out themselves, or they hesitate to ask for support. But success isn't about proving what you already know. It's about getting results.

And getting results means using every resource available—coaching, tools, and networks that help you go further, faster.

Why These Resources Matter Now

You've done the work. You've built your roadmap, executed the Plays, and established the habits that lead to consistent achievement. But success isn't a one-time event. It's an ongoing process that demands sustained effort and consistent refinement.

These resources exist to help you:
1. Sustain the progress you've made
2. Accelerate your momentum toward even bigger achievements
3. Reassess and adapt as new challenges and opportunities emerge
4. Stay connected to a community of people focused on continuous growth

The following resources are here to help you sustain your momentum and accelerate your success, with support systems, tools, and a community built specifically for people like you. I'll continue adding to these, because I'm still on the journey too.

You already have advantages. Now, use every available resource to accelerate your success.

Know Thyself—Take the Smartness Assessment Privately and Confidentially

Success begins with self-awareness. If you haven't yet taken the *Smartness Assessment*, now is the time. This proprietary tool identifies your enablers, disablers, and mixed factors, providing a personalized roadmap to accelerate your progress.

- Access the assessment at: *www.MySmartness.com/Assessments/*
- Use the discount code: *SmartnessBook-2025* to take it for free ($198 value).

Take this step: understand your true starting point and begin building the future you envision. You can scan the QR code below to be taken to the assessments page.

Get a Deeper Understanding of Each Smartness Factor

From the *Smartness Assessment*, you'll broadly identify which of the *Smartness Factors* enable, disable, or have a mixed impact on your success, giving you a high-level view of your enablers and disablers. A mixed impact means your behavior shifts between enabling and disabling modes over time or in different situations. For example, you may take decisive action in familiar situations but hesitate when facing uncertainty.

However, knowing which factors affect you isn't enough—you must understand exactly how. If Action Orientation is a disabler, is it due to haste, procrastination, or overthinking? Likewise, if it's an enabler, pinpointing how it benefits you can help you achieve greater success. These details aren't available from the high-level *Smartness Assessment*. You need to take the individual *Smartness Factor Assessments* to uncover them.

Each of the assessments, like the Action Orientation Assessment, analyzes your mindset, behaviors, and patterns to reveal what's driving or hindering your success. If overthinking stalls your progress, recognizing it allows for targeted improvement.

With these insights, you can make informed choices: what to maintain, modify, or improve—and what to leverage or mitigate.

Take any of the *Smartness Factor Assessments* to dig deeper—whether to understand your enablers and disablers or to uncover why a factor appears as mixed in your *Smartness Assessment Report*. Access them at *www.MySmartness.com/Assessments* to gain clarity on your *Smartness Factors* and achieve greater success.

Learn in Other Formats

I have laid out my current thinking in this book. Books may or may not be your thing. For those who learn best through listening, I'm creating an audiobook. You can listen to these transformative insights while you're jogging or driving. For further details, please visit www.MySmartness.com/books.

The Smartness AI Bot

Artificial Intelligence is here. The *Smartness AI Bot* leverages this book, hundreds of references, my latest thinking, and cutting-edge research. It lets you interactively complete exercises and seek guidance, with monthly updates to reflect new insights, research, and AI advancements. Learn more at www.MySmartness.com.

Smartness Stories: Inspire & Be Inspired

We're collecting real stories of Smartness in action—successes, failures, breakthroughs, and lessons—across all 21 Smartness Factors. Share your own experience: what worked, what didn't. Then explore how others have developed and used their Smartness—what they tried, how it went, and what they learned. Get inspired, gain ideas, and build your own Smartness at www.MySmartness.com/Stories.

Smartness Camps: Where You Develop Your Smartness by Doing

Smartness Camps are where you learn to develop and use your Smartness by doing. You'll work on yourself and with others—sometimes inside the room, sometimes in the outside world. Each session focuses on one or more of the 21 Smartness Factors. Some exercises are structured, others open-ended. All of them are built to help you practice how to use Smartness to think better and act more effectively in real situations.

Together, they'll help you build and apply your Smartness. You'll leave more confident to take on the world—and better equipped to turn your intelligence and other advantages into real achievement.

The Smartness Podcast

And speaking of audio—get your podcast app ready. The *Smartness Podcast* is coming your way. It will be a deep dive into each of these transformative *Smartness Factors*, complete with insights from people who've walked the talk or experts on them. It will also address other aspects that could be useful on your journey to become an achiever. Learn more at: www.MySmartness.com/podcast

Get Fresh Content Regularly to Keep You Growing

Now, if you like to sip your morning coffee while reading useful articles, then you might enjoy my:

1. Weekly iAchiever Newsletter. You can subscribe to this fluff-free newsletter at this signup link: iAchiever Weekly Newsletter signup - https://bit.ly/iAchieverNewsletter
2. Blog posts at www.MySmartness.com/blog
3. LinkedIn Posts at www.linkedin.com/in/mitramiyer

They'll keep you in the loop about everything related to the *Smartness Factors* and more.

The Smartness Book Club

This book is just the beginning. I'm constantly uncovering new insights—through talks, discussions, *Smartness Assessment* data, and conversations with members and experts—that can accelerate your success.

To help you keep growing, I've launched the *Smartness Book* Club. As a member, you'll get exclusive access to evolving content, including new chapters, fresh insights, and segment-specific mini-books.

Every month, I'll share the latest research, newly identified *Smartness Factors*, and updates from our growing assessment database. You'll stay current, informed, and ahead of the curve—among the first to access new insights and targeted resources as they're released. Club members also get direct access to these insights and opportunities to discuss them with me and the community. You can learn more at www.MySmartness.com under OFFERINGS.

Derivative Books for Specific Segments

This book was written specifically for smart people who want to close the gap between intelligence and achievement. I also offer additional resources for those who want to go deeper into specific areas—whether you're a tech professional, a leader, an immigrant, or navigating unique challenges in your career or life. These targeted resources are optional add-ons designed to help you apply *Smartness* in specific contexts.

Smartness Circles: Growth-Focused, Not Commerce-Focused

We're building Smartness Circles in cities and professions—small, invite-only peer groups for people committed to applying Smartness in real life. These aren't sales funnels or coaching programs. No pitching. No promotions. Just real people developing Smartness—together, in real life.

Every self-policed Smartness Circle begins with a clear pledge: commit to personal Smartness development and mutual support. Members must sign a Code of Conduct—zero tolerance for agenda-pushing or prospecting. Violators are banned—permanently. One strike. You're out.

I'm creating these Smartness Circles to connect people, not to monetize them. While I will offer paid Smartness Camps and advanced coaching separately, Smartness Circles are strictly for personal development—not for prospecting, coaching, or client-building.

Want to start or join a Smartness Circle in your city? Request an intro at: www.MySmartness.com/SmartnessCircle

Smartness Camps

Live, immersive experiences where you can work with others to develop and apply your Smartness in real-world situations. Each session focuses on one or more of the Smartness Factors. While I lead them, they aren't lectures—they're live labs to develop your capabilities and accelerate your success. Learn more at: www.MySmartness.com/SmartnessCamps

The Smartness Community

I recognized that we need a community of people on a similar journey where you can be yourself, comfortably discuss your challenges, and have people who will support you and hold you accountable. You know that finding such people who are on a similar journey of transformation is very difficult. They may be around you, but they won't reveal themselves. That's why I created the *Smartness Community*, a vibrant space of people committed to achieving more in their personal and professional lives. Think of a time when community support made a significant difference in your life. Think of how a similar group can enable your greater success. Learn more at: www.MySmartness.com/programs.

Personalized Coaching: Group & Individual

If you value personal guidance, I offer both group and one-on-one coaching. This isn't generic advice. These sessions are customized to your (or your group's) unique *Smartness Factors*, using your *Smartness Assessment Reports* to provide actionable steps and ongoing guidance on maximizing your enablers and overcoming your disablers. You will also get my absolute latest thinking and the newest tools that may not be in the book.

- **Group Coaching**: Collaborate with peers and learn in a structured setting.
- **One-on-one Coaching** – Personalized sessions to address your unique *Smartness Factors*.
- **For coaching details,** visit: www.MySmartness.com under Offerings & Programs.

Final Thought: Turning Smartness into Lasting Success

This book, along with the companion *Smartness Playbook*, gives you the knowledge, tools, and strategies to leverage what you have to achieve what you want. But tools alone won't create success—only your commitment to act and your persistent actions can.

> *Achievers are not recognized for their ambitions but by their achievements.*

You know that *Smartness* isn't a fixed trait, and you need to know how to develop, apply, and improve it for the rest of your life. Are you committed to putting it into action?

As a smart person, you've likely relied on intelligence to get you this far. But *Smartness* is what will take you further. Now, you must decide:

- Will you act with urgency or let time slip away?
- Will you build momentum or let hesitation stall your progress? Small, daily wins will build momentum and boost your confidence.
- Will you step into your full potential or settle for less than you're capable of?

> *If you want to become an achiever, act with urgency and build momentum. Otherwise, it will fade away like another broken New Year's resolution.*

For many, the biggest barrier to success isn't lack of opportunity—it's fear: fear of failure, fear of judgment, fear of stepping outside of what feels comfortable, and maybe even fear of doing anything at all, because doing nothing feels very comfortable. But fear itself is a choice.

Maintain Your Momentum

- **Reassess Your Progress Regularly**
  Retake your *Smartness Assessment* every 90 days to stay sharp on your Enablers, Disablers, and Mixed Factors. Fresh insights drive better actions.
  www.MySmartness.com/Assessments/Smartness
- **Stay Engaged in the Smartness Community**
  Connect with others committed to achieving more. Stay accountable, share insights, and keep learning. www.MySmartness.com/programs
- **Use the Tools That Keep You Moving Forward**
  Leverage the Podcast, Book Club, AI Bot, and Personalized Coaching to accelerate your success. www.MySmartness.com

Smartness is a lifelong advantage—but only if you keep applying it. You've done the hard part. Now make this process part of your life.

Achievement isn't accidental. Neither is *Smartness*.

You've closed the gap between knowing and doing. This is just the beginning.

Keep the Conversation Going

1. LinkedIn: https://linkedin.com/in/MiTRamiyer (MiTRamiyer)
2. Twitter/X: @MiTRamiyer
3. Instagram: MiTRamiyer
4. YouTube: www.youtube.com/mitramiyer
5. Website: www.MySmartness.com
6. Email: info@*iSmartandSuccessful*.com

Thank you for making this book a part of your journey to greater achievements. Your best days are ahead of you, because you've chosen to act with *Smartness*.

"If a growth mindset was a breakthrough in thinking, Smartness is a breakthrough in achieving."

~ Ram V. Iyer

www.ingramcontent.com/pod-product-compliance
Lightning Source LLC
Chambersburg PA
CBHW030447100526
44580CB00001B/13